General Motors and the Nazis

General Motors and the Nazis

The Struggle for Control of Opel,

Europe's Biggest Carmaker

Henry Ashby Turner, Jr.

Yale University Press

New Haven and London

Published with assistance from the Mary Cady Tew Memorial Fund.

Set in Garamond and Stone Sans types by The Composing Room of Michigan, Inc.

Printed in the United States of America by Sheridan Books.

Library of Congress Cataloging-in-Publication Data
Turner, Henry Ashby.
General Motors and the Nazis : the struggle for control of Opel, Europe's biggest
carmaker / Henry Ashby Turner, Jr.
    p.   cm.
Includes bibliographical references and index.
ISBN 0-300-10634-3 (cloth : alk. paper)
1. Opel, AG—History.   2. Automobile industry and trade—Germany—History.
I. Title.
HD9710.G44O648 2005
338.7′629222′094309043—dc22
2005001370

A catalogue record for this book is available from the British Library.

The paper in this book meets the guidelines for permanence and durability of the
Committee on Production Guidelines for Book Longevity of the Council on Library
Resources.

10 9 8 7 6 5 4 3 2 1

Contents

Preface

Throughout the twelve years of the Third Reich the largest automotive manufacturing firm in Germany and indeed in all of Europe, Adam Opel AG, was the property of the General Motors Corporation. During the Second World War, while GM was serving as one of America's chief arsenals, its German subsidiary supplied large quantities of war equipment to Hitler's armed forces. Opel produced key components for one of the most deadly warplanes of the Luftwaffe as well as the truck model most heavily relied upon by the German army. These, and an array of additional weaponry made by Opel, were used against the armed forces of the United States and its allies. In producing war materials for the Third Reich, GM's German subsidiary made extensive use of unfree labor.

These facts have given rise to a number of grave accusations against General Motors. Its executives have been depicted as pro-Nazis who colluded with Hitler's regime to equip the Third Reich for conquest. They have been charged with covertly exercising control over Opel even after Germany declared war on the United States and with continuing to do business with the enemy in defiance of American laws.

They have been accused of divided loyalties and of cynically profiting from both sides of the conflict by producing war materials for the Third Reich as well as for the United States.[1]

With the goal of assessing the validity of these accusations and setting the record straight, this book examines GM's relations with Opel and the German government. It was made possible by a documentation project that I directed during the years 1999–2000 under the sponsorship of the General Motors Corporation. Initiated by GM in response to pending class-action suits on behalf of victims of forced labor against American corporations that had owned German firms during the Third Reich, the project was designed to locate all available relevant records and provide information to GM. To that end, GM granted full and unrestricted access to its files and those of its subsidiaries. The relevant records of GM, Opel, and some of the corporation's other foreign subsidiaries were copied onto compact discs and cataloged, along with those located in other repositories, in a compact-disc database. Upon completion of the documentation project, a complete set of the discs, designated as the General Motors–Opel Collection, was donated by GM to the Manuscripts and Archives Division of Yale University's Sterling Memorial Library, where all are available to other researchers.

This book was not commissioned by General Motors. It was written after the documentation project was completed and without any financial support from GM. Its contents were seen by no one at GM prior to publication. It is therefore an independent undertaking by the author, who bears sole responsibility for its contents.

Many helpful individuals have contributed to this study. The documentation project was made possible by the labors of a staff of able young Yale historians who participated in locating the thousands of records included in the GM-Opel Collection and preparing the database guide: Pertti T. Ahonen, Charles B. Lansing, John S. Lowry, David B. Posner, Mary E. Sarotte, Douglas E. Selvage, Brian E. Vick, and Heidi Walcher. David Hayward, Günter Neliba, Anita Kugler, Hans Pohl, and Dirk Riesener generously shared information from their own researches. Robert C. Weinbaum, John G. Rahie, and Brigitte H. Wolin of the General Motors Corporation legal staff provided tireless assistance in locating documents, as did Ralph Greb of the Opel legal staff. Gerald D. Feldman, Richard F. Hamilton, Harold James, Robert O. Paxton, Helmut Walser Smith, and Judith and Warren Spehar read earlier drafts and provided invaluable advice.

Chapter 1 GM's Costly Subsidiary
Sags with the Slump, Then Soars
under the Swastika

At the height of the economic boom of the 1920s, General Motors president Alfred P. Sloan decided the time was ripe for a major commitment by the corporation to the European market. Elevated to his post in mid-decade after masterminding GM's recovery from a financial crisis, Sloan had built the firm into America's largest automotive producer and one of the country's biggest enterprises. In the course of 1928, GM captured close to 40 percent of the American market and realized profits of well over a quarter of a billion dollars from the sale of more than 1.8 million trucks and cars. That autumn, during a European trip to survey possible locations for a large-scale subsidiary, Sloan decided upon Germany. The prospects for production and sales there seemed highly promising. After a shaky beginning, the republic established after the First World War had stabilized, giving the country a functioning democratic government. Germany was once again a respected member of the international community. It was complying with the terms of the Treaty of Versailles, was meeting its reparation obligations, and had been accorded membership in the League of Nations. Adolf Hitler's National Socialist Party languished on the fringe of politics, having obtained less than 3 percent of the vote in the most recent national election. The German economy had recovered rapidly after currency stabilization had put an end to runaway postwar inflation five years earlier. Foreign investment capital had poured in, mainly from the United States. Many sectors of industry had attained or surpassed prewar output, and the trends pointed to further expansion. This was especially true of the German automotive industry, which in the estimate of GM stood at about the level attained in the United States before the war. Whereas there was one car for every five Americans in 1928, one for every thirty-eight Britons, and one for every forty-three Frenchmen, the corresponding number for Germany was a hundred and thirty-four. With rising incomes stimulating demand for cars, the makings of an enormous expansion appeared to be at hand. Situated in the middle of Europe, Germany could also serve as a base for production of vehicles for export to the rest of the continent. In short, that country seemed an ideal location for expansion of GM's European operations.[1]

General Motors had previously sought to tap into the German market by shipping motors and other parts of its American models to assembly plants in that country and combining them with locally made components. That arrangement, similar to GM's practices in many other countries, enabled the firm to economize on shipping costs and also to circumvent Germany's protective tariffs, since auto parts were subject to lower import levies than finished vehicles. But this approach provided only a partial solution to the obstacles posed by high German import duties, and the limited number of vehicles that it brought to market precluded the economies of scale that only on-the-spot assembly-line production could provide. Moreover, the end products were essentially GM's American models, which were both more costly to purchase and more expensive to maintain than most European vehicles. A German auto tax that varied according to engine cylinder volume imposed an added handicap on the marketability of American models. Earlier in 1928, furthermore, German import duties on auto parts had been increased, giving rise to concern that prohibitively high rates might follow and eventually choke off automotive imports altogether. If GM were to expand its share of the continental market, Sloan and his colleagues concluded, the company would have to find a way to produce vehicles there on a large scale, including smaller models suited to European conditions.

While in Germany, Sloan visited the plant of the family-owned Adam Opel firm in Rüsselsheim on the south bank of the Main River between Frankfurt and Mainz. What he saw there impressed him very favorably. Opel was the largest manufacturer of motor vehicles outside the United States. It towered over the fragmented German automotive industry, producing nearly 45 percent of the trucks and cars made in that country, accounting for more than a quarter of domestic sales and leading in exports as well. With some twelve thousand on its payroll, the firm was one of Germany's largest employers, and its 3.5 million square feet of factory floor space placed it among the biggest by that measure as well. During the 1920s its management had invested heavily in up-to-date American machinery and adopted advanced production methods developed in the United States, including the assembly line. Opel had also pioneered in the manufacture of small cars. Since 1924 the firm had successfully marketed at an unprecedentedly low price a compact, two-seat, four-cylinder "tree frog," whose bright green finish broke with the practice of painting cars black. Moreover, the firm had taken the lead in establishing an extensive network of dealerships that provided reliable maintenance and repair service for purchasers of its vehicles.[2]

Finding the owners of Opel favorably disposed to a sale, Sloan negotiated an option to purchase the company while he was in Germany. When scrutiny by a GM study group yielded favorable findings, the option was exercised in March 1929. General Motors bought 80 percent of the shares of Opel stock and secured the rest two years later when the owners exercised an option to sell the remainder. The total purchase price came to slightly over $33,3 million, a sum equivalent to more than a third of GM's overall after-tax profits in the depression-plagued year of 1931. At a time when the American economy was contracting drastically, Opel represented a significant commitment of GM's financial resources. Its acquisition far overshadowed the corporation's purchase in 1925 of a small British automotive firm, Vauxhall, for a little over $2.5 million. The German firm thus became GM's largest foreign holding and the bellwether of its overseas operations, which comprised some two dozen assembly plants and sales outlets around the world.

In acquiring Opel, GM not only entered the German auto industry at the very top but also became the owner of one of the country's most venerable and best-known manufacturing companies. Its founder, Adam Opel, had launched the firm in 1862 by establishing a successful sewing machine factory in Rüsselsheim. In 1888 he added the highly lucrative manufacture of bicycles—then a hugely popular innovation—the best known of which was called the Blitz (lightning). The firm would continue to make bicycles until 1937, for much of that time as the world's largest producer. After Adam Opel's death in 1895, his sons took over the firm and in 1899 marketed its first automobile, which was

General Motors president Alfred P. Sloan (sixth from right) with Opel executives at the Rüsselsheim factory, next to the monument to founder Adam Opel, after purchasing the firm for GM in 1929. To the right of Sloan is Wilhelm von Opel, until then head of the family firm. Courtesy of Adam Opel AG.

soon followed by a line of trucks that would also come to bear the designation Blitz. The Opel brothers financed the firm's expansion mainly from its profits and kept it a family-owned enterprise until late 1928. Then, following the option taken by GM, it was incorporated as the *Adam Opel Aktiengesellschaft,* and shares with a nominal value of 60 million marks were issued.[3]

Recognizing that foreign ownership might prove a handicap at a time of heightened nationalism in Germany, GM strove to preserve an appearance of independence for Opel. At the time GM officials spoke publicly of the purchase in terms of an "agreement of association" or "alliance" between the two firms and sought to downplay the fact that an outright acquisition had occurred. Formally, Opel remained a wholly separate entity under German corporate law, with GM's role limited to that of owner of all the stock. As sole shareholder, however, GM determined the composition of the Supervisory Board (*Aufsichtsrat*), which was analogous to the board of directors in an American firm. By way of indicating continuity with the firm's past, the two surviv-

Aerial view of the Opel factory at Rüsselsheim on the Main River, between Frankfurt and Mainz. Courtesy of Adam Opel AG.

ing sons of Adam Opel were installed as members. The elder, Wilhelm von Opel, received the title of chairman, the younger, Fritz Opel, bore that of deputy chairman until his death in 1938. But during the early years of GM's ownership, executives from its ranks far outnumbered the German members of the board. Since most of the American members worked and lived in the United States and rarely—in most cases never—attended board sessions, GM's majority was therefore more a potentiality, available in case of need, than a functioning reality. The board determined the composition of the Directorate (*Vorstand*), the small executive group that wielded actual operational authority under German corporate law. The Directorate's conduct of the firm was reviewed regularly by the board, as was its annual report, which was routinely approved. Ultimate authority rested with the yearly shareholder meetings, at which representatives of GM voted all the stock and could dismiss or reconstitute the Supervisory Board and reject the Directorate's annual report. Dividends—all of which went to the American corporation—had to be authorized by the shareholder meetings.[4]

In spite of the firm's conformity with German corporate structure and the prominent presence of the Opel brothers and other Germans in its upper ranks, the *Adam Opel Aktiengesellschaft* functioned as a wholly owned subsidiary of GM. Leadership of the Directorate was assigned to the senior GM executive at the firm, who was assisted by one, at most two, other Americans. He reported to General Motors Overseas Operations, headquartered in New York, and carried out instructions from his superiors there. The first GM executive assigned to head Opel's management was a naturalized American citizen of German origin, and the move from Detroit to Rüsselsheim posed no linguistic problems for him. After only a year, however, he was replaced by the first of a succession of Americans who had little or no knowledge of the German language. The same was the case with most of the GM engineers assigned to the firm for various periods of time, so that internal memoranda had to be circulated in both English and German.

The American executives assigned to Opel exercised wide-ranging discretionary authority. Under Sloan's leadership, GM operated on a managerial principle of "co-ordinated decentralization" that reserved control over allocations of capital to the central leadership but otherwise left most decisions to the corporation's various divisions, which were monitored by a hierarchical system of committees. The Americans at Opel were, however, from the outset heavily dependent upon the German members of the managerial staff, who far outnumbered them. Of necessity, they had to rely upon these colleagues for information about what was happening at the firm and elsewhere in the country as well as for communications with employees and government officials. Returning to the United States frequently for vacations and for consultations at GM's New York headquarters at a time when trans-Atlantic sea travel required a week or more each way, the American executives were absent for substantial periods of time. As a result, those charged with responsibility for Opel exercised at best a tenuous control over the firm.[5]

General Motor's major German investment quickly turned sour. The timing of the purchase could hardly have been worse. Even before the Wall Street crash of late 1929 plunged the world into the Great Depression, the German economy began to sag badly. When GM assumed control of Opel in the spring of that year, the Americans found that the firm was burdened with bank overdrafts equivalent to more than three million dollars. By mid-December Opel sales had fallen so far that the new management shut down the plant for two weeks and sent the workers home without pay. A modest profit was realized for 1929, thanks to stronger sales during the early months. But the following year unit production dropped by nearly a quarter. As a result, the company suffered losses equivalent to more than three million dollars in 1930, in part because of costly plant expansion and modernization projects launched when prospects still seemed bright. Losses were reduced during the following two years, but only by means of drastic layoffs, shutdowns, reduced workweeks, and economies achieved by manufacturing many components previously purchased from suppliers. In 1932 unit sales nevertheless stood at less than half the level of 1928. Because of Opel's ability to export its vehicles through GM's worldwide international sales network, it experienced a less severe contraction than most German automakers. But red ink nevertheless continued to flow. To keep Opel afloat, GM had to borrow funds in the United States to finance a $4.25 million loan for the company and deposit another $3.85 million in German banks to shore up its credit. Through these and other infusions of funds, GM's investment in its faltering German subsidiary grew to some $42 million by 1932, a year when the American corporation's profits shrank, under the impact of the Depression, to only $165,000. General Motor's largest overseas unit had not only failed to prove profitable but was becoming a financial drain on its hard-pressed owner.[6]

On top of its other German woes, GM found itself without the option of liquidating its investment in Opel in order to recover at least part of its multi-million-dollar outlay. To stem the flight of capital during a major banking crisis in the summer of 1931, the republican government of Germany imposed stringent currency exchange controls. Henceforth, marks could be used to purchase dollars or other foreign currencies only with government permission and then only on a very limited scale and usually at highly unfavorable exchange rates. Originally conceived as a temporary response to an emergency, these controls were repeatedly tightened as the Depression deepened and would remain in effect until well after the Second World War. General Motor's major investment was, as a result, locked into Germany. The huge Opel factory, its machines and skilled workforce, could not be moved elsewhere. Since the currency controls drastically reduced the market value of Opel stock outside Germany, its sale for convertible currency would entail prohibitive losses on GM's investment. The stock could be sold for marks, but that would leave the problem of finding alternate ways to invest the proceeds within Germany at a time when virtually all of that country's economy was profoundly depressed. Because of Opel's losses, the stock was yielding no dividends, but even if the firm's performance should improve, the prospects for converting the profits into dollars would remain uncertain because of the currency controls. By the end of 1932 the investment opportunity in Germany that was so alluring only three years earlier had come to seem highly dubious, if not downright disastrous.

At the end of January 1933 German politics took a fateful turn when backroom political intrigue led to the appointment of Adolf Hitler as chancellor at the head of the government. There is no record of GM's reaction to that surprising development, which came just as Hitler's party was rapidly losing strength after several years of electoral successes. But the swift consolidation of Nazi rule could scarcely have been encouraging for the American owners of Opel as spokesmen of that hypernationalistic party had long inveighed against the presence of foreign businesses in Germany. This was particularly the case with regard to the auto industry. Even before Hitler came to power, an automobile club headed by a Nazi had exacted from its members a pledge not to buy foreign cars. Nazi hostility focused, moreover, on the foreign ownership of the venerable Opel firm, especially after the firm's management refused in 1932 to allow use of the auto racing track and grandstand on its factory grounds for a Hitler election campaign rally. By contrast, according to an American observer in Berlin, the new factory that the Ford Motor Company had launched at Cologne from scratch in 1930 was largely spared such hostility, presumably because of Hitler's admiration for Henry Ford but also because its establishment had not involved the takeover of a German firm.[7]

Because of Opel's production of army vehicles during the First World War, prominent Nazis viewed its return to German hands as militarily desirable. In 1932 Hitler's henchman Hermann Göring had bluntly informed an American Embassy official in Berlin that the Nazis would not allow Opel to remain under U.S. control after they attained power. Hitler himself had, however, assured an American journalist four months before attaining power that he saw no problem with Opel's American ownership since the firm generated work for Germans and, instead of importing automobiles, made them with German materials. The sincerity of that statement was, to be sure, open to question. It was made in the course of an interview in which Hitler clearly sought to cultivate respectability abroad by countering fears that a Nazi regime would repudiate private debts owed to foreigners and confiscate property they owned in Germany. He did not repeat that view for home consumption, nor did he silence expressions of hostility toward Opel on the part of other Nazis.[8]

When rumors circulated in the wake of Hitler's installation as chancellor to the effect that the Opel brothers were seeking to repurchase the firm, the Nazi press applauded the prospect of its restoration to German ownership. Those same papers expressed misgivings, however, about losing the export advantages that Opel enjoyed because of its connection with GM's worldwide marketing system at a time when Germany desperately needed foreign exchange in order to pay for the imported food, raw materials, and other commodities on which the country was heavily dependent. But the rumors of a German repurchase quickly proved groundless, and as events would demonstrate, the Nazi leadership proved sufficiently rational to recognize that the economic drawbacks of wresting Opel from its American owner would outweigh any political gains.[9]

It must have come as a great relief to GM executives when Chancellor Hitler indicated publicly not only that in his case Nazi xenophobia did not necessarily extend to cars but also that he intended to give the auto industry as a whole favored treatment. Less than two weeks after taking office, following a speech at the opening of the annual Berlin auto show, Hitler ostentatiously visited the Opel display and allowed himself to be photographed while examining the company's new models. In a regime that relied heavily on symbolic gestures, publication of this photo served as a signal that, despite Nazi antiforeigner rhetoric, Opel would be permitted to continue under GM ownership. In his speech, moreover, Hitler left no doubt about his enthusiastic support for the auto industry, which he termed the most important of the time. To spur the industry's development, he called for reductions in the high taxes the republic had imposed on car sales and proclaimed a major program of road building to encourage the use of cars and trucks. Addressing the session of the German parliament that granted him sweeping authority in late March, the man who was well on the way to becoming a dictator pledged to use his new powers to promote automotive travel and transport.[10]

Actions soon followed Hitler's words. During the spring of 1933 the tax on new car purchases was eliminated and levies on sales of used cars were eased significantly. In June the new regime, drawing on preparations begun by the republican government, announced plans for a nationwide network of four-lane, median-strip highways to augment Germany's antiquated road system. In September construction on the first stretches of this autobahn commenced amidst much fanfare. Stimulated by the government's measures, the auto industry spearheaded the remarkable recovery of the German economy that boosted the popularity of the Nazi regime by virtually eliminating within a few years the mass unemployment that had idled a quarter of the workforce and contributed so importantly to Hitler's rise.[11]

Opel drew handsome benefits from the economic upswing that marked the early years of the Third Reich. Beginning with the spring of 1933, new orders for cars and trucks flooded in. In the course of the year, the firm sold almost twice as many vehicles as in 1932 and surpassed predepression highs. During the next two years sales more than doubled again, as Opel outstripped not only the rest of the German auto industry but also the laggard performance of GM in the United States. By 1934 the firm's share of the German car and truck market had risen to almost 40 percent, and its portion of automotive exports had reached 64.8 percent. The company's workforce, which had declined by about half to a low point below six thousand in 1930, again topped ten thousand by the summer of 1933 and swelled to nearly seventeen thousand in 1934.[12]

Throughout the peacetime years of the Third Reich, Opel continued to prosper. Rigorous management, advanced production line techniques, and implementation of GM technology maximized efficiency. An increase in the variety of car models in line with GM's practices and the introduction of new small cars at low prices as well as larger, more expensive models spurred sales, both within Germany and in export markets. Passenger car sales hit a peak of 118,850 in 1938, far more than recorded by any other German company. Before the beginning of the war the following year, sales were well on the way to topping that figure. Despite the high corporate taxes imposed by the Nazi regime, rising profits were achieved, bolstered by sizeable government export subsidies. Beginning with 1935, annual dividends began to be declared at a rate of 6 percent of the face value of the stock, which was increased two years later to 8 percent, in both cases the maximum permitted by Nazi laws. The American firm's ugly German duckling of only a few years earlier had become a goose laying golden eggs in the Third Reich.[13]

Opel's gold remained, however, in large measure tantalizingly beyond the grasp of GM. By the time the first dividends were declared, the Nazis had tightened currency controls to an extent that made their conversion into dollars possible only in very limited amounts and at highly disadvantageous exchange rates. Foreign money generated by Opel exports to other countries had to be exchanged for nonconvertible marks, in line with the German government's practice of seizing convertible currency in order to allocate it to purchases abroad of strategic materials needed for armaments and other politically determined purposes. Some of the dividend marks that began to accumulate in a GM account at Opel were sold for dollars to American purchasers who needed money in Germany, but this yielded only discouraging knockdown prices. To GM's dismay, the restrictions imposed by the Nazi regime had the effect of reducing the dollar returns on the American corporation's large investment in Opel to a fraction of what they would have been in the absence of those controls.[14]

In 1936 an extortionary German government measure turned Opel into a drain on GM's own dollar reserves. As part of a drive to curtail Germany's ballooning trade deficit, the authorities in Berlin prohibited the firm from using marks to purchase foreign currency needed to pay for the imported rubber required to make tires for its cars and trucks. Faced with the prospect of its subsidiary producing cars and trucks unmarketable for lack of tires, GM found itself forced to advance what by 1939 came to more than $3.5 million dollars to purchase rubber for Opel. Lengthy negotiations with the Economics Ministry led to a complex agreement designed to enable GM to recoup some of those dollars. General Motors was permitted to use limited amounts of its dividend marks to buy Opel vehicles for sale in countries with convertible currencies. It was also allowed to purchase Opel-made wheels for use on Chevrolets produced in the United States as well as to buy items such as pencils and sandpaper from other German firms that could be used by GM in the United States and elsewhere. When those arrangements failed to produce significant results, further dispensations allowed GM to recover additional profits by means of barter. Limited amounts of Opel dividend marks were, with the consent of the Economics Ministry, used to purchase from other German firms a variety of finished products, including knitting machines, printing presses, and Christmas tree ornaments. General Motors then sought, with varying degrees of success, to resell those goods profitably in the United States. The dollar yields were, however, curtailed by stipulations requiring that as much as half the purchase price of the German finished goods must be paid in dollars or other convertible currencies. The resulting complicated transactions also failed to match profit expectations and burdened GM with considerable overhead costs. When the British wartime blockade of German ports put an end to shipments of German goods to the United States and elsewhere, GM was left with a sizeable cash deficit in the Opel rubber account.[15]

Indirect gains in convertible currencies derived from Opel exports provided GM with partial compensation for the frustratingly low dollar returns from its German subsidiary. By buying cars, trucks, and spare parts from Opel and reselling them abroad at often considerable markups, GM's other foreign subsidiaries reaped profits in currencies that could be used to purchase dollars. So successful were Opel's vehicles in international markets that their sales generated the larger part of the net income of GM's other European subsidiaries, in effect keeping those components of the American corporation's worldwide network in business. In all, these transactions netted GM approximately $7 million in the course of the prewar years. Because of the unsettled conditions of the time, however, those funds were credited to reserves rather than being recorded by GM as income.[16]

Taken together, the dollars derived from these various stratagems prior to the U.S. entry into the war represented a meager return on GM's large investment in Opel. By the time Hitler declared war on the United States in December 1941, close to half of GM's Opel dividends had been converted by various methods into nearly $1.5 million. But only part that money amounted to net profit for the American firm as a result of its dollar losses in the rubber transactions. Particularly frustrating was the large volume of mark-denominated Opel dividends that remained bottled up in Germany. By late 1941 these totaled over ten million marks, the equivalent of nearly $2.5 million at the exchange rate that had prevailed before the currency controls were imposed. A GM internal report of 1940 exaggerated in claiming that the American corporation's direct dollar return on its large investment in Opel amounted to "practically nil" after a decade of ownership, but the yield was unquestionably very disappointing.[17]

Unable to extract Opel's profits from Germany on satisfactory terms, GM chose to let most of its dividends remain with the firm. A large part, along with the far greater undistributed profits, was reinvested to expand and modernize Opel's production facilities. When plant expansion was curtailed by government controls designed to divert building materials to rearmament and other projects favored by the Nazi regime, the GM men in charge of Opel dealt with excess liquidity by purchasing shares of other German industrial firms. Those investments in turn yielded still more profits. By the end of 1937 Opel's declared net worth had ballooned to almost triple that of the next largest German auto firm, Daimler-Benz, and nearly four times that of Ford's German subsidiary. Although GM continued to list Opel as an asset at the purchase price, an internal analysis of 1940 estimated the subsidiary's value as of the end of the previous year, including reserves, at $86.7 million, well over double GM's initial investment. It was by far the biggest automaker not only in Europe but in the world outside the United States.[18]

As they watched Opel grow in value and its unconverted dividends accumulate, GM executives consoled themselves—and their American shareholders—with the hope that a return to more normal conditions in Germany would some day enable them to convert into dollars the impressive profits generated by their major investment in that country. As they would soon discover, that proved a woefully illusory hope. In the meantime, with GM's capital locked into Germany, its costly subsidiary remained a hostage of Hitler's regime.

Chapter 2 Opel and GM Adapt
to the Third Reich

After gaining power, Germany's new rulers strove through coercion, intimidation, and infiltration to bring all institutions and organizations into conformity with their ideology. Ruthlessly utilizing governmental authority and the violence unleashed by some of their fanatical followers, the Nazis swiftly imposed tyrannical rule on the country. Despite its American ownership, Opel did not escape the effects of the resulting pressures.

At Rüsselsheim, the Nazis quickly made their influence felt by capturing control of the factory council, the representative body established under the republic to give employees an institutionalized means of asserting their rights. Prior to the Third Reich, democratic socialists had predominated in Opel's council, while communists held a minority of the seats. But when a new council was elected in late March 1933, just after Hitler had consolidated his grip on power by extorting sweeping powers from the national parliament, Nazi candidates gained a narrow majority. The balloting was less than free; the socialists were subjected to harassment, and communist candidates were excluded altogether. But the resulting domination of the factory council gave Hitler's followers a foothold within Opel that they were quick to exploit in the interest of their party and the new regime.[1]

With Nazis now speaking in the name of Opel's employees, the American-led management broke with the German firm's nonpolitical traditions and acquiesced in the use of the Rüsselsheim factory for agitation on behalf of the new regime. This began on May 1, the government-proclaimed "Day of Labor" designed to preempt the traditional socialist demonstrations. That morning Opel's workers assembled in the plant's large central courtyard, some wearing Nazi uniforms, to hear the party member who had recently been installed as chairman of the factory council deliver a speech from a podium in front of a massive swastika banner. The following day the regime forcibly suppressed Germany's socialist trade unions, which had hitherto represented most organized workers. Six weeks later, Opel workers again gathered, this time to hear a speech by Jakob Sprenger, the regional party chieftain—Gauleiter—who had recently been appointed by Hitler as governor of the state of Hesse, where Rüsselsheim was located. Henceforth, such compulsory political assemblies became routine at the Opel plant. So did loudspeaker relays of Hitler's radio speeches to the assembled workers.[2]

Under pressure from the Nazis, other aspects of plant life at Opel were soon brought into line with the regime's ideology. The firm's annual series of evening lectures for employees, which had previously provided talks by experts about cultural and scientific topics of general interest, became a forum for political indoctrination. The employee library was purged of books regarded as politically unacceptable and stocked with new ones that reflected the party line. The monthly in-house company magazine, *Der Opel Geist* (The Opel Spirit), quickly adopted an affirmative stance toward the new regime. Beginning in 1934, Nazi labor officials participated directly in its editing. As a result, its pages abounded with praise for the regime and the dictator, who was accorded personal credit for the upturn in Opel's economic fortunes. In keeping with terminology favored by the new regime, the title of the magazine was twice altered, in 1934 to *Opel Werksgemeinschaft* (Opel Plant Community) and in 1936 to *Der Opel-Kamerad* (Opel Comrade). With each succeeding year, it became more intensely politicized, as did similar publications of other German firms, which agents of the regime also subjected to sustained surveillance.[3]

Although life at the Opel plant conformed in many respects to the "new spirit of the time," the company was less close to the Nazi regime during the first years of the Third Reich than appearances suggested. None of the German managerial staff had belonged to Hitler's party before it came to power. It was

Der führer,

der die deutfche Wirtfchaft im abgelaufenen Jahr aus tieffter Not rettete. Ihm wollen wir in der feften Zuverficht auf einen weiteren Aufftieg auch im kommenden Jahr treue Gefolgfchaft leiften.

Opel's in-house magazine quickly came under the influence of the Nazis, who gained a majority in the workers' council of the Rüsselsheim factory after Hitler came to power. Courtesy of Adam Opel AG.

difficult, however, for an automobile manufacturing firm to remain aloof from the National Socialist Motor Vehicle Corps, an auxiliary organization of the ruling party that promoted the products of the auto industry. Like other German auto firms, Opel became a patron of the Corps, which offered instruction in driver skills and vehicle maintenance through a nationwide network of units. Opel employees were encouraged to join the Corps' local unit, whose activities were featured in the company magazine. Trucks were loaned to the local unit and to an affiliated storm trooper (*Sturmabteilung* or SA) unit and, adorned with markings proclaiming them as Opel products, served as rolling advertisements. Opel also provided financial support for driving schools operated by the Corps. During the first year of the regime, some of the firm's German managerial staff became members of the Corps. Although that did not entail becoming a Nazi, the sales manager during the 1930s later claimed that his involvement in the Corps on behalf of Opel resulted in his eventual party membership.[4]

Hostility toward foreign-owned companies, fanned by Nazi propaganda in the hypernationalistic atmosphere of the Third Reich, posed an increasingly troublesome problem for the GM executives charged with responsibility for Opel. In response, they resorted to a strategy of what they privately referred to as "camouflage" designed to minimize the outward appearance of American control. In 1934 the Supervisory Board, which had previously consisted of seven Americans and two Germans, was reconstituted on a basis of parity, with four seats for each. Since only one of its American members was stationed at Opel and the others rarely, in most cases never, traveled from the United States to attend meetings, the German members constituted a de facto majority. Parity was also instituted in the Directorate that stood at the head of the firm's management, leaving Germans and Americans represented in equal numbers. In major departments within the firm, titular authority was assigned to Germans, although effective control remained with the GM men. Increasingly, the Americans withdrew from public roles, leaving day-to-day representation of the firm, including contacts with the government and the Nazi Party, to a German member of the Directorate, Rudolf Fleischer, who was also Opel's treasurer. By 1936 the exalted title of general director, which had previously been bestowed on the senior American executive at Opel, had dropped out of usage. As a consequence, it was no longer easy for outside observers to discern from the firm's corporate personnel whether Americans or Germans wielded ultimate authority. This "false façade," as one GM official described it, did not, however, deceive Nazi activists rankled by foreign ownership of Germany's biggest carmaker. In a speech to Opel employees at the Rüsselsheim plant, a local party official spoke caustically of the GM managers and predicted that the Americans would soon be gone, leaving the firm once again fully in German hands.[5]

With the rapid imposition of a one-party regime, relations with the Nazi officials who now controlled all governmental authority became a persistent problem for the GM executives charged with responsibility for Opel. They could rely for some help on the chairman of the Supervisory Board, Wilhelm von Opel, who was usually referred to as the *Geheimrat,* an honorific title bestowed upon him during the last stages of the Empire that collapsed at the end of the First World War. At age sixty-two, he joined the Nazi Party in the spring of 1933, along with other officers of the national association of automotive companies, in response to the measures taken by the new regime to promote the industry's interests. After the Second World War he would claim that he had consulted with GM executives at Opel before taking that step, but he provided no proof of that. The Americans raised no objections to his party membership, however, which was convenient under the circumstances. In his figurehead role as chairman of the Supervisory Board, the Geheimrat was repeatedly called upon to represent the firm on public occasions involving important Nazis. It was he who usually welcomed party and government officials when they visited the Rüsselsheim plant, and it was he who showed the company's new models to Hitler when the dictator inspected Opel's displays at the annual Berlin auto shows. On such occasions, the Nazi Party membership button on the Geheimrat's lapel undoubtedly counted as a plus.[6]

Because of Geheimrat von Opel's tardy entry into the party, there were limits to the political insulation he could provide for the company. Those Nazis who had joined the party before Hitler's acquisition of power, when it had been a struggling opposition movement, looked down upon such latecomers as untrustworthy opportunists seeking to horn in on the spoils of the victory won by the "old fighters." That was especially so when, as in the case of the Geheimrat, those latter-day members played no active role in the party. Nazi officials from humble origins also resented privileged members like the Geheimrat, who owed their prominence to their wealth and parentage. Such was the attitude of the most important Nazi in the region where Opel's Rüsselsheim plant was located, Gauleiter and Hessian state governor Jakob Sprenger. A former postal employee, he ruled over the regional government in dictatorial fashion, which put him in a position to cause the company difficulties whenever it needed official consent for such matters as building permits or authorization to purchase land. When such problems arose, Geheimrat von Opel was of little or no use

Geheimrat Wilhelm von Opel, son of the founder of the firm and
chairman of Opel's board under GM's ownership. Courtesy of Adam
Opel AG.

since Sprenger made no secret of his disdain for him, pointedly snubbing him
on visits to the Opel factory and otherwise shunning him.[7]

More valuable as political lightning rods in the Third Reich than latecomer
Nazis like the Geheimrat were "old fighters" whose early membership in the
party entitled them to wear a special golden party emblem in their lapels. Nazis
of that sort who had knowledge of the higher reaches of business were rare and
much sought after by German companies as political shields during the early
years of the Third Reich. In 1934 just such an individual was added to Opel's
Supervisory Board. He was Carl Lüer, a thirty-seven-year-old veteran of the
First World War with a doctorate from the University of Frankfurt and some
business experience. He had joined Hitler's party in 1927 at a low point in its
fortunes, presumably out of conviction but apparently without experiencing

Carl Lüer, Nazi "old fighter," was added to Opel's
board after Hitler came to power. Courtesy of Adam
Opel AG.

any of the hardship or sacrifice implied by the designation "old fighter." During
the following years, while employed by various banks and business firms as well
as serving as a teaching assistant at the University of Frankfurt, Lüer promoted
Nazi ideas about economic policy in lectures to party organizations and in articles in party publications. These activities brought him to the attention of
Gauleiter Sprenger, who became his patron and included him in a planning
staff that prepared the way for a Nazi takeover. Afterward, Lüer was installed by
the Gauleiter as president of the Frankfurt Chamber of Industry and Commerce following the Nazis' ouster of the officers elected during the republic.
Exploiting the considerable powers of that quasi-governmental body, Lüer participated during the regime's first year in a purge of Jews and opponents of
Nazism from commercial and industrial associations and even from some private companies. For these accomplishments, he was rewarded with a number of
prominent posts, including a university professorship for which he lacked the
normal academic credentials.[8]

Under interrogation by American investigators in 1947, Lüer recalled being approached with the offer of a seat on Opel's Supervisory Board by the firm's German treasurer, Rudolf Fleischer, and the American Graeme Howard of GM's overseas operations division. His comparative youth, undistinguished career, and lack of any experience with the automotive industry were, in their eyes, clearly outweighed by his political connections. As they had undoubtedly heard, possession of the golden lapel emblem reserved for "old fighters" could bestow political influence on even nondescript individuals. The extent to which GM's executives were aware of the unsavory nature of Lüer's activities on behalf of the Nazi regime remains unclear. In any event, no one seems to have raised objections to his appointment. As Cyrus Osborn, one of the Americans assigned to Opel, later put it, Lüer was "our point of contact with the Gauleiter." Eventually, however, he would come to play a far greater role.[9]

The addition of an "old fighter" to the board did not reflect endorsement of Nazi anti-Semitism by Opel. The firm gave way to that aspect of the ruling party's ideology only reluctantly and under pressure from the authorities. During the early years of the regime, to be sure, it was not always easy to establish the extent to which private companies had to comply with Nazi racist ideology in order to avoid trouble with the country's new rulers. Calls by various Nazi organizations for Germans to refuse to do business with Jews, for example, posed a dilemma for Opel since sales of cars to Jews were just as profitable as those to non-Jews. In hopes of clarifying the regime's position, the firm's treasurer, Rudolf Fleischer, took up the matter with Gauleiter Sprenger in the fall of 1935. Asked whether Opel should continue to sell cars to Jews, the Gauleiter replied that if a Jew was willing to pay for a car, the company should attempt to sell him two instead of merely one. Asked whether Opel should continue to service cars made by the firm that were owned by Jews, Sprenger replied that this obviously must be done. If any Opel dealers refused to meet the contractual obligations to service cars owned by Jews, Sprenger recommended firing them. He was himself prepared, the Gauleiter added, to take strong measures against any Nazis in his sphere of competence who attempted to interfere in such matters.[10]

As the Gauleiter left no doubt, the commercial success of one his region's largest industrial firms took precedence for him over a thoroughgoing application of Nazi anti-Semitism to the business sphere at a time when the regime was focused on reducing unemployment. Having secured his approval for sales and services to Jews in Hesse, Opel's management sought to stave off attempts by local Nazi organizations elsewhere in the country to wring from the firm's dealerships pledges to refrain from doing business with Jews. The surviving records make it impossible to determine the extent to which these efforts were successful. It is clear, on the other hand, that Opel's sales division sought to shield the company from anti-Semitic boycotts by instructing dealers to specify in their advertisements that the company was a German firm and that none of its stock was in Jewish hands.[11]

As Opel's management soon learned, the Nazis regarded selling to Jews, which yielded profit to the seller, as altogether different from buying from Jews, which profited the latter. From the earliest days of the regime, party members had to pledge not to patronize Jewish businesses and to encourage others to refrain as well. As a result, Opel dealerships that were owned by Jews soon became targets of hostility on the part of local Nazi organizations. Such was the case with the large and prosperous Jewish-owned dealership in nearby Frankfurt am Main, which served not only as the city's sole sales outlet for Opel vehicles but also as the distributorship for the surrounding region. Like all of the firm's dealerships, it was a separate, independently owned firm, in this case a corporation. In mid-1935 local Nazis demanded arrangements that would enable them to circumvent the Frankfurt dealership when purchasing Opel vehicles. They also complained that the Jewish owner, Viktor Haas, sought to conceal his continuing control by assigning 49 percent of the stock to his wife and transferring 51 percent to Fritz Opel. Throughout the ensuing year, this matter remained a source of friction between Opel's management and the Hessian Nazis. It was finally resolved in July 1936, when the firm gave way and informed the authorities that Haas had withdrawn from any participation in the dealership and sold all his remaining shares to the Opel brothers.[12]

After the Second World War, Haas, who had returned to Germany from exile in the United States, voluntarily submitted a statement to the denazification court handling the case of Adam Bangert, who as Opel's sales manager had joined the Nazi Auto Corps and then, in 1937, the party itself. Haas described Bangert as an old and loyal friend who had resisted Nazi efforts to deprive him of his dealership for as long as possible. He added that Bangert had done the same for other Jewish Opel dealers who were presumably also eventually forced out by the repeated waves of Nazi "Aryanization" that plundered the property of Jewish businessmen in the course of 1930s. But as Haas's own case reveals, Opel's management lacked the means to shield these victims from their persecutors.[13]

Like many others in Germany, Opel's executives initially underestimated the seriousness with which the Nazis took their anti-Semitism. This became apparent in June 1933, when the task of introducing Gauleiter Sprenger's first speech to the company's workers was assigned to a member of the Directorate who was of Jewish ancestry, Dr. Manfred Wronker-Flatow. Not surprisingly, the Gauleiter reacted angrily. In October, Wronker-Flatow, a Berlin lawyer who had risen rapidly at Opel after GM took over, was quietly removed from the Directorate. Not long thereafter, he was reassigned to GM's New York headquarters. Since Wronker-Flatow had been the only "non-Aryan" member of the Directorate, his departure made Opel's top management immune to Nazi racist objections. Several lower-level members of the German managerial staff remained at their posts, however, despite Jewish ancestry on their part or that of their wives. After the end of the Third Reich, they credited their German superiors with repeatedly fending off Nazi agitation for their removal, presumably with the knowledge of Opel's American executives. Perhaps revealingly, such deviations from the regime's racial policies went unmentioned in Opel's response in the summer of 1936 to a questionnaire in which a Nazi agency peremptorily demanded the identification, under oath, of employees as either "Aryan" or "non-Aryan." Wronker-Flatow's removal from the Directorate was, however, duly reported in the response.[14]

In view of the fact that the metalworking trades central to the manufacture of motor vehicles were not a common career choice for German Jews, it is not surprising that only one member of the Opel production workforce was Jewish. In response to a query in the Nazi questionnaire of 1936 about the number of non-Aryan employees, the firm's answer was "one member of the workforce with Mosaic religion in subordinate position," a formulation that avoided the racist terminology of the Nazis. The individual in question, who went unnamed in the questionnaire, was, from all indications, a thirty-five-year-old metallurgist named Willy Hofmann, who had been employed at the Rüsselsheim factory since 1930. Despite mounting Nazi efforts to purge Jews from the economy and despite Opel's having identified him as Jewish in the 1936 questionnaire, Hofmann remained in his job until the end of June 1938. At that point the personnel office, which GM's executives at Opel left to their German colleagues, dismissed him in compliance with Nazi demands. Jobless and without prospects of employment in Germany, Hofmann turned for help to Cyrus Osborn, Opel's chief American executive. Upon learning of his plight, Osborn urged him to apply for a job at GM's British subsidiary, Vauxhall Motors. In a letter to Vauxhall, Osborn explained the situation and gave a British colleague to understand that Hofmann was "quite a good lad." After delays occasioned by British immigration restrictions and Hofmann's month-long incarceration in a

Nazi concentration camp following the "crystal night" pogrom of November 1938, he, together with his wife and daughter, reached England in March 1939 to begin work at Vauxhall.[15]

For the "Aryan" workers at Opel, Nazi rule brought radical changes in the conditions of employment, just as it did at factories throughout Germany. Having abolished collective bargaining by crushing the independent trade unions, the new regime set about curtailing the gains organized labor had made under the republic. By law, employees now became "followers," obliged to render obedience to a plant leader (*Betriebsführer*), a new title initially assigned by Opel's management to the firm's German treasurer, Dr. Rudolf Fleischer. The assertive factory councils (*Betriebsräte*) of the republican period, which had been freely elected, were replaced by compliant, party-dominated bodies (*Vertrauensräte*). Candidates were nominated by Nazi organizations and, after concurrence by the plant leader, submitted to employees for ratification on a yes-or-no basis that effectively predetermined the outcome. A nationwide Nazi organization, the Labor Front, served as the official spokesman for workers and sought by a combination of manipulation, paternalism, and symbolic egalitarianism to keep labor appeased and to promote the regime's commitment to a classless society. A new codification of Opel's plant rules, which was put into effect in 1934, specified that all employees were required to join the Labor Front, but enforcement by the firm's management appears to have been lax.[16]

As a consequence of these developments and Opel's rapidly expanding production, which provided welcomed jobs for thousands of previously unemployed workers, labor-management relations caused no significant problems at the firm during the Third Reich, in sharp contrast to GM's protracted and often violent conflict with unions in the United States. An additional factor, to be sure, was knowledge on the part of the workers that the repressive power of the Nazi regime stood ready to intervene at the slightest hint of insubordination on the part of labor. This became evident in June 1936 when around 260 workers at the Rüsselsheim factory interrupted production on the chassis assembly line for about twenty minutes to go to the administrative offices to protest a reduction in their earnings as a consequence—it would later be determined—of a shortage of raw materials. Alarmed by the commotion caused by the protesters, a policeman who happened to be passing by the factory notified local party officials. They at once called in the dreaded secret police, the Gestapo, who conducted an exhaustive on-site investigation that same day. At the insistence of the Gestapo, all the workers involved in what was declared a violation of the regime's prohibition of strikes were summarily dismissed from their jobs by

Opel that evening. Among them were a sizable number of members of the Nazi Party and its storm trooper auxiliary, the SA. Seven of the workers, including two Nazi "old fighters," were placed under what was known in the Third Reich as protective arrest, a euphemism for indefinite incarceration without recourse to law.[17]

Besides penalizing the targeted workers and intimidating the rest, these reprisals by the Nazi authorities caused Opel's management considerable difficulties. The mass dismissals had a far more disruptive effect on production than had the brief incident itself. Since the German economy was approaching full employment, workers with the skills needed to fill the jobs of those dismissed were in very short supply in a tightening labor market, and the regime discouraged firms from raiding each other's skilled workforces. In order to fill the vacant posts, Opel had to hire on short notice more than two hundred inexperienced replacements and transfer to the chassis line workers from its bicycle division, thereby disrupting the production schedule there. In the course of the summer, permission was eventually secured from the authorities to rehire, with loss of seniority, most of those dismissed. But some three dozen who were suspected by the Gestapo of participating in a Marxist conspiracy remained banned. In August the firm suffered another setback as a result of what may have been retaliatory worker sabotage when some hundred and fifty motors were ruined by a mysterious nighttime building flood and another ten were disabled by removal of parts. Although the consequences of these incidents for Opel were in no way commensurate with those suffered by the workers involved, the company's management learned that it was not immune to the intrusion of arbitrary Nazi power.[18]

Hitler's regime made itself felt at Opel in still more insidious ways. After the installation of the Nazis in power, employees who belonged to the ruling party or sought its favor were enlisted as spies. They reported anti-Nazi slogans scrawled on walls within the factory and denounced anyone who expressed views critical of the regime or its leaders, often with severe consequences for those so targeted. This political scrutiny was heightened when, as a result of pressure from the local Nazi authorities, one Heinz Riller, who held officer rank in the Nazi SS elite corps, was appointed chief of the Rüsselsheim plant's security force in 1937. He soon established an elaborate internal espionage system that kept him informed of any behavior or remark that could be regarded as subversive. As numerous postwar testimonies reveal, Riller dealt ruthlessly with those who stepped or spoke out of line.[19]

No full record of Riller's activities at the Rüsselsheim plant has survived, but the case of Dr. Heinrich Hermann Koretzky, a white-collar employee at the plant's forge, provides a chilling example. In August 1937 Koretzky was suddenly arrested and consigned, without any judicial procedure, to a Gestapo prison in the city of Darmstadt, fifteen miles southeast of Rüsselsheim. As his sister recalled after the war, when she asked Riller for an explanation, he informed her that her brother had been overheard to state that it was "a shame that Göring had not been killed in the war." Riller further specified that Koretzky had declined to contribute to the Nazi Winter Help charity fund, refused to buy copies of an anti-Semitic magazine, and subscribed to—and read—foreign newspapers. When Koretzky's sister, who was not permitted to visit her brother, went to the Darmstadt prison the following week to take him some personal items, she was informed that he was dead, having hanged himself in his cell the previous night. When she requested help from a German manager at Opel in seeking information about her brother's death, he informed her that he could find no record of the case. An American GM engineer at the plant counseled her to be careful about what she said and warned her that he was powerless to protect her from the Gestapo.[20]

In addition to acquiescing to Nazi surveillance and intimidation of Opel's workers, the firm's management joined the rest of German industry in routinely paying financial tribute to the country's new rulers. That practice began during the first year of the Third Reich, when companies across the country found themselves besieged for contributions by a multiplicity of party organizations hungering for the spoils of victory. In an effort to escape this onslaught, which frequently verged on extortion, spokesmen of industry secured Hitler's approval in the spring of 1933 for establishment of a central collecting agency, the Adolf Hitler Fund, which would dispense the money raised to components of the party at the dictator's discretion. Originally conceived as a one-time expedient, the fund became a permanent feature of the regime, a kind of party tax that yielded more than fifty million marks a year by the latter half of the 1930s. A labor-intensive firm like Opel was required to contribute a sum equal to 0.03 percent of its yearly payroll, which with the rapid growth of the workforce mushroomed into a six-figure annual budgetary item by the mid-1930s.[21]

Other contributions by Opel to Nazi causes were, like the Adolf Hitler Fund, less than voluntary. Sizable payments were made each year to the annual Winter Help charity. Established during the regime's early stages to provide help during the winter months for the millions left jobless by the Depression, Winter Help, like the fund, became in effect a permanent levy, despite the sharp decline of unemployment. Nor did the Hitler Fund prove an effective shield from additional solicitations by party organs. By the late 1930s lower-echelon party units were increasingly ignoring the fund's claim to exclusive solicitation rights, so that Opel was subjected to additional requests for contributions. Appeals from local party authorities capable of causing troublesome difficulties for the firm amounted to veiled extortion, and the firm's responses suggest a policy of limiting expenditures in such instances to a minimum regarded as sufficient to avoid arousing the ire of the requestors. Asked in 1939 to pay 150,000 marks toward the cost of a new building for Gauleiter Sprenger's headquarters in Frankfurt, Opel's Supervisory Board approved a donation of half that amount. As a prominent and wealthy party member, Geheimrat Wilhelm von Opel was also frequently called upon to reach into his own pocket in response to solicitations on behalf of various party organizations.[22]

Like other German companies, Opel sought, whenever possible, to derive commercial advantage by associating its products with the rulers of what was, during the peacetime years, an increasingly successful and popular Nazi regime. This was particularly the case with the car industry as a consequence of Hitler's well-known enthusiasm for the automobile. On the occasion of the dictator's birthday in April 1938, Opel presented him with a gleaming new model of its top-of-the-line limousine, the six-cylinder Admiral. With much fanfare and less than complete accuracy, it was proclaimed vehicle number 500,000 to roll off the assembly line since the beginning of the regime. But neither that gesture nor the gifts and loans of cars to various Nazi organization by Opel's sales division succeeded in shaking the preference of Hitler and other Nazi grandees for the products of the Daimler-Benz Corporation. Abundant newsreel footage and widely distributed photographs of the dictator and other Nazis riding in Mercedes-Benz limousines amounted to massive free advertising, which identified that firm with the country's rulers and contributed significantly to its rapid growth during the 1930s. Opel could at best strive for some secondary exposure. At the annual Nazi Party congresses, which were accorded extensive pictorial publicity by the regime, the company's sales division had to content itself with loaning cars for use by foreign diplomats and other guests, while Hitler and his henchmen were repeatedly photographed and filmed in large, lavishly appointed convertible limousines supplied by Daimler-Benz. Less expensive Opel vehicles nevertheless proved attractive among subaltern and auxiliary units of the party. During the years 1933 to 1938 those units reportedly purchased more than three thousand of the firm's cars and trucks.[23]

Some of Opel's retained earnings that were invested within Germany during the latter half of the 1930s reflect deference to the holders of political power. To a large extent, that was involuntary. Like other German firms, the company extended what amounted to credit to the government by accepting in lieu of payment for cars and trucks certificates redeemable against future taxes. Because Nazi law required that corporate dividends in excess of 6 percent be invested in nonnegotiable Reich bonds yielding a rate of interest considerably below the prevailing market rate, appreciable sums had to be loaned to the government on these terms after Opel's dividends were raised to 8 percent beginning in 1938. A portion of the undistributed profits was also invested in bonds of the Reich and in the Nazi-sponsored Hermann Göring Works, which was intended to free Germany from dependency on imported iron ore by producing steel from low-grade domestic ores. The regime left no doubt that industrial firms were expected to provide the capital needed to launch that huge undertaking, and refusal to do so, particularly by a foreign-owned company, risked incurring the disfavor of those who wielded political power. In a report to GM, the American manager of Opel explained that bonds of the Reich and the Göring Works had been "purchased as a result of direct pressure by the Government on all industry."[24]

In seeking to adapt to the Nazi regime, the Americans in charge of Opel reflected the outlook of GM's senior executive, Alfred P. Sloan. Writing to a shareholder, he explained his views about how an international business should conduct itself abroad:

> Now I believe that if an international business such as General Motors engages in the commercial activity of any country with the idea of making a profit . . . it has an obligation to that country, both in an economic sense as well perhaps as in a social sense. It should attempt to attune itself to the general business of the community; make itself a part of the same; conduct its operations in relation to the customs, and design its products so as to meet the needs and viewpoint of each community, so far as it can. I believe further, that that should be its position, even if, as is likely to happen and particularly as was the case during the past few years, the management of the Corporation might not wholly agree with many things that are done in certain of these countries. In other words, to put the proposition rather bluntly, such matters should not be considered the business of the management of General Motors. . . .
>
> . . . an international business operating throughout the world, should conduct its operations in strictly business terms, without regard to the political beliefs of its management, or the political beliefs of the countries in which it is operating.[25]

Sloan appended an important qualification to this statement of principles. An American company engaged in business abroad should, he wrote, "govern its operations, wherever they may be, in accordance with the foreign policy of the United States." Throughout the 1930s, however, the hesitant and ambiguous reactions of the American government to the Third Reich provided GM's executives with little or no guidance applicable to their management of Opel or their relations with the Nazi authorities. Indeed, it is questionable whether one can speak of a coherent U.S. policy toward Germany until well after the war began in Europe. Among American diplomats and policy makers, a widespread belief that unjust treatment of Germany after the First World War was the source of European instability vied with revulsion at the methods of Nazi rule, giving rise to ambivalent responses to Hitler's early challenges to the status quo. Within the senior ranks of the State Department a deep division developed between those diplomats who believed that Hitler could be appeased by economic concessions and those who held that nothing short of force could deter him from an attempt to dominate Europe, if not the world. In any event, as no one was more aware than President Roosevelt, the ascendancy of isolationist sentiment at home precluded vigorous or sustained American political involvement in European affairs.[26]

The only sphere in which Nazi practices collided directly with American foreign policy was the regulation of trade. In hopes of resuscitating international commerce, the Roosevelt administration strove to surmount the protectionist barriers that had been erected around the world in response to the Depression by promoting what was called "the open door" through insistence upon multilateral, most-favored-nation trade principles. That effort by the Americans encountered stiff resistance from the German government, which insisted on bilateral balancing agreements designed to enable the Nazi regime to exercise control in order to contain a mounting negative balance of trade and channel foreign exchange generated by German exports into the purchase of imported goods approved of by the regime. An impasse therefore developed between the two governments. But rather than jeopardize the economic benefits to the American economy generated by ongoing trade with Germany, the State Department—which opposed government intervention in foreign commerce— refrained from objecting when American firms complied with Berlin's restrictive trade rules. State Department officials privately expressed disapproval in 1934 when the head of GM's overseas division, James D. Mooney, expressed a readiness to enter into bilateral barter deals with Germany, but no official objections were registered against the expedients employed by GM in the management of Opel. Neither the use of dollars to pay for the importation of rubber into Germany to supply tires for Opel vehicles nor the American corporation's resort to barter arrangements in an effort to recoup those dollars drew a rebuke from Washington. Even when Opel was later pressed into the production of armaments for the German military after the outbreak of the war in Europe, the American government took no action.[27]

One of the GM executives assigned the task of dealing with the problems of doing business in the Third Reich was Graeme Howard, general manager of the corporation's overseas operations. Unlike his colleagues, he took a special interest in Germany, having attended schools in Berlin and Heidelberg while his father, a professor at Stanford University, spent time at universities there. Although Howard's office was located in New York, he visited Rüsselsheim from time to time and kept an eye on developments there. In the spring of 1936 he warned his superiors that "it would be extremely short-sighted to offend or reap the ill will of the German government" in view of the fact that GM's large investment in Opel was locked into Germany "in the form of bricks, mortar, equipment, working capital, personnel and good will." Seeking to reassure his superiors about political conditions in that country, Howard then posed what he characterized as a "fantastic analogy":

> Assume that the United States had been defeated in a long, costly war, that Japanese, Mexican and Canadian troops had occupied a fifth of her territory, that Americans had gone through a wild, tragic period of currency inflation, that huge indemnities had siphoned out invaluable working capital, that the country was at the eleventh hour of turning to communism, that morally, financially and economically the nation approached bankruptcy—and that at that moment a Leader, a Theodore Roosevelt, a Wilson, or a Lincoln arose, who fired the imagination of the people by his sincerity, forcefulness and effectiveness; that this Leader reduced unemployment from six million to two million, brought back general prosperity and, but above all, brought back America's self respect and pride as a nation.

As a result of the Third Reich's achievements, Howard assured his colleagues, "Germany to a man and woman is behind Hitler and his objectives of equality and peace."[28]

Although Howard's analogy was indeed fantastic and revealed little awareness of the effects of Hitler's rule on German life, his positive assessment of its record was by no means exceptional at the time. Numerous citizens of other countries who subscribed to democracy at home found much to admire—particularly from afar—in the Germany of 1936. By many measures, Hitler seemed the most successful ruler of the day, and from all indications his regime enjoyed broad, if by no means unanimous, support among the German public. Whereas the Western democracies were still plagued by depression and chronic joblessness, Hitler had presided over a remarkably swift economic recovery that was well on the way to achieving full employment. Without recourse to arms, he had successfully defied the victors of the First World War by renouncing, in 1935, the disarmament they had imposed on Germany and by sending German troops into the demilitarized Rhineland shortly before Howard committed his views to paper. No aggression against other countries seemed at hand, and no ruler in Europe pledged himself publicly more often—or more cynically—to preservation of peace than Adolf Hitler. With Germany hosting the Olympic games and cultivating international respectability, his regime was on its best behavior in 1936, so that persecution of political foes and Jews was temporarily soft-pedaled. In short, the brutal, criminal face of Nazism had not yet fully revealed itself when Graeme Howard penned his positive assessment. Not long thereafter, Howard would come, as a consequence of subsequent developments and trying personal experiences, to deplore the lawlessness of the Nazi regime and its persecution of Germany's Jews.[29]

By 1936, after three years of Nazi rule, Opel and the GM executives in charge of it had undergone a far-reaching adaptation to the Third Reich. Faced with a ruthless regime and a company workforce the Nazis had brought under their control, the Americans responsible for the firm had acquiesced in the politicization of factory life and intimidation of their employees. To cope with the xenophobia promoted by the regime, they had withdrawn into the background and sought to conceal the firm's foreign ownership. As political insurance, they had bestowed a prominent post on a Nazi with strong party credentials. They had bowed to pressure to remove Jews from Opel's payroll, although where possible they arranged employment at GM operations elsewhere for such victims of Nazi racism. They had authorized the less-than-voluntary financial contributions and loans that the wielders of dictatorial political power routinely extorted from German firms. Although they had been unable to find a satisfactory solution to the currency controls that kept GM from fully reaping the gains generated by Opel, they had thus far successfully protected the American corporation's ownership and sustained the profitable conduct of business by its subsidiary. They would soon learn, however, that adaptation did not guarantee protection against those who wielded power in a totalitarian dictatorship.

Chapter 3 GM Fumbles the Volkswagen, Gains a Truck Factory, Identifies Foes and Friends

In a speech at the Berlin auto show in March 1934 Hitler called for the development of a small car so inexpensive to purchase and operate that millions of Germans with modest means could afford to own one. His proposal, quickly labeled "Volkswagen" by the press, eventually led to a vehicle of revolutionary design that would in fact make car ownership possible for multitudes, and not merely in Germany. That would be achieved, however, only well after the end of Hitler's catastrophic regime. At the time he launched the Second World War, the Volkswagen project had yet to produce a single car for the civilian market, and its factory was quickly enlisted for military production. Nevertheless, the prospect of easy access to car ownership contributed to the popularity of the Third Reich at home. For the GM executives at Opel and their counterparts at other German automotive firms the issues raised by Hitler's endorsement of a car for the masses proved both enticing and problematic.[1]

Opel had much to lose or gain from Hitler's proposal. Since the 1920s the firm had invested heavily in the development of small cars, and in 1934 it offered the cheapest models available in Germany. If a more inexpensive car made by a competitor with government endorsement should capture that sector of the market, Opel stood to sustain significant losses. On the other hand, the firm seemed in a strong position to take advantage of Hitler's proposal. As Germany's largest carmaker, equipped with the latest American assembly-line technology, Opel expected to be able to lower the cost of its smallest car still further through engineering refinements. If that car could gain official recognition as the Volkswagen, additional price reductions would be made possible by economies of scale resulting from high-volume sales.

Hitler himself gave Opel grounds for optimism by visiting the company's stand at the 1934 auto show, where its smallest model was on display at the low price of 1,990 marks. A two-door, four-passenger miniature sedan of conventional boxlike body lines, it had a four-cylinder motor generating eighteen horsepower. Hitler made no public statement about the car, but the Nazi Party newspaper published a photograph of him scrutinizing the display model with a caption indicating that he had shown particular interest in the "Opel-Volkswagen." According to the accompanying article, whereas several small cars made by other firms displayed features pointing the way to a Volkswagen of the future, Opel's smallest model already incorporated many of the essential requirements, including exceptional reliability. By summer, the view that Hitler favored Opel for his pet project was being voiced in leading German automotive circles.[2]

These encouraging signs did not escape the attention of James Mooney, the head of GM's overseas operations. In hopes of gaining government endorsement of Opel's small car as the Volkswagen, he requested a meeting with Hitler. The German Foreign Ministry advised the chancellor not to receive Mooney, lest the American press for guarantees that Opel would not be nationalized. Nevertheless, Hitler, who seldom passed up opportunities to speak with automotive experts, made himself available. On May 2, 1934, Mooney, accompanied by the chief GM executive at Opel, R. K. Evans, and the firm's treasurer, Rudolf Fleischer, met with Hitler at the Reich Chancellery in Berlin. Also present were Hitler's commissioner for economic questions, Wilhelm Keppler, and future foreign minister Joachim von Ribbentrop, then head of the Nazi Party's foreign affairs branch.[3]

Mooney later recounted that before leaving his hotel for the Chancellery he had practiced raising his right arm in the Nazi salute before a mirror and then delivered it upon entering Hitler's office, only to find the dictator emerge from behind his desk to shake hands in relaxed fashion. In the course of the ensuing conversation, he and his colleagues found Hitler avidly interested in automotive developments. What had been scheduled as a fifteen-minute meeting

Der Führer im Gespräch mit Geheimrat Dr.-Ing. e. h. Wilhelm von Opel auf dem Opel-stand der Automobil-Ausstellung 1937

Hitler, who regularly visited the Opel displays at the annual Berlin auto shows, in conversation with Wilhelm von Opel in 1937. Courtesy of Adam Opel AG.

lasted an hour and a half, as Hitler deluged his visitors with questions. In an effort to win his endorsement of their small car as the Volkswagen, they offered the dictator a proposition. Opel would be prepared, they informed him, to lower the price of that vehicle to 1,400 marks, a level previously regarded as inconceivable. That could be achieved, they stated, if sales of at least 100,000 cars could be guaranteed, if dealers' commissions were limited to 15 percent, and if there were no increase in the price of the necessary materials and components.[4]

Mooney came away from this encounter with Hitler very optimistic about gaining his endorsement for Opel's small car. The June issue of GM's overseas operations magazine gave prominent display to an article about the meeting obviously inspired by him. The chancellor had proved, it stated, "as easy and satisfactory to talk to as any intelligent business man, with no air of bureaucracy about him." In the course of their conversation, he had shown "a remarkable grasp of the fundamentals of the industry and a keen desire to know more." Most important from the standpoint of GM, Hitler was reported in the article to have characterized Opel's smallest model "as his conception of the true 'Volkswagen,' the car for the German masses, the goal which he had expressed at automobile shows and elsewhere." The day after the meeting, the article continued, Opel's Rudolf Fleischer was summoned back to the Chancellery by Keppler, who gave him a list of additional questions at Hitler's request. Later, Mooney would recall spending most of that day at his Berlin hotel, preparing written responses to Hitler's questions. But despite these encouraging developments, GM's hopes of capturing the Volkswagen project for Opel were soon dampened. Hitler failed to respond to the Opel proposal, even after Mooney sent him an effusive letter of thanks for their meeting. The dictator's silence apparently aroused fears that the GM magazine article had gone too far, and the management in Rüsselsheim ordered the destruction of all copies that had reached Germany.[5]

Meanwhile, Opel's competitors were taking steps of their own in response to Hitler's call for a small, inexpensive car. The prospect of losing a potentially large portion of the car market to a low-priced vehicle mass-produced with government backing greatly alarmed the other auto companies. To some of the auto executives, Opel seemed the most likely beneficiary because of its size and advanced assembly-line production. But they also feared the alternative of a government-controlled enterprise dedicated solely to producing a Volkswagen. They therefore embarked upon a strategy designed to head off both these possibilities by collaborating to capture the Volkswagen project for the automotive industry as a whole. To that end, the manufacturers' Automotive Association allocated half a million marks to commission a little-known engineer named Ferdinand Porsche to explore for six months the feasibility of a small, inexpensive car of the sort proposed by the dictator. Most auto executives remained skeptical about the possibility of ever producing a car costing anything approaching the thousand-mark price figure that had quickly become linked with the idea of a Volkswagen. If Porsche's project failed, they hoped that would be the end of the matter. But if he arrived at promising results they wanted to be in a position to share in the manufacture of any new vehicle he developed. Hopelessly outnumbered, Opel's representatives in the Automotive Association reluctantly joined in supporting what the chief GM executive at Rüsselsheim privately referred to as "this piece of monkey business." But, like Auto-Union, the other major manufacturer of small cars, Opel remained skeptical about Porsche's chances of success and served notice of its intention to proceed with independent efforts to produce a Volkswagen of the sort Hitler envisioned.[6]

Despite these setbacks, Opel soon received what its managers took to be an authoritative offer of sole rights to the Volkswagen project. When Hitler first heard of Porsche's plans for a small car in October 1934, his initial reaction was negative, primarily because of the unorthodox placement of the engine in the rear of the vehicle, which he dismissed as unsafe. Accordingly, his adviser Wilhelm Keppler, who had maintained contact with Opel after Mooney's meeting with Hitler, informed the company in November that the government had no interest or confidence in the Automotive Association's joint undertaking with Porsche. Only Opel, Keppler gave the firm's management to understand, was considered "capable of undertaking and carrying out the work which the Chancellor desires done." To that end, Keppler proposed that Opel establish a new factory devoted to the production of the kind of small, inexpensive car Hitler wanted. He made this proposal contingent, however, on a major proviso. In line with the government's wishes to situate as many important manufacturing firms as possible beyond the reach of enemy bombers in the event of war, Opel would have to build its new factory several hundred miles to the east of the company's Rüsselsheim plant. To facilitate this, Keppler held out a number of inducements, including generous tax write-offs for investments in new equipment and exemption from regulations restricting manufacturers of finished goods from producing the components they needed rather than buying them from suppliers. When Opel's spokesmen pointed out the impractical aspects of establishing a new plant at such a distance from the company's base, Keppler warned that if the firm did not accept the proposal, "somebody else would be instructed to undertake the project."[7]

Apprised of Keppler's offer, Mooney pledged GM's cooperation in a telegram sent from New York in mid-December to the chief American executive at Opel. He added, however, a suggestion that may well have eventually cost Opel the Volkswagen project and that would launch the company on a very different endeavor with major effects on its future. The best place to build a Volkswagen was, he observed, the Rüsselsheim factory "due to natural advantages and grooved-in organization." He therefore suggested freeing up space there for that undertaking by transferring the manufacture of larger cars and trucks to the new factory in central Germany proposed by Keppler. Informed of Mooney's suggestion, Keppler responded that it met with approval in official circles in the capital. Urging prompt adaptation of the Rüsselsheim plant for development of a Volkswagen, he indicated that there were no objections to the site proposed by Opel for a new factory for truck and large car production, the small city of Brandenburg, thirty-seven miles west of Berlin. Before proceeding further, Opel asked for endorsement by Hitler himself. After several suspenseful weeks Keppler reported at the end of January that the Führer had approved the establishment of a new factory at Brandenburg and its use for truck production. Keppler included no assurance of support by Hitler for development of a Volkswagen by Opel, but he stated that the dictator cautioned against proceeding hastily with the company's small-car project and urged thorough study and preparation.[8]

With this apparent encouragement from the highest political quarter, Opel's bid for the Volkswagen seemed well on the way to success in early 1935. By that time, it was becoming clear that Porsche had encountered serious practical difficulties with his project and would not be able to meet the spring deadline the Automotive Association had set for completion of his design. Skepticism about his prospects for designing a suitable vehicle had been widespread in the industry from the outset and was on the increase because of his slow progress. With the path seemingly clear, Opel intensified its efforts to improve its smallest model and reduce its price to the level of 1,400 marks proposed to Hitler the previous year. Development of an improved version, designated as the P-4, was pushed ahead at he Rüsselsheim factory. It provided twenty-three horsepower with low fuel consumption and low exposure to the registration tax based on the size of cylinder displacement. But although some body modifications were made, the P-4 essentially retained the conventional lines of the older model. In November 1935 it was introduced at the record low price of 1,650 marks, which made it by far the cheapest German car.[9]

As GM and Opel soon learned, there could be no reliance on Adolf Hitler's

James D. Mooney and Wilhelm von Opel with the Opel P-4, the small car GM hoped would gain Hitler's endorsement as the Volkswagen. Courtesy of GM Media Archive.

word. Unbeknownst to them, Porsche, who sought to escape dependence on the Automotive Association and establish a factory to manufacture a Volkswagen of his own design, had managed to gain the dictator's attention and was well on the way to winning his backing. In February 1935 Hitler used what had become his annual speech to the Berlin auto show to proclaim that preliminary designs for a German Volkswagen had been completed by an unnamed "designer genius." He added that the first models would be ready for testing by the second half of the year. As he did so often, Hitler exaggerated wildly. Far from achieving a workable design, Porsche continued to fall behind the schedule he had agreed to in his contract with the Automotive Association. Hitler's words were nevertheless taken as an endorsement of the designer's project, which enabled him to obtain renewed financial support from the association by claiming that the government would finance the continuation of his project if his contract was not renewed. In August, the leaders of the association agreed to protect Porsche's project by withholding information about his designs from Opel.[10]

In spite of these discouraging developments, Opel's executives continued to view Porsche's project as impractical and sought to convince the other auto manufacturers to withdraw their financial support. At a meeting of the Automotive Association's committee on the Volkswagen in February 1936, Opel's representative, Rudolf Fleischer, argued that innovative design alone would not suffice to achieve a Volkswagen and that Porsche was not equal to the task. Production of a car that could be marketed at the targeted price could be achieved, he insisted, only by an established, experienced auto manufacturer, not by an experimental laboratory like Porsche's. Calling for reliance on the market to resolve the matter, Fleischer left no doubt that Opel still considered itself a contender. But partly out of deference to the apparent wishes of the dictator and partly out of fear that the Volkswagen project would fall into Opel's hand if Porsche failed, the other companies continued their support of the designer's laboratory. Despite this setback and complaints by Porsche, Opel pressed ahead with efforts to preempt the small-car market by lowering the price of its P-4 model.[11]

Porsche would, of course, eventually win out in the competition for the Volkswagen. The key to his success lay in gaining sustained personal access to Hitler. As he repeatedly demonstrated, the designer had no qualms about making exaggerated claims and allowing the dictator to indulge in unrealistic fantasies. He also turned to his advantage Hitler's mistrust of the established auto firms, which the dictator held responsible for Germany's laggard motorization. Most important, he stirred Hitler's fancy with his design for a radically different vehicle with swooping, aerodynamic body lines and a compact air-cooled rear engine. By comparison, Opel's P-4, with its conventional design and boxy body, seemed hopelessly antiquated. After seeing one of Porsche's experimental models, Hitler claimed credit for the Volkswagen project sponsored by the Automotive Association in his speech at the February 1936 Berlin auto show. When he praised "the genius of the designer in charge of it," there was no longer any doubt about who was meant. The dictator seemed, however, to leave open the question of who would make the Volkswagen when he referred in his speech to "the eventual producers."[12]

Criticism by Porsche's financial patrons in the Automotive Association of his conduct in executing his project served only to confirm Hitler's mistrust of the industry and heighten his admiration for the pioneering designer. After observing test-drives of two of Porsche's cars in July 1936, he assured the designer of his full support. In typically grandiose fashion, Hitler envisioned construction within nine months of a huge factory headed by Porsche that would be able to produce Volkswagens by the time of the 1938 auto show. He projected its productive capacity at 100,000 cars a year but saw output eventually rising to 300,000 annually. Ignoring economic realities, Hitler convinced himself that the price of the car designed by Porsche could be held to 990 marks, a point on which no one dared contradict him. This would require, he estimated, an investment of 80 to 90 million marks, whose source he neglected to specify. He spoke vaguely of the possibility of a publicly financed enterprise and also of providing funds of his own to enable Porsche to accelerate his experiments more rapidly than was possible on the limited budget set by the Automotive Association. Hitler also let it be known that the Volkswagen was to be a "purely national matter" in which "factories oriented to America" should play no role. When the leaders of the Automotive Association heard of Hitler's wishes, they excluded Opel from their meeting of July 1936, at which the organization, bowing to Hitler's wishes, renewed its financial support of Porsche.[13]

Although no official endorsement of Porsche's project followed, reports during the summer of 1936 of Hitler's growing enthusiasm for it delivered a crushing blow to Opel's Volkswagen hopes. That turn of events was particularly distressing, coming as it did just as the company announced it would lower the price of its P-4 model to 1,450 marks as of September, a level only 50 marks more than the figure proposed to Hitler two years earlier. In hopes of eliciting a sympathetic hearing for Opel's small car, Mooney sought another meeting with the dictator. But when he arrived in Berlin late in September, accompanied by his aide Graeme Howard, Edwin K. Palmer, the senior GM executive at Opel, and Rudolf Fleischer, he was informed that Hitler was elsewhere and unavailable. Mooney and his colleagues had to settle instead for a meeting with Keppler, who grew evasive when the subject of the Volkswagen was broached after discussion of other matters. Opel's management then set forth its case for the P-4 in a memorandum for Hitler, which Fleischer personally attempted to deliver to the Reich Chancellery in Berlin. When he was informed that Hitler was at his alpine retreat in Bavaria, Fleischer traveled there and submitted the memorandum to the chief Chancellery aide. About three weeks later the aide returned it with a noncommittal message to the effect that Hitler had taken note of it with great interest.[14]

As Opel's executives discovered, the Volkswagen had become a hypersensitive issue in the German capital as a result of Hitler's involvement. Although the dictator repeatedly expressed boundless enthusiasm for Porsche's design, he took no steps to effect the ambitious measures he had sketched out during the summer of 1936. Without an official commitment on his part, no one in the government was willing to do anything about it. The resulting lack of clarity about the Volkswagen issue frustrated the management of Opel and the GM executives in charge of the firm. In private, high-level officials in Berlin doubted the soundness of Porsche's plans, and the minister of transportation on one occasion publicly expressed the view that Opel was best suited to produce a Volkswagen quickly at the lowest possible price. But no one in the government would discuss the matter with Opel's representatives in economic terms on the grounds that it had become a "purely political issue." Unless access could be gained to the dictator, GM's men at Rüsselsheim concluded that Opel was effectively shut out of whatever future the Volkswagen might have.[15]

Only after many behind-the-scenes maneuvers in the murky realms of high-level Nazi politics would the issue of who was to build the Volkswagen be settled in Porsche's favor. He eventually achieved his goal by forging an alliance with the powerful Nazi Labor Front that enabled him to escape his financial dependence on the Automotive Association and obtain the capital needed to launch construction of a huge factory dedicated to production of a Volkswagen of his design. By late 1938, when only prototypes existed, eager would-be car owners began making advance installment-plan payments against a price of 990 marks for a vehicle initially designated as the "strength-through-joy" car to echo a slogan of the Labor Front. Before any models were delivered, however, the factory was converted to war production.[16]

Despite Porsche's successes, Opel's management continued for a time to nurse diminishing hopes that the designer might eventually fail to produce a practicable car cheaper than the P-4 or that Opel might be called upon to mass-produce a car designed by him. After an initially promising market performance, however, sales of the P-4 sagged sharply during 1937. Moreover, the car's rock-bottom price of 1,450 marks made it unprofitable in the absence of the hoped-for high sales volume that would have resulted from its official recognition as the Volkswagen. Continuation of the P-4 also hampered production and sales of a newer, somewhat larger, more stylish sedan, the Opel Kadett. It was introduced in late 1936 at the more profitable price of 2,100 marks in response to improving economic conditions and would become Germany's best-selling car of its class by 1938. In May 1937 Opel's Volkswagen hopes suffered yet another setback when the company's German production manager resigned to join Porsche's staff. The recruitment by Porsche of some two dozen skilled Opel employees followed. In the fall of 1937, after consultation with GM chairman Sloan, the corporation's men at Opel finally laid to rest the company's bid for the Volkswagen by discontinuing the P-4.[17]

Any chance Opel had to capture the Volkswagen project was probably lost early on, when Mooney suggested that the new factory in central Germany proposed by Keppler in late 1934 for production of a small, inexpensive car be

Introduced in 1936, the Kadett replaced the P-4 as Opel's low-price car and quickly became a market success. Courtesy of GM Media Archive.

used instead to make trucks. Had Opel obtained official authorization at that point to announce publicly the construction of large new factory dedicated to realization of a Volkswagen, that might conceivably have doomed Porsche's prospects by leading the Automotive Association to withdraw its financial support from his fledgling venture. Success would have by no means been certain, however, even if Keppler's consent for such an announcement could have been obtained. In the Third Reich, governmental decisions turned on the whims of a dictator for whom the doublecross was standard procedure.[18]

Although GM and Opel failed in their bid for the Volkswagen, the new factory at Brandenburg proved a considerable consolation prize. Construction of the buildings, financed in part by a ten-million-mark credit from a consortium of German banks, was launched in the spring of 1935 and completed on a crash basis by the end of August. Mooney's idea of producing large cars there was abandoned, and Opel's entire truck assembly line, its machines and workmen, were transferred to Brandenburg that autumn. In early January 1936 the first truck, a model that since 1931 bore the designation "Blitz"—originally coined for Opel bicycles—rolled off the assembly line. The results quickly exceeded all expectations. Sales of trucks nearly doubled in 1936 over the previous year, when production had taken place at Rüsselsheim. Opel's share of domestic truck sales rose from less than a third in 1934 to close to 40 percent by 1937.

During those years passenger car output at Rüsselsheim also increased substantially but at a slower rate, and when demand for cars temporarily flagged, steadily rising sales of the trucks made at Brandenburg sustained the firm's profits. The addition of the new plant swelled the company's workforce from around seventeen thousand in 1934–35 to almost twenty-seven thousand by 1938.[19]

Opel's burgeoning truck sales were spurred in part by the crash German rearmament program launched after Hitler renounced the disarmament clauses of the Versailles Treaty in March 1935. Even before then, cordial relations had developed between Opel's management and the army. Concerned about the vulnerability of factories in western Germany to aerial attack, the officers in charge of procurement had immediately seen military advantage in Mooney's proposal to devote the projected new plant in central Germany to the truck production that was their primary interest rather than to a Volkswagen. At a meeting in Berlin in January 1935 with representatives of Opel, they enthusiastically endorsed that option. The following month, they offered assurances that establishment of a truck factory in Brandenburg would "automatically bring about a more active business connection" with the army procurement office, even though they were not at that time in a position to make any specific guarantees. That prediction was swiftly borne out once the new factory began operations in 1936, as orders for trucks, many fitted out to military specifications as personnel carriers, mounted. No complete record of transactions with the military is available, but internal Opel working documents indicate that nearly 17 percent of Blitz trucks were sold to the army in 1937 and 29 percent in 1938, when those sales came to over six thousand. Even before the war began, the army had become by far the biggest customer for Opel's Blitz trucks.[20]

Since military contracts were not subject to competitive bidding during the Third Reich and often required numerous costly modifications of standard designs, truck sales to the army proved financially very advantageous for Opel. According to a 1938 company analysis, the profits per unit exceeded those from civilian sales by more than 40 percent. Selling to the military authorities had drawbacks, however, as they could prove to be imperiously demanding customers. Their insistence that absolute priority be accorded to military orders was sometimes difficult to reconcile with orderly manufacturing procedures. In 1937 Opel had to disrupt its carefully scheduled truck assembly line and invest several million marks of its reserves in order to comply with the army's demand that the company accelerate development of a special four-wheel-drive model.[21]

Opel's new truck factory in Brandenburg, opened in 1936, was a by-product of the company's unsuccessful bid for the Volkswagen project. Courtesy of Adam Opel AG.

Opel's three-ton Blitz truck, made in large numbers at the Brandenburg factory, became a favorite of the German army during World War II. Courtesy of Adam Opel AG.

General Motors and Opel had no realistic alternative to accepting orders from the German army for its vehicles. Refusal by a foreign-owned company to fill military orders for its products would have occasioned difficulties in any country, but in the Third Reich the consequences would have been especially dire for Opel. By the time the Brandenburg factory began operations, the Nazi regime had wrapped the country's economy in a tight web of controls that gave the government the power of life and death over manufacturers. Hitler's implementation in late 1936 of a four-year plan designed to gear the economy for war created a huge, all-pervasive bureaucratic apparatus assigned the task of reducing Germany's dependence on imports and channeling strategic materials into rearmament. As a result, in order to purchase steel and other essential materials, either for vehicle production or plant expansion, Opel had to secure permission from agencies and boards established by the four-year-plan administration to control their allocation. The authorities thus commanded virtually unlimited means for crippling retaliation against any firm that offended them.

The vulnerability of Opel to government pressure had became abundantly clear in late 1936 when the authorities in Berlin withdrew permission to use marks to purchase imported rubber needed for tires. Faced with the prospect of seeing their two factories idled and warned that the government "would know how to appraise the company's patriotic attitude," GM's men concluded that they were dealing with "a veiled threat of confiscation" and swiftly capitulated, turning to GM for dollars to cover rubber purchases. When the Nazi boom gave rise to near full employment in the latter half of the 1930s, even labor came under government control, so that henceforth additional skilled workers could be recruited only with official permission. If needed elsewhere for strategically important production, Opel's workers could be commandeered by government order. As Mooney explained to GM chairman Sloan in 1938, "Practically nothing can be done for operating the business without government sanction." Under such circumstances, refusal to accept military contracts would have predictably resulted in damaging consequences, especially for a foreign-owned firm like Opel. In the view of Graeme Howard, the matter was starkly simple: "Opel, among other duties to the State, has a duty to provide whatever the Army requires . . ."[22]

Even before the German authorities began extorting dollar outlays from GM by forcing it to pay for the rubber needed by Opel, some executives of the corporation were considering ways to shield their German subsidiary from discriminatory treatment arising from its American ownership. In the spring of 1936 the two top officials of GM's overseas operations, Mooney and Howard, discussed the possibility of removing the foreign taint from Opel by acquiring German partners through the sale of a minority of Opel stock. Howard proposed spreading the minority portion of Opel stock widely among 25,000 or more German shareholders. Such a broad native constituency, he argued, would enhance Opel's chances to capture the Volkswagen project, which still seemed at the time still very much alive, since Hitler had not yet thrown his full backing to Porsche.[23]

Nothing came of these ideas because the most powerful figure at GM, Alfred P. Sloan, ruled out any sale of Opel stock. The difficulties of dealing with minority stockholders, especially if they were foreigners, far outweighed in his view the problems arising from Opel's American ownership. If GM were ever to sell Opel stock it should, he insisted, dispose of the majority and retreat to the status of a minority shareholder, leaving the management to others. But Sloan foresaw no need for such a step, which would leave GM with the problems of how to invest elsewhere in Germany the marks gained from a sale of stock and how to ensure that Opel, with Germans in control, would continue to serve as a prime source of vehicles for other GM's overseas subsidiaries. Nor did Sloan fear confiscation by the German government, except in the case of war, which he did not regard as an imminent danger. He remained confident that GM had invested wisely in Opel and expressed the view that "nothing the world could do" could stop the German people, "a strong virile nation," from finding "their place in the sun." "When Germany does overcome her difficulties, as she eventually will," Sloan predicted, "then General Motors will be in a position to take advantage of the hard work and progress which has been made during the past seven or eight years in the form of profits which are transferable to America."[24]

Sloan and the GM executives responsible for Opel remained hopeful that increased German-American trade would provide a solution to the problem of the millions in Opel dividends denominated in marks that remained tantalizingly beyond GM's reach because of German currency controls. If American import duties on German goods could be lowered, they contended, the result would be the accumulation of German-owned dollar reserves in the United States that would facilitate the conversion of Opel's frozen mark dividends into American currency. General Motors therefore publicly applauded Secretary of State Cordell Hull's policy of seeking to lower trade barriers by means of reciprocal agreements with other countries. Negotiations between Washington and Berlin quickly reached an impasse, however, when the Germans rejected the multilateral, most-favored-nation principle espoused by the United States and continued to insist on bilateral barter-and-quota clearing arrangements of the kind used by the Nazi regime to manipulate trade with other countries for its purposes. Frustrated by the resulting lack of progress, Graeme Howard angered the secretary of state in the spring of 1939 with a speech in which he advocated suspension of the most-favored-nation principle in the German case. In a book he published the following year to the acclaim of the magazine of GM's overseas division, Howard rejected the most-favored-nation principle as impractical and advocated acceptance of bilateral trade as the norm of the future.[25]

Although GM's executives strove to treat Germany like any other country, they had come by the late 1930s to recognize that the political situation there posed especially vexing problems. "Legal rights have lost their meaning in a large degree in Germany today, particularly as applied to the situation in which we find ourselves," Graeme Howard observed in 1938. "Laws," he wrote, "are interpreted by judges in the spirit of the times and the current emotions of the Party, rather than according to the specific and clear meaning of the law." As for the Nazi Party, it had become in Howard's view "an almost hopeless barrier to overcome," a view shared by other GM executives. Petty Hitlerites, hostile to foreigners in general, especially resented American ownership of Germany's biggest carmaker and sought whenever possible to make difficulties for Opel by accusing the company, among other things, of employing Jews or doing business with them. Another source of trouble was the trade board for the auto industry established under the Nazi four-year plan to control access to scarce resources. Dominated by representatives of Opel's competitors, the board repeatedly used its sweeping authority in ways that the GM executives regarded as discriminatory. In 1938 the trade board even sought—unsuccessfully—to foil a challenge by Opel to the makers of luxury cars by invoking government calls for a reduction in the number of car models in an effort to force the company to halt production of its new top-of-the-line sedan, the Admiral.[26]

"To have the law on one's side is essential and useful," Howard concluded, "but the greatest use is in having influential friends who could be relied upon to support General Motors in obtaining those rights recorded in the written law." To promote such contacts, Opel established a special office in Berlin that served as liaison with government agencies. When GM and Opel executives visited Berlin, appointments with officials charged with implementing the government's economic policies were arranged for them. Because many career civil servants at both the Economics Ministry and the Reich Bank were free of Nazi xenophobia, the cordial relations that resulted proved useful to the men in charge of Opel. On his visits to Germany, GM's James Mooney assiduously cultivated Hjalmar Schacht, who headed both the ministry and the bank until

Hermann Göring's growing control over economic policy undermined his influence.[27]

Shared interests facilitated Opel's relations with the Economics Ministry. A major problem for ministry officials was Germany's dwindling supply of the foreign currencies needed to pay for the imported resources without which the country's economy could not function. They therefore sought to ensure that nothing interfered with Opel's robust export sales, which generated significant amounts of badly needed foreign currency. In line with currency control regulations, the firm's foreign income was in effect confiscated by the government, which then compensated Opel with marks that were augmented by sizable export subsidies but could not be exchanged for dollars or other currencies without official permission. Recognizing that Opel's export successes depended on its access, as a GM subsidiary, to the American corporation's international network of sales outlets, officials of the Economics Ministry dreaded the possibility that GM might abandon Opel rather than expend still more unrecoverable dollars on its behalf. They therefore authorized GM to recoup some of the dollars it was forced to expend to purchase imported rubber by using frozen dividend marks to buy Opel automotive products and other German finished goods that could be used by GM elsewhere or resold for dollars in the United States. When the initial terms of these arrangements failed to yield satisfactory results, ministry officials proved accommodating in arranging modifications in the American corporation's favor.[28]

Well-disposed, cooperative civil servants often proved very helpful, but as Graeme Howard informed Mooney in the spring of 1938, the German military was GM's "best bet" for friendly support. Until Hitler purged its top ranks in 1938, the army was the sole component of the national government free of complete Nazi control. Even after that purge, much of the officer corps still consisted of career soldiers who, like many professional civil servants, did not view the world through the distorting prism of Nazism. Deals struck with army officers for large purchases of trucks produced by the new Brandenburg factory provided Opel not only with lucrative business but also with sustained contact with highly placed military personnel. The resulting mutually advantageous business relations gave rise to cordial after-hours socializing, which soon included officers of the air force as well. The manager of the Opel dealership in Berlin, Eduard Winter, proved especially adept, Howard assured Mooney, at cultivating the "Army crowd" and the "Air Force crowd." As early as the spring of 1935 an internal Opel communication had referred to these military contacts as "our Berlin friends."[29]

Amicable relations with key military officers repeatedly proved useful to the men in charge of Opel. When local officials in Brandenburg obstructed expansion of Opel's truck factory, the firm surmounted their opposition by invoking military authorization. When restrictions on the use of building materials imposed by the four-year-plan administration stood in the way of construction of new production facilities necessitated by mounting orders for trucks, military officials repeatedly interceded to make the needed cement and iron available. When the automotive industry trade board that advised the authorities with regard to allocations of government-controlled supplies of metals resisted Opel's requests for the steel it needed for production of its vehicles, a branch of the four-year-plan administration headed by an army colonel intervened to authorize the company to "jump over the heads" of the board and obtain special allocations of steel. When a growing shortage of skilled labor caused problems for the Brandenburg plant, its designation by the military authorities as a factory of "urgent importance" accorded it priority claims on scarce workers. The military could also provide valuable symbolic support. Since Opel was the target of repeated Nazi denunciations because of its foreign ownership, a visit to the Rüsselsheim plant in the spring of 1936 by the defense minister, General Werner von Blomberg, bestowed a welcome military seal of approval on the firm.[30]

As events would soon demonstrate, amicable relations with high military officers and career civil servants constituted valuable cards that GM and Opel could, in time of need, play to good effect in the poker game of Third Reich politics.

Chapter 4 A Nazi Grasp for Opel
Is Fended Off

In the spring of 1938 Graeme Howard was circuiting the globe on an inspection tour of the corporation's worldwide network of factories and sales outlets in his capacity as general manager of overseas operations. Tall and slim, with the wavy hair, clipped mustache, and the chiseled features of a film star of the time, Howard was, at forty-two, a veteran of GM's overseas empire. He had joined the company seventeen years earlier, soon after graduating from Stanford University and Harvard Business School. Rising through the ranks in posts at GM branches in Great Britain, Denmark, India, and Singapore, he had been assigned to the corporation's New York headquarters in 1931. Upon disembarking from a steamer in Bombay in early April 1938, Howard found a telegram awaiting him from Cyrus Osborn, the chief GM executive at Opel. The message so alarmed him that he immediately cancelled his plans for a month-long trip to Europe by sea and hurried to Rüsselsheim. Chartering a plane to Karachi, he then connected to other flights that enabled him to reach Germany in what was, for that time, the remarkably short span of four days. Although he had never been assigned to Opel, Howard was returning to a coun-

Graeme K. Howard of General Motors Overseas Operations defended General Motors' ownership of Opel against Nazi encroachment. Courtesy of GM Media Archive.

try well known to him from his school days there. He arrived equipped with a rudimentary command of the German language and some familiarity with German ways. These were to prove valuable assets, as he quickly found himself facing challenges that dispelled his earlier illusions about Nazism and threatened to shake GM's control over Opel.[1]

In Rüsselsheim, Howard's colleague Osborn was locked in a bitter feud with the senior German member of Opel's Directorate, the firm's treasurer Rudolf Fleischer. Osborn, too, was a veteran GM executive who had joined the firm fifteen years earlier. A heavy-set, stolid engineer, he was a graduate of the University of Cincinnati who began his GM career in the service department of the overseas branch, then managed the corporation's Swedish subsidiary for two years before returning to the United States to head GM's engineering department. Assigned to Opel as second in command in 1936, he became the senior GM executive there a year later at age forty. In that capacity, he suffered what he regarded as a succession of demeaning slights on the part of Fleischer and came to suspect that the German was seeking to gain control over the firm. In March 1938 Osborn's patience had come to an end, and he telegraphed Howard, who was then in Australia, that Fleischer must be dismissed. At Howard's request,

Osborn agreed to put the matter off until his colleague's scheduled arrival in Germany five weeks hence. But in his April telegram, received by Howard in Bombay, Osborn indicated that an unpardonable incident made immediate action imperative. In a speech to Opel personnel at the Rüsselsheim factory, a local Nazi Party official had, without being challenged by Fleischer, made disparaging remarks about GM and intimated that termination of American ownership of the firm would be only a matter of time. Upon Howard's arrival, Osborn told him in no uncertain terms that either Fleischer or he must go.[2]

Although Osborn and Howard would come to regard Fleischer as a tool of the Nazis, this was not the case at the outset of what would become a major crisis in Opel's management. Rather than being political in origin, the trouble between the German treasurer and Osborn arose from a spheres-of-authority dispute of the sort that frequently develops in large, complex organizations. Their clash was, however, complicated by Nazi legislation. In keeping with the regime's "leadership principle," German firms were required by law to appoint a plant leader (*Betriebsführer*). Holders of that post were granted sweeping authority over employees, who were enjoined to accord them virtually unconditional obedience. Most German firms bestowed the title of plant leader on their top executives, but the necessity of creating such a conspicuous post at Opel posed a problem for GM because the appointment of an American would undermine GM's policy of camouflaging its ownership. The post was therefore assigned to Fleischer, who was regarded as a loyal and trusted GM man. A forty-three-year-old veteran of the German army who had been wounded and captured by the Russians, he had completed a doctorate in law at the University of Leipzig after the war before taking a job in New York, where he began work at GM's overseas office in 1925. With the intent of becoming an American, Fleischer applied for citizenship but was unable to complete the required residency period before being transferred to GM's assembly plant in Germany two years later. Assigned to Opel in 1931, he rose rapidly in the finance department, becoming a member of the Directorate in 1932 and company treasurer in March 1933. Fluent in English and conversant with American ways, Fleischer had enjoyed cordial relations with GM executives. In their correspondence, some of the latter addressed him in letters as "Dear Doc."[3]

During the early years of the Third Reich, the Americans at Opel found it convenient, in keeping with their policy of camouflaging GM's ownership, to rely on Fleischer to handle most contacts with the government and the Nazi Party. A hard-working, uncommunicative man, he preferred to make decisions on his own rather than engage in time-consuming meetings with colleagues. As a result, Opel's affairs became increasingly concentrated in his hands. Within the Rüsselsheim plant he supervised a broad range of matters, including the factory security force that exercised surveillance over the employees. He also conducted most of the firm's external correspondence, including its communications with GM, often without consulting either his American or German colleagues. When personnel decisions were pending, GM executives in the United States sought his advice about candidates, even for the highest body at Opel, the Supervisory Board. But despite his increasingly dominant role, Fleischer remained, in the corporate structure of the firm and in the eyes of GM, merely Opel's treasurer and one member of the Directorate. Since those positions did not reflect the extent of his de facto authority, he increasingly invoked his title of plant leader, which commanded considerable respect in the Germany of the Third Reich. That Nazi-imposed post occupied no place in Opel's managerial structure, however, and was referred to as "social 'Führer'" in GM usage.[4]

Initially, the expansion of Fleischer's role met with acquiescence on the part of the GM men assigned to Opel. That changed, however, with the appointment of Osborn as head of the firm's management in 1937. An ambitious man, he chafed at Fleischer's control over matters he believed should be under his authority. In the autumn of 1937 Opel's Supervisory Board sought to placate Osborn by reviving the title of general director—the usual designation for chief executives of German corporations—and bestowing it on him. That step in turn offended Fleischer, who disliked taking orders from an American who was two years younger than he was and who lacked the prestigious title of *Doktor.* For his part, Osborn resented the prominent role Fleischer had come to play on occasions that brought Opel to public view. When important Nazi officials came to speak at the Rüsselsheim plant, it was increasingly Fleischer who, in his capacity as plant leader, introduced them. When the company's seventy-fifth anniversary was celebrated in the summer of 1937, Plant Leader Fleischer delivered the main address. When Hitler visited the Opel display at the annual Berlin auto show in 1938, Fleischer assumed the role of company spokesman, to the irritation of Geheimrat Wilhelm von Opel, who, although present, was shunted aside. A photograph of Fleischer explaining a new Opel model to Hitler, with the Geheimrat looking on sourly, dominated the cover of the next issue of Opel's in-house magazine. By the spring of 1938 relations between Osborn and Fleischer had become so strained that the American began assembling documentation on Fleischer's activities at his home, fearing that his office at Opel was no longer secure. Word of their estrangement soon spread through the company's managerial ranks and reached the ears of government officials

Der Opel-Kamerad

WERKZEITSCHRIFT DER ADAM OPEL A.G. / RÜSSELSHEIM A.M.

9. Jahrgang   März 1938   Nummer 1

Der Führer im Gespräch mit Geheimrat W. von Opel und Betriebsführer Dr. R. A. Fleischer vor dem „gläsernen" Kadett. (Dahinter von links nach rechts, teilweise verdeckt, die Vorstandsmitglieder Hoglund, Bangert und Stief.)

Rudolf Fleischer, Opel's German treasurer and plant leader, explaining an Opel Kadett with a glass hood to Hitler at the 1938 Berlin auto show as Wilhelm von Opel looked on. Courtesy of Adam Opel AG.

and military officers in Berlin, complicating the conduct of business and awakening fears of a debilitating split within the company along American-German lines.[5]

Although Osborn wanted Fleischer fired at once, Howard hesitated to take that step. Soon after his arrival, the treasurer gave him to understand that he had no intention of stepping aside and could count on the backing of Carl Lüer, the Nazi "old fighter" on the Supervisory Board, who had close ties to the powerful regional party chieftain, Hessian Gauleiter Jakob Sprenger. Fleischer further indicated that the other German board members, as well as officials of the Nazi Party and the government, had been apprized of his concerns. He was, Fleischer added, under obligation to keep all these influential individuals fully informed of further developments. This came as something of a shock for Howard, as Fleischer had previously displayed no Nazi proclivities. In spite of the multiple advantages that membership in the party would have brought him, he had not joined. He had, indeed, privately expressed misgivings about policies of Hitler's regime to his American colleagues. His speeches to Opel audiences had been free of Nazi ideology, and he had on occasion shielded employees from persecution by party officials. His communications with Howard in April 1938 left no doubt, however, that he was quite willing to invoke political protection in an effort to hold on to his prestigious, well-paying job at Opel.[6]

Faced with the threat of political retaliation and the possibility of a rebellion by the German members of the Supervisory Board, Howard asked two German attorneys—one a Nazi Party member—to clarify the legal questions involved. Their findings greatly diminished the scope and significance of Fleischer's authority as plant leader. In large corporations such as Opel, they reported, Nazi law assigned the responsibilities of plant leader collectively to the managing directorates, which could, if they wished, then delegate the post to one of its members. That law not only subordinated the post to decisions of directorates but also restricted the plant leader's sphere of responsibility to labor relations and the social welfare of employees. Production, sales, and other commercial transactions lay outside the competence of the plant leader. As Howard observed, the position was therefore functionally comparable merely to an American corporation's vice president in charge of labor, personnel, and social relations. The attorneys also pointed out that a new law adopted the previous year authorized the supervisory board of a corporation to appoint a chairman of its directorate. Moreover, that law empowered the chairman to override the rest of the managing directorate in the event of a difference of opinion. In effect, the bearer of that title thus wielded potentially absolute authority over a firm's management so long as its supervisory board refrained from withdrawing the appointment. Howard's goal therefore became the appointment, by Opel's Supervisory Board, of Cyrus Osborn as chairman of the firm's Directorate. He also set out to ensure a majority on the board by adding reliable GM men. To strengthen their hand, he and Osborn paid a visit to the American ambassador in Berlin and arranged for him to inspect the Rüsselsheim plant during the second week of May. Their meeting with the ambassador, Howard assured Mooney, "will be known in all responsible official quarters in Germany, and as such, let us say, 'can do no harm.'"[7]

Howard's next step was to assure himself of support from Opel's German managers. In individual consultations, he asked nine of them to take part in a review of the company's overall course by responding confidentially to a set of questions devised by him. He was not disappointed. Under a barrage of flattering remarks on Howard's part about Germany, the Nazi regime, and its Führer, the German managers produced the responses he wanted. They unanimously agreed that GM's acquisition of Opel and its assignment of American personnel to the company had been beneficial. Asked whether a chairman of the Directorate should be appointed and, if so, whether the post should go to an American with experience on the production side of the firm—which Osborn had—they responded similarly. They also agreed there was no need to continue to camouflage Opel's foreign ownership. The way was thus smoothed for appointment of enough reliable GM men to ensure firm majorities, an arrangement that was especially important in the case of the Supervisory Board, which had the authority to determine the composition of the Directorate and appoint—and remove—Osborn as its chairman.[8]

On April 20 relations between Osborn and Fleischer reached the breaking point. The occasion was the presentation of one of Opel's new luxury limousines, the Admiral, to Hitler on his birthday. As arrangements were being made to deliver the car to Hitler in Berlin, Fleischer questioned the need for Osborn's presence. When the American insisted it would be insulting if Opel's general director did not personally present the car, Fleischer gave way and agreed they should both go. But when, on the twentieth, Osborn went to the lobby of their Berlin hotel at the hour when he understood they were to meet to drive together to the Chancellery, he found that Fleischer had already left. Hurrying on foot to the Chancellery, Osborn found himself, to his chagrin, left on the street outside the closed gates while Fleischer alone presented the car to the dictator in the courtyard of the building. A photo of Fleischer with Hitler and the car was promptly spread across the cover of an issue of Opel's company magazine.[9]

Der Opel-Kamerad

WERKZEITSCHRIFT DER ADAM OPEL A.G. · RÜSSELSHEIM A.M.

9. Jahrgang   April 1938   Nummer 2

Dem Führer zum Geburtstag: der 500.000ſte ſeit der Machtübernahme gebaute Opelwagen

Rudolf Fleischer presenting an Admiral limousine to Hitler on the dictator's birthday in 1938. Courtesy of Adam Opel AG.

Seeking a reconciliation between Osborn and Fleischer, Howard arranged for them to meet with him a few days later, on neutral ground, in Paris. For three days he served as a mediator as the two sought to resolve their differences. When they had finished, he and Osborn agreed that "sufficient extenuating circumstances had been exposed during the discussion to permit a renewal of confidence in Dr. Fleischer." The treasurer also relented, agreeing to consult closely with Osborn and to respect the American's right to deal with anyone outside the firm, including the Nazi Party and the government. Fleischer further promised to take measures in the future to prevent inappropriate political speeches at Opel. He also acquiesced in the appointment of a veteran German production manager, Heinrich Wagner, as deputy plant leader, to relieve Fleischer of some of his burdensome duties. Both rivals concurred on the need to expand the membership of the Directorate and require it to meet regularly. And much to Howard's relief, Fleischer voiced no objection to Osborn's appointment as its chairman.[10]

As he later confided to his chief, James Mooney, Howard came away from Paris less than confident that the crisis at Opel had been permanently resolved. He and Osborn had assented to the agreement only out of expediency, he explained. The meeting had not dispelled their misgivings about Fleischer, and they felt no "warm glow regarding the gentleman's loyalty or character." Nevertheless, the two Americans had decided that in view of "the practical realities of the situation" it was wisest to "stretch a close decision" and allow Fleischer "to start up with a clean page," as Howard put it. But in their view, the German had been assigned a status of "outward reinstatement but inner probation." They were ready to trust him, but only "as long as we could see him under an arc light and we had the gun." As for Fleischer, he, too, apparently doubted whether his problems with GM had been laid to rest, for just a week later he joined the Nazi Party.[11]

Having negotiated what amounted to a shaky truce, Howard set about arranging for enactment of the agreed-upon changes at a session of Opel's Supervisory Board scheduled to coincide with the annual shareholder meeting in late May. Since he was the sole American board member then in Europe, he had to guard against opposition by the four German members. He therefore prepared a lengthy presentation designed to leave the impression that the firm's problems had been resolved to the satisfaction of all concerned. Osborn's appointment as chairman of the Directorate was depicted as highly advantageous and in conformity with the Nazi leadership principle. Aware that his words would in all likelihood reach the eyes of Nazi officials, Howard went out of his way to compensate for being an American. Invoking his childhood experiences there, he described himself as "an admirer and friend of Germany" and "a strong supporter of Germany's eminently just aspirations." He would, he added, therefore "regard it as a privilege throughout our discussion, to speak as one of you." As for GM, Howard announced that despite the minimal returns realized on its large investment in Opel, the American firm "has an abiding faith in Germany's ultimate destiny under the able leadership of Chancellor Hitler."[12]

Drawing on his presentation, Howard sounded out each of the four German members of the Supervisory Board separately. He found Nazi "old fighter" Carl Lüer initially reserved about the proposed changes. Lüer quickly proved much more responsive, however, when Howard suggested an expanded role for him at Opel that would substantially increase his financial remuneration. Lüer could be counted upon, Howard concluded, for "a certain amount of neutral assistance." When Howard sounded out Geheimrat von Opel, he was pleased to learn that the elderly chairman of the Supervisory Board was very critical of Fleischer and highly supportive of Osborn's elevation to chairman of the Directorate. The Munich banker Franz Belitz also indicated his willingness to approval Osborn's appointment. Only the younger Opel brother, Fritz, proved uncooperative, objecting that the proposed changes would strip the firm of its German character. At the conclusion of his consultations in mid-May, Howard reported to Mooney in a coded trans-Atlantic telephone call that he had the votes of three of the four German board members. He was not, however, assuming victory. His task, he warned Mooney, was comparable to "going down dark alleys in a strange city with certain unscrupulous personalities around." Of particular concern to him was the possibility of intervention by "the Frankfurt government crowd," an allusion to the headquarters of Gauleiter Jakob Sprenger.[13]

Howard's apprehensions were quickly borne out. The morning after his telephone conversation with Mooney, Fleischer informed him that the Gauleiter wanted to see him at his office in Frankfurt. An early member of the Nazi Party, Sprenger had been installed by Hitler as Gauleiter in 1927 and made governor of the state of Hesse after the Nazi takeover. One of only two of the thirty-two Gauleiters with such dual authority, he was the dominant political figure in the region where Opel's headquarters and main factory were located. A typically unscrupulous Nazi upstart, Sprenger strove to expand his authority at every opportunity. His ambitions repeatedly embroiled him in disputes with other Nazi officials, from which he usually emerged victorious and with increased power. Deeply resentful that the largest manufacturing enterprise in his realm was in

Jakob Sprenger, Nazi Gauleiter of Hesse who sought to wrest control
of Opel from General Motors. Courtesy of Adam Opel AG.

American hands, he welcomed the possibility of bringing Opel under the control of a German, such as Fleischer, who would be beholden to him. As governor of the area surrounding Rüsselsheim, he was already in a position to exert
pressure on Opel, but a powerful agent in its top management would give him
a potent lever inside the firm.[14]

Howard arrived at Sprenger's office at the appointed time on May 18 and was
kept waiting for half an hour, which he took as a calculated affront. Finally admitted to the Gauleiter's office, he found not only Sprenger but also his entire
staff as well as Opel Supervisory Board member Carl Lüer, who owed his rise to
prominence to Sprenger's patronage. Based on what he had heard from Fleischer and Lüer, Howard had, as he explained to Mooney afterward, expected "a
pleasant little meeting" at which the Gauleiter would apologize for the offensive speech at Opel by one of his subalterns that had triggered the crisis at the

firm. Instead, he found himself the target of an angry tirade. The meeting was, he informed his boss, "an absolute frame-up and conducted along third-degree lines. . . . There was no friendliness . . . and no courtesy. . . . It was a cut-and-dried affair, with hostility and suspicion sticking out all over."[15]

The Gauleiter began by angrily announcing that he had received from Lüer the memorandum that Howard had submitted to the German members of the Supervisory Board. Dismissing it as "the report of a lawyer," he complained that it showed "no appreciation whatsoever for the spirit and the problems of Germany." Sprenger then stated that he would not consent to Osborn's appointment as chairman of Opel's Directorate and that any such appointment "was definitely out." Caught completely off guard, Howard was at a loss about how to respond to the Gauleiter's verbal assault. Although his knowledge of German enabled him to grasp the meaning of Sprenger's heated words, he pled an inability to understand the language and requested another meeting when he could be accompanied by an interpreter. Reluctantly, the Gauleiter consented, but he warned that his mind was definitely made up and that he was agreeing to another meeting merely to make sure his reasons were understood. After only fifteen minutes, the encounter came to an icy end.[16]

Howard concluded from this ambush that Gauleiter Sprenger had designs on Opel and that both Lüer and Fleischer were in league with him. In Fleischer's case, that amounted in Howard's eyes to a double-cross, which rendered meaningless the agreements so painstakingly reached in Paris. If no countermeasures were taken, he feared that Osborn would resign, that the other Americans at Opel would follow suit, and that the German members of the Supervisory Board would lose all respect for GM and give in to political pressure from the Gauleiter. "In a nutshell," he later wrote to Mooney, "General Motors would be through, and the Company would be in the hands of Dr. Fleischer, his patron Prof. Lüer, and the local political crowd." Although Howard refrained from mentioning it, he could hardly have been unaware that, should this happen, a heavy share of responsibility would be laid at his own door by his superiors at GM. With his career on the line, Howard opted for a frontal attack, the first stage of which was to fire Fleischer. But he and Osborn realized that their suspicions alone would not suffice to bring the German members of the Supervisory Board to consent to the dismissal. They therefore decided to make use of several recent minor incidents to construct a case for Fleischer's termination.[17]

A letter Fleischer had written to the local army authorities became the centerpiece of the Americans' accusations against him. In it, he had complained that military security had been breached by communications between the foreigner Osborn and Colonel Adolf von Schell, who was in charge of vehicle procurement, about the specifications of a truck that was on order for army use. Since neither the colonel, who experienced unpleasant repercussions in Berlin, nor Osborn had been contacted directly by Fleischer in the matter, they reacted angrily, as did the colonel's superiors. Upon learning of Fleischer's letter, Osborn went to Berlin to apologize to the colonel, who, he was pleased to discover, shared his indignation against Fleischer and approved of the planned changes in Opel's management. The list of offenses by the German treasurer thus began with the accusation that he had underhandedly denounced both an officer of the German army and Opel's top executive. The Americans further accused Fleischer of deficient regard for the interests of GM. In responding to a Nazi complaint about the marketing of Opel cars through a Jewish-owned dealership in South Africa, Fleischer had, they reported, informed the automotive association that such matters were under the sole control of GM and contended that the American corporation had proved unresponsive to complaints from Opel on that score. Finally, a letter from the *Vertrauensrat,* the Nazi-dominated panel of employee spokesmen at the Rüsselsheim factory, setting forth a long list of complaints about working conditions and fringe benefits was invoked as evidence that Fleischer had been negligent in discharging his responsibilities as plant leader.[18]

Armed with this hastily assembled indictment, Howard assumed the offensive. Swallowing his distrust of Lüer, he requested an appointment with him. When they met, as Howard later explained to Mooney, he acted "the part of a naäve American and generally the part of a fool." He set forth the accusations against Fleischer as evidence that the treasurer had "made a sucker" not only of GM's men but also of Lüer and the Gauleiter. Fleischer must, he insisted, be fired. By way of strengthening his position, Howard handed Lüer a copy of an extensive set of accusations against Fleischer prepared by Osborn in advance of the Paris meeting. When Lüer, who appeared shaken, asked whether that document could be passed along to the Gauleiter, Howard assented. He asked Lüer to inform Sprenger that he preferred to settle the matter locally, but should that prove impossible, he would "take up the matter personally and forcefully with Messrs. Göring and Hitler," so that "it might be in the interest of the Gauleiter himself if he and I could straighten out this thing right here in Frankfurt."[19]

Upon hearing that Sprenger was ready to see him again, Howard resolved to avoid a repetition of the Gauleiter's earlier tirade by going on the attack himself. He prepared a speech that he had translated into German and then rehearsed "in exactly the same way that an actor would rehearse a part in a drama." His confidence was bolstered by assurances from Eduard Winter, the Opel dealer in Berlin who had become the firm's liaison with the military, that Fleischer could not count on support from the senior ranks of the army and that General Georg Thomas, who was in charge of the army's economic mobilization office, would not object to Osborn's appointment as chairman of Opel's Directorate.[20]

When Howard met with Sprenger for a second time on May 20, once more in the presence of the latter's staff and Lüer, he again pleaded linguistic problems, this time as grounds for reading from his prepared German text, which he had carefully larded with flattery for the Gauleiter. He began what he later described to Mooney as a particularly important move "in this poker melodrama" by recapitulating the events that had led to the Paris consultation and the agreements reached there. The result had been, he wrote, that GM had "washed the slate clean" for Fleischer. He then set forth the fresh incidents "which have absolutely destroyed our confidence in Dr. Fleischer." By way of suggesting that the Gauleiter would risk trouble with the military hierarchy if he sided with Fleischer, Howard laid particular stress on the charge that the treasurer had deeply offended a highly placed army officer in Berlin by underhandedly denouncing him, an action he described as "inexcusable." Resorting to bluff, he invoked that incident as added justification for the plan to upgrade Osborn's role at Opel, claiming that Osborn had, in offering apologies to the colonel, assured him that the Supervisory Board would at its next meeting put an end to the "internal friction" in the firm by appointing him chairman of the Directorate.[21]

Howard also dwelt at considerable length on the letter of complaint by Opel's panel of employee spokesmen, in effect accusing Fleischer of having failed, as plant leader, to live up to the standards of Nazi labor policies. Leaving unmentioned the fact that GM's men had chosen Fleischer as plant leader, Howard went on to question his qualifications for that post. As someone whose experience had been "exclusively of a clerical and financial character," the treasurer was, he argued, "not one of the men." The plant leader of a large manufacturing firm should be, he stated, "a man who has grown up from the ranks, who knows how to use his hands, who knows what it means to stand by a machine for eight hours a day, for six days a week." Howard added that both Osborn and Heinrich Wagner—the German manager who had been appointed deputy plant leader in keeping with the Paris agreement—were "men who have worked as laborers and understand labor."[22]

After accusing Fleischer of deliberately affronting Osborn by excluding him from the presentation of the Admiral limousine to Hitler the previous month, Howard went on to contend that the treasurer had systematically sought to prevent contact between Opel's American executives and Nazi Party and government officials, including the Gauleiter himself. By way of warning Sprenger that GM's men were nevertheless well connected in high places, Howard then recited a list of important government officials and military officers in Berlin with whom Osborn, Mooney, and he had been in contact. Among these was none less than Adolf Hitler, who had, Howard explained, personally assured GM's men that "in National Socialistic Germany exactly the same treatment, exactly the same duties and exactly the same rights would be extended to Adam Opel A.G. as is the case with every German company." He then added that the very next week he would himself be traveling to the capital "to pay my respects and renew my contacts with various officials."[23]

Having put the Gauleiter on warning that GM had powerful friends, Howard delivered his punch lines. GM was not without fault, he conceded, but its mistake had been "to place undeserved trust in one of our employees, a man who places personal advantage and ambition above all else; a man who abuses the friendship of his associates; a man who uses the fine name of the Party for his own selfish ends." Because of these transgressions, Howard announced, "Dr. Fleischer's services with Adam Opel A.G. will be terminated on May 25th," the day when Opel's shareholder meeting and that of its Supervisory Board were scheduled to take place. Treating Fleischer's dismissal as an accomplished fact and omitting any suggestion that the Gauleiter's approval might be needed, Howard then posed a crucial question: would Opel be denied a right extended to all other companies in Germany, the right to appoint a chairman of its Directorate "in accordance with the new Leader spirit of Germany?"[24]

Thrown onto the defensive by Howard's assertiveness, Sprenger responded in conciliatory fashion. He had no wish, he indicated, to interfere in those aspects of Opel's affairs that did not concern him. He therefore conceded that the firm's Supervisory Board had the right to appoint anyone it might choose— whether German or American—as chairman of the Directorate. While admitting that Fleischer might not be blameless, the Gauleiter expressed high regard for him, as well as continuing concern about the position of plant leader at Opel. He needed more time, Sprenger concluded, to hear Fleischer's side of the matter and to review the whole situation more fully. When Howard pointed out that the Supervisory Board was scheduled to meet only five days hence, they agreed, at Sprenger's suggestion, to consult again at noon on the day before the Opel meetings. They then parted with what Howard described in his report to Mooney as "the greatest show of courtesy and friendliness on both sides." In summing up his assessment of the exchange with the Gauleiter, Howard reported: "I had let him understand in a diplomatic way that I considered General Motors had certain rights, that we had many important friends, and that we damned well intended to fight for our rights,—all of which might eventuate in a situation from which he might derive little credit. This of course was pure bluff on my part, but which bluff I thought useful and justified, since I had the intuitive impression that there was considerable bluff on the Gauleiter's part." His exchange with Sprenger, Howard observed, had resembled a poker game in which one player can, by raising the stakes—sometimes solely on the basis of a bluff—succeed in bringing others to capitulate.[25]

When the two men met on May 24, this time with no one else present, Sprenger raised the stakes. As Howard by then knew, the Gauleiter had in the interval spent two days in Berlin, accompanied by Lüer and Fleischer, consulting with government and military officials. Reading aloud from the text of a letter addressed to Howard, Sprenger announced that his position was based on consultation with Nazi Economic Minister Walther Funk. Dismissing the most recent accusations against Fleischer as unfounded, he contended that there was no reason why good will on both sides could not restore the previously harmonious relations. While conceding that Opel was legally entitled to appoint a chairman of its Directorate, he pointed out that such a step was not required by law and strongly warned against it. Should Osborn be appointed chairman and become the paramount manager, Sprenger warned, Opel would be branded as a purely American firm in the eyes of German purchasers of vehicles. And that, he ominously added, would be "by no means favorable for the development of the enterprise." He proposed instead that Osborn content himself with the title of general director and that Fleischer, as plant leader, exercise independent authority over Opel's relations with the government, the party, and the army.[26]

Sprenger ended his statement with an ultimatum: if the course he had proposed could not be immediately followed, he demanded that no changes in Opel's management be discussed by the firm's Supervisory Board the following day, so as not to preempt a decision by Minister Funk. He threatened, that is, government intervention in the internal affairs of Opel unless his wishes regarding the composition of its managerial personnel and the allocation of authority within the firm were implemented. As Howard recognized, acceptance of these demands would set a precedent that could lead to an ongoing decisive voice for the Gauleiter in Opel's affairs. He therefore sought a compromise. Holding his ground on Fleischer's dismissal and Osborn's appointment as chairman of the Directorate, Howard conceded that no one unacceptable to the Gauleiter would be appointed to replace Fleischer as plant leader. As this was not required by law, it amounted to a significant concession. He then presented Sprenger with the names of four German members of Opel's managerial staff who would be acceptable to the firm as plant leader and invited him to choose one of them. Taken aback by this unexpected move, the Gauleiter withheld an immediate response. The meeting ended inconclusively, but with his threat of political intervention still in effect.[27]

Howard's efforts to stave off the Gauleiter's grasp for control over Opel's management now hinged on his obtaining the backing, the following day, of the four German members of the Supervisory Board for Fleischer's dismissal and Osborn's appointment as chairman of the Directorate. He was therefore alarmed to learn on the morning of the twenty-fifth that Lüer had asked the German members to caucus at the Rüsselsheim factory prior to the session of the full body. The previous day Howard had won from both Opel brothers assurances of their support for the motions he proposed to submit to the board, but he feared they might renege if subjected to political pressure by the Gauleiter through Lüer. The remaining German board member, Munich banker Franz Belitz, was an unpredictable factor, having been on vacation in Italy for three weeks. In hopes of winning Belitz's support, Howard dispatched his American assistant to the Frankfurt airport meet the private plane flying the banker from Italy with instructions to use the drive to Rüsselsheim to inform him of the charges against Fleischer and the planned actions by the board. When Belitz arrived at Opel headquarters, Howard had the banker brought directly to him. He then sought to "convert him to the true faith" while preventing him from attending the caucus of German board members under way on an upper floor of the Opel headquarters building.[28]

As Howard feared, Lüer's application of political pressure proved effective. By telephone from the room where the caucus was taking place, Geheimrat Wilhelm von Opel informed him that he had changed his mind in view of the Gauleiter's opposition. After repeated messages inviting Belitz to join the caucus had, on Howard's orders, gone undelivered, the Geheimrat appeared to request the banker's attendance. Concerned lest he be faced with unanimous opposition from the German board members, Howard intervened. As he later recounted in his report to Mooney, "I turned upon Dr. Belitz and challenged him as to why it was necessary to hold this private 'fix-up everything' meeting between just the German Board members, when I was under the impression that he had come to attend a Board meeting and not to a private preliminary frame-up." Howard then demanded that the board convene at once to deal with the scheduled agenda. When it became clear that Belitz was unwilling to join the caucus, the Geheimrat "trotted back to the private session upstairs" and returned with his brother Fritz and Lüer.[29]

Still facing the possibility of being outvoted by the German board members, Howard resorted to a tactical move designed to give him leverage over them. Instead of holding the annual shareholder meeting before the Supervisory Board met, as was customary when the two were scheduled for the same day, he reversed the sequence and convened the board first. This forced the German members to vote on the measures he proposed in the knowledge that if they dissented they might well not be re-elected at the shareholder meeting to follow, since Howard would, on behalf of GM, control all the stock. He thus gambled that their personal interests would prevail over the political pressure that had been brought to bear by the Gauleiter. The Geheimrat, he knew, would be highly reluctant to lose the title of chairman of the Supervisory Board of the firm that bore his family name. His brother Fritz, Howard believed, would be similarly averse to risking the loss of his title of vice chairman and his membership on GM's board of directors. Howard regarded Franz Belitz as interested primarily in money and was thus confident that the banker would not risk jeopardizing the sizable annual honorarium paid to members of the firm's Supervisory Board. Even Lüer, Howard believed, would be loath to lose his place on the board in view of his recent appointment as a director of the Dresdner Bank, one of whose major clients was Opel.[30]

Howard's ploy worked. In the ensuing three-hour, stormy meeting of the Supervisory Board, over which he presided, he achieved everything he sought. Lüer initially balked at firing Fleischer, and Geheimrat Opel wanted to leave that step to the shareholder meeting in order to evade responsibility for it. But when Howard nevertheless insisted Fleischer must go, it was agreed to seek a voluntary resignation. The board therefore offered the treasurer a very generous financial settlement that would provide him with full salary not only for the remainder of 1938 but also for the entire following year, as well a sizable bonus. When Lüer and Belitz communicated that proposition to Fleischer, he readily accepted it, thus showing himself not to be, as Howard and Osborn had feared, merely an agent of Gauleiter Sprenger. His resignation was unanimously accepted. Although both Lüer and Belitz expressed doubts about the appointment of Osborn as chairman of the Directorate, a motion to that effect also carried unanimously, as did one to expand the size of that body by adding GM men nominated by Howard. Four of its seven members would henceforth be American, and two of the German members were regarded by Howard as loyal, the third as neutral.[31]

At the close of the Supervisory Board session, Howard convened the shareholder meeting, at which he and a GM attorney from New York voted all of Opel's stock to approve the measures he sought. The firm's by-laws were revised to assign primacy to the chairman of the Directorate. The holder of that post was authorized to override a majority vote of that body on his own authority but required to consult with the Supervisory Board before overriding a vote of two-thirds or more. The German members of the Supervisory Board were rewarded for their compliance with re-election and an increase in their annual honoraria. Howard, Mooney, and Sloan were continued as members of that body, and two GM men stationed in Europe were added. This ensured GM a five-to-four majority as opposed to the previous four-to-four alignment.[32]

It was essential, Howard explained afterwards to Mooney, to maintain a GM majority on the Supervisory Board because there could be no reliance on the German members. But although the four had previously "worked as a unit," they had now been "irreconcilably split." Lüer's influence on the others had, he assured Mooney, "now been broken." "I find it exceedingly difficult with even the most Christian attitude to say anything in his favor," he added. "His game throughout was dirty and underhanded. The best one can say about him is that he is a tough baby." Lüer was, he concluded, "crooked and a terrific liability." Although Howard still rated the Opel brothers as assets for the firm because their family name provided useful German cover, he warned Mooney that "we cannot count on them for serious outside help—neither will take risks or has guts." Both brothers were, according to Howard, "cork-screws" who would "require constant re-charging in the matter of courage." As for Franz Belitz, Howard noted that the banker had "two primary interests, the one the pay-off, and the other, not to stick his neck out." Belitz had therefore hesitated and listened when he was "propositioned by the opposition." But once he saw that GM would not give way, he had fallen into line. To ensure Belitz's future compliance, Howard confided to Mooney that "in addition to his regular Board duties, he will work on a special assignment basis with Mr. Osborn on various matters, for which services he will be additionally and separately compensated." Belitz was now, Howard confidently predicted, "a fellow conspirator with his hand definitely thrown in on our side." By way of an additional safeguard against trouble from the Supervisory Board, Howard informed Mooney that he had arranged the appointment of GM's longtime Berlin attorney, Heinrich Richter, as secretary of that body. Richter's presence at future meetings would, he was confident, serve "as a restraining and chilling influence upon the German members, should they be inclined to pull a fast one."[33]

At the close of the meetings of May 25, 1938, Graeme Howard had fended off Gauleiter Sprenger's efforts to bring political pressure to bear in order to assert authority over Opel. He had successfully asserted GM's right to choose and dismiss the managerial personnel of Opel as well as to bestow paramount executive authority on one of its own men at the firm. He had preserved the appearance of German-American harmony while ensuring GM majorities in both the bodies that controlled the firm. Afterwards, he exaggerated somewhat in contending that a "conscious plan" had been "well organized to obtain control of Adam Opel A.G." and that GM had been "unquestionably . . . on the verge of loss of control" over its subsidiary. The clumsy, last-minute effort by Lüer to exert political pressure on behalf of Gauleiter Sprenger scarcely amounted to a well-calculated plot. There can, however, be no question that the American corporation's hold on Opel would have been greatly weakened had Howard been unable to win the backing of the German members of the Supervisory Board. He later assured Mooney that although he had refrained from openly threatening them with loss of their posts, he had been fully prepared to end their roles at Opel if they had refused to give unanimous approval to all the items of his agenda. He admitted, however, that he had been "most anxious not to provoke this situation, as that would have implications and potentialities dangerous to the maximum degree." Such surely would have been the consequence of a wholesale dismissal of the German Supervisory Board members, a development that Gauleiter Sprenger would doubtless have sought to exploit in order to bring still greater pressure to bear on Opel.[34]

Although Howard's success was appreciable, it had been achieved only after a harrowingly narrow scrape. In order to achieve his aims, moreover, he had defied the Gauleiter, something that was unlikely to be forgotten or forgiven. And in his effort to placate Sprenger he had, by offering him a veto over the choice of Opel's next plant leader, provided the ambitious Nazi chieftain with a lever that would enable him to launch yet another attempt at gaining influence over the firm.

Chapter 5 The Gauleiter Is Thwarted but Not without Consequences

In June 1938 Graeme Howard left Rüsselsheim for London, where communications with GM would not be subject to Nazi surveillance. There he laid out a strategy for coping with Gauleiter Sprenger's designs on Opel in a lengthy report to Overseas Operations chief Mooney. General Motors was, in his estimation, in an "excellent tactical position" despite his having agreed to accord Sprenger a voice in choosing a new plant leader. Since Opel's Directorate held legal authority over any appointment to that post, GM's tightened control over that body assured it a veto when a decision became necessary. Meanwhile, there was no pressing need to appoint a successor, as Heinrich Wagner, the loyal German manager who had been installed as Fleischer's deputy after the Paris meeting, was doing the job ably on a provisional basis. Discussion of the matter with the Gauleiter could therefore continue indefinitely, and GM need be "in no particular sweat" to make a replacement appointment. The essential point, Howard emphasized, was to avoid the mistake that had given rise to the problems with the Gauleiter. That mistake lay in assigning the post of plant leader to Fleischer, who as treasurer headed a department of the firm and was a member of the Directorate. If the next the plant leader were denied such managerial roles, Howard predicted, whoever held the post would be rendered impotent.[1]

Before leaving Germany, Howard had moved swiftly to implement this strategy. Two days after the May 25 meetings, a company press release and internal memoranda announced Fleischer's resignation, the expansion of the Directorate, and Osborn's appointment as its chairman. On the same day Howard sent a letter to the Gauleiter by messenger. Cordial in tone and concluding with the "Heil Hitler!" then common in German correspondence with officials, the letter sought to soften the news of the Gauleiter's setbacks. Osborn's elevation was only briefly mentioned. Fleischer's departure was characterized as "voluntary retirement" as the result of a "friendly understanding." But by way of indicating that Fleischer's acquiescence had been influenced by material considerations, the letter spelled out in detail the specifics of his abundant financial compensation. Howard also announced the appropriation of 1.5 million marks to Opel's worker welfare fund and invited the Gauleiter to inspect the Rüsselsheim plant. Only in a postscript did he address what he well knew was the still unresolved question of who would succeed Fleischer as plant leader. Seemingly as an afterthought, he indicated that he and Osborn would be ready at any time to clear up "the question of who is best qualified" to fill that post.[2]

Sprenger responded immediately and angrily in a letter delivered to Howard the next day by a member of the Gauleiter's staff. He expressed regret at Fleischer's departure but made no attempt to challenge it. He also refrained from contesting Osborn's appointment as chairman of the Directorate, although he accused Howard of violating what he claimed had been a promise to make no personnel changes in Opel's management without his approval. Sprenger embarked upon a new line of attack, however, by asking that Howard confirm to him that Opel's policies regarding the role of the plant leader were in conformity with his specifications regarding that post. Its occupant must, he claimed, be coequal to the chairman of the Directorate and serve as the company's liaison with the party and the government. The plant leader must enjoy independence in the execution of his duties and be required to consult with the chairman of the Directorate only about measures involving financial expenditures. If these specifications were not already set forth in Opel's statutes, Sprenger insisted that they be included. Only after he had been assured on this score would he be willing to discuss a successor to Fleischer.[3]

In an exchange of letters that followed, Howard sparred with the Gauleiter about the extent of the plant leader's authority. The holder of that post, he contended, was coequal to the chairman of the Directorate only within a "special sphere" that encompassed relations with the Nazi Party—but not the government—and promotion of the welfare of the company's employees. The "general conduct of business," including production, sales, finance, and engineering, lay outside that sphere, he insisted. In short, Howard sought, as he later explained in his London report to Mooney, to reduce the post of plant leader to the equivalent of GM's vice presidency for labor relations by denying its occupant any voice in managerial decisions. Reaffirming his agreement that a successor to Fleischer should be someone acceptable to the Gauleiter, Howard stated that if he and Osborn could reach agreement with Sprenger on a candidate, the matter could be quickly resolved. He also reminded the Gauleiter that he had submitted to him the names of four German managers at Opel who were suitable for the job. For his part, Sprenger dropped his claim to a veto over all managerial appointments at Opel but persisted in his demand that the plant leader be accorded the broad authority he had specified.[4]

In Howard's letters to the Gauleiter, a new factor increasingly assumed a prominent place: the military. Addressing those aspects of Opel's operations that he contended lay outside the next plant leader's sphere of responsibility, Howard gave the following examples in a letter of June 3: "the sale of trucks to the Army, the design of a particular product for the Army, the furnishing of assistance to the Air Force in the way of specific equipment or in the way of lending them assistance in the manufacture and design of planes." Those words were not unrelated to what occurred during a trip Howard and Osborn had made to Berlin earlier that week. The purpose of their two-day trip, Howard later explained to Mooney, was to quell any unfavorable reactions in the capital to the changes in Opel's management by "consulting with various important personalities." Whatever other individuals Howard and Osborn may have contacted during their stay in Berlin, the only ones specified in Howard's report to Mooney, aside from the American ambassador, were all German military officers. Moreover, judging from that report, those meetings, which were arranged by Eduard Winter, the Opel dealer in Berlin, must have filled much, if not all, of the two days.[5]

Upon arrival in Berlin, Howard and Osborn first called on the most important army officer from the standpoint of industry: General Georg Thomas. As head of the Economic and Armaments Office of the armed forces, Thomas was in charge of overseeing contracts with private firms for procurement of the equipment required for the military build-up that was consuming an ever-greater portion of the Reich's expenditures. Reading from a prepared statement in German, Howard gave Thomas GM's version of the events at Opel and then responded to questions posed by the general. "The upshot of the half hour's visit," Howard reported to Mooney, "was the fortification of a most helpful, co-operative and understanding friendship for General Motors and Adam Opel A.G. on the part of General Thomas—a very decent chap." Howard and Osborn then met with the head of army intelligence, who accepted their apologies for what they characterized as Fleischer's underhanded denunciation of Colonel von Schell. When they called on the colonel himself he congratulated them on the dismissal of Fleischer and presented them with an order for two thousand Blitz trucks. Afterward, Howard wrote to General Thomas, expressing gratitude for his "benevolent and loyal treatment" of Opel and GM and promising full cooperation with him and the German government in the future.[6]

Having satisfied themselves that Opel's relations with the army were in order, Howard and Osborn turned their attention to the air force. With the assistance of Eduard Winter, they hosted a dinner for the two most important generals in the Luftwaffe, Erhard Milch, state secretary in the Air Ministry, and Ernst Udet, the First World War flying ace who was in charge of technical development. The following day the two Americans were in turn invited to lunch by Milch and Udet at the newly opened Air Ministry building. As Howard reported to Mooney afterward, "we had a very nice luncheon, did a little serious drinking, and reviewed many business matters." Preferring not to commit these business matters to paper, Howard promised to inform Mooney about them orally. In the meantime, he left no doubt that cordial relations had been established with the men who were building Hitler's air force.[7]

The exact nature of the business matters Howard and Osborn discussed with Milch and Udet remains unclear, but surviving documents reveal one of the results. After the two Americans returned to Rüsselsheim, preparations were secretly set in motion there for construction, at the request of the Air Ministry, of a new plant for production of special gears designed to control the propeller speed of a Mercedes-Benz airplane engine in which the ministry was very interested. For generals Milch and Udet, such a plant held out the prospect of access to advanced American technology, as Opel engineers were routinely sent to the United States to acquaint themselves with the latest techniques under development at GM.[8]

On Opel's side, the gear plant project was not regarded as a normal commercial venture. As Osborn explained to his superiors in America the following year in belatedly seeking their approval, only a modest profit could be foreseen.

The rationale for the project lay, he made clear, in the political sphere: "In the interest of the protection of our entire investment in Germany, it has become necessary for us to co-operate with high and important government departments in the furtherance of certain of their projects." The project was, that is, a concession to the Air Ministry in hopes of gaining a shield against the designs of Gauleiter Sprenger on Opel. Headed by the second most prominent figure of the Nazi regime, Hermann Göring, the ministry must have seemed ideal for that purpose.[9]

At the time, the decision to build the gear plant was made by Howard and Osborn without informing GM's leadership in the United States or seeking its approval. Obtaining approval would have taken weeks, if not months, because of the ponderous procedures of GM's hierarchical committee structure, and Howard and Osborn were urgently seeking immediate leverage against the Gauleiter. There also seemed to be no need to submit to GM the usual appropriation request for use of Opel reserve funds. The cost of the gear plant could be covered, Howard and Osborn were led to believe, by a combination of subsidies from the Air Ministry, tax write-offs, and reallocation of funds earlier committed by the army for a vehicle project regarded by Opel as a failure. They therefore acted on their own in line with GM's decentralized managerial practices, which accorded wide discretionary authority to its executives unless significant amounts of corporation money were involved.

Upon his return from Berlin, Howard lost no time in letting Gauleiter Sprenger know about GM's new friends in high places. In his letter of June 3 he reiterated his narrowly restrictive view of the plant leader's authority and objected to Sprenger's having earlier questioned the right of Opel's management to do business with the Air Ministry without approval by Fleischer's eventual successor. "Might I suggest," Howard wrote, "that in view of the several confidential discussions which we have had with General Milch and General Udet, particularly over the last Tuesday and Wednesday, that this might possibly better be a subject for verbal discussion rather than writing, at which time Mr. Osborn and I should be only too pleased to advise you that Mr. Osborn's confidential assistance has been specifically requested by General Milch and General Udet." He was sure, Howard added, that Sprenger "would wish not to lay down any regulations which would prevent providing the Air Force with the specific assistance which they have personally requested from Mr. Osborn." Without explicitly stating it, Howard was warning the Gauleiter that if he persisted in interfering in such matters he would run the risk of incurring the wrath of Air Minister Hermann Göring.[10]

Obviously daunted by this warning, Sprenger wrote to Howard on June 4 to deny any intention to meddle with Opel's internal affairs. Dropping his demand for a revision of Opel's statutes, he expressed the view that the division of responsibilities between the plant leader and the Directorate should be left to mutual cooperation. Relieved at the conciliatory tone of Sprenger's letter, Howard chose to overlook the fact that it concluded with a reiteration of the Gauleiter's earlier sweeping specifications regarding the plant leader's role. In a cordial acknowledgment, he therefore gave cause for future difficulties by assuring Sprenger that "in principle we find ourselves in entire agreement with the thoughts therein expressed."[11]

Late on the afternoon of June 7 Howard and Osborn met with Sprenger in Frankfurt at his invitation. He informed them that none of the four German managers whom they had suggested as plant leader would be acceptable and that he wanted an outsider for that post. The two Americans expressed doubt that GM would understand why no one suitable could be found within Opel's managerial ranks. Howard added that he was sure Sprenger would not want to awaken the impression that he was imposing a government commissar on Opel, a step that could shake confidence in the firm on the part of its employees and its network of dealerships. He then brought the Gauleiter to admit that he had not interviewed Opel's four candidates and secured his agreement to do so. Howard also substituted for one of those names that of Hanns Grewenig, the manager of the company's Brandenburg truck factory, who, unlike the others, was a Nazi Party member and would therefore be less easy to disqualify. To the distress of Osborn, however, Howard conceded that if no one suitable could be found within the company, an outsider would be acceptable.[12]

The meeting concluded with an agreement to postpone a decision on a successor to Fleischer until after Sprenger's return from an extended trip abroad. Afterwards, the two Americans joined their host and his staff at a protracted meal marked by repeated rounds of "wine tasting" that lasted until six the following morning. In the course of the night, Sprenger used the occasion to introduce to the Americans his candidate for the post of plant leader, Wilhelm Avieny. A former bank clerk who had joined the Nazi Party in 1931 and held officer rank in the SS, Avieny had, with the backing of Sprenger, gained control over a government-owned bank in the region. He was obviously a political lackey, without any experience whatever in the automotive industry—a person wholly unacceptable to GM's men at Opel.[13]

By the time the Gauleiter returned from his trip in late July, Howard was back in New York, leaving Cyrus Osborn to cope with the problem of a successor to

Fleischer. Since he had only a shaky command of German, Osborn relied heavily upon a German aide for translation when he met with Sprenger at the end of the month to discuss the matter. In a carefully drafted statement that his aide read aloud in German, he marshaled an array of arguments against an outsider as plant leader and in favor of appointing someone from within who was already thoroughly familiar with the firm and its ways. He added that he knew an excellent Opel manager who was a National Socialist, a reference to Hanns Grewenig. In the conversation that followed, Sprenger, who larded his remarks with allusions to how helpful he could be to Opel if it cooperated with him as well as to unspecified difficulties for the firm if it did not, continued to insist that no one but Aviny would be acceptable to him. The right plant leader, he argued, could be of great value to the firm in negotiations with the authorities in Berlin about such matters as steel allocations, a point on which he claimed he and Howard had earlier agreed. As a consequence of the long delay, Economics Minister Walther Funk was, Sprenger warned, growing impatient and would soon make the appointment himself if an agreement were not quickly reached.[14]

During this meeting with Osborn, Sprenger posed a major additional demand: he insisted that the new plant leader must also be appointed deputy chairman of Opel's Directorate, a point he claimed Howard had conceded during the lengthy nocturnal discussions of early June. Such an arrangement would have accorded the plant leader just the sort of role in Opel's management that Osborn and Howard were determined to rule out. Among other things, it would mean that during the often lengthy trips of the senior GM executive at Opel to the United States, the plant leader would have become acting chairman of the Directorate, in command of that post's extensive authority. Osborn therefore firmly denied knowledge of any such a concession and secured Sprenger's agreement to adjourn their discussion until the following day so that he could check with Howard about the matter by trans-Atlantic telephone.[15]

When Osborn called on Sprenger again on the morning of July 29 he assumed the offensive. He could still not accept, he began, the view that none of Opel's German managers was suited to be plant leader and that an outsider must therefore be appointed. As for making the holder of that post deputy chairman of the Directorate, he reported that Howard had assured him by phone from New York that a misunderstanding must have arisen if Sprenger had gained the impression that he had approved such an arrangement. Howard had also denied having suggested that the plant leader should play a role in Opel's dealings with the authorities in Berlin in such matters as steel allocations. Sprenger protested that he was concerned only with promoting the in-

Cyrus R. Osborn, chief GM executive at Opel, 1937–1940,
successfully frustrated Gauleiter Sprenger's designs on the
firm. Courtesy of Adam Opel AG.

terests of the company and stressed how useful the kind of advance information
often available to him would be for Opel if he could work with a plant leader
who had his full confidence. Since his proposals were apparently being ignored,
however, he saw no purpose in further negotiations and indicated that he
would have to refer the matter to the "competent authorities in Berlin."[16]

Despite this threat, Sprenger hedged on stands he had taken earlier when
Osborn requested clarification on three central points. Asked whether he definitely insisted on the need to appoint an outsider as plant leader, the Gauleiter
merely stated that this was his opinion. He insisted, however, that Howard had
agreed to accept an outsider if he found none of the German managers suitable. Questioned about whether he insisted that the plant leader be made
deputy chairman of the Directorate, Sprenger avoided a flat confirmation, re-
plying that he regarded this as advisable. Asked whether the unspecified diffi-

culties for Opel he had mentioned the previous day concerned that firm alone and were therefore discriminatory, he avoided a direct answer and spoke instead of the overall problems of the German economy. Once again, he stressed how useful the kind of information he could supply would be for the firm. The meeting ended inconclusively, with Osborn reiterating his view that the best solution would be appointment of a plant leader from within Opel's managerial staff.[17]

Sprenger's retreat proved only temporary. In a forcefully worded letter to Osborn in early August he repeated and even expanded his demands, effectively invoking two concessions made by Howard before his departure. As the Gauleiter correctly pointed out, Howard had expressed "complete agreement" with his letter of June 4, in which he set forth his sweeping version of the plant leader's authority. Sprenger reminded Osborn that in the course of their lengthy nocturnal conversations in Frankfurt in early June, Howard had conceded that if none of the firm's German managers proved acceptable to the Gauleiter, GM would accept a plant leader from outside. Sprenger then went on to claim falsely that it had also been agreed that Opel's by-laws should specify that the new plant leader would be deputy chairman of the Directorate and thus second in command at the firm. He had, Sprenger informed Osborn, discussed these matters with the Economics Ministry during the previous days and received instructions to hold to his position and insist upon appointment of a plant leader who would enjoy his full confidence. Characterizing his negotiations with Howard as binding, the Gauleiter called upon Osborn to confirm his interpretation of what had been agreed upon. The matter was urgent and brooked no delay. He must have a final decision at once.[18]

Osborn concluded from Sprenger's letter that the concessions made earlier by Howard placed him at a grave disadvantage. Especially damaging was Howard's expression of readiness to accept an outsider as plant leader, which put Sprenger in a position to force someone of his choice on the firm simply by rejecting everyone nominated from within Opel by GM. When Howard made that concession in June, Osborn had immediately sought to offset his colleague's words by pointing out to Sprenger the damaging effects an outside appointment would have on company morale and expressing confidence that a suitable candidate could be found among Opel's staff. But the concession had been made, and the Gauleiter's letter left no doubt that he was determined to hold GM to it. That, together with Sprenger's renewed insistence that the plant leader be made deputy chairman of Opel's Directorate and his claim that the Economics Ministry stood behind his demands, led Osborn to decide that it was futile to continue negotiations with the Gauleiter without help from higher governmental officials. He therefore again headed for Berlin in the second week of August.

In the capital Osborn played Opel's export card. He took his case to the second in command at the Reich Economics Ministry, State Secretary Karl Brinkmann, a non-Nazi known to be well disposed to the private sector. The state secretary was preoccupied with the problem of acquiring sufficient foreign currency to pay for essential imports in the face of a steep decline in German exports. Because Opel's export sales were booming as a result of its products' access to GM's worldwide marketing network, the firm was an exception to the overall pattern. Its rising yields of foreign currency, which were turned over to the government in return for heavily subsidized compensation in marks, represented a precious national asset from the perspective of the ministry. Anything that might call into question GM's commitment to Opel would be most unwelcome. In Brinkmann, Osborn found a sympathetic ear when he explained his problems with the Gauleiter. Upon his return to Rüsselsheim, he wrote to the state secretary, thanking him for the opportunity to present his side of the dispute and enclosing copies of his correspondence with Sprenger and his notes on their meetings. He also included a memorandum setting forth in detail his reasons for rejecting the Gauleiter's demands.[19]

As agreed upon with Brinkmann, Osborn also sent off a lengthy letter addressed to Economics Minister Funk. Writing on behalf of GM, he stressed the large amounts of foreign currency brought into the German economy by Opel and its development into a major exporter through its connection with GM. He also claimed that GM had, through Opel, rendered significant help to the German armed forces. Overstating GM's role in the American air industry considerably, Osborn claimed that it had placed all of its patents at the disposal of the Air Ministry and was providing the latter with an advanced gear plant as well as a development plant for carburetors. He gave no specifics about Opel's usefulness for the army but pointed out that War Minister von Blomberg had personally visited the Rüsselsheim factory to convey his appreciation. Having set forth this exaggerated version of GM's importance for Germany's military, Osborn proceeded to lay out the reasons for his unwillingness to accept Gauleiter Sprenger's demands. Appointment of an outsider as Opel's plant leader against the wishes of its management would, he warned, unavoidably be perceived as imposition of a commissar by the government. It would amount to a discriminatory measure that would damage morale within the firm and shake public confidence in it. He refrained from spelling out the full extent of the possible negative consequences, but his line of argument suggested strongly that, if the Gauleiter got his way, the flow into Germany of foreign currency generated by Opel's exports would be imperiled.[20]

To support his argument against discriminatory treatment, Osborn pointed out in his letter to Funk that Hitler himself had assured GM's representatives in 1934 that Opel would be treated on an equal footing with other German corporations. He added that if the government wished to take over the firm, GM would be willing to negotiate a sale, but only on the understanding that the purchase price must cover the American corporation's total investment and be paid entirely in dollars—conditions that Osborn knew would be ruled out by Germany's foreign currency policies. Referring to assurances he had received— presumably from State Secretary Brinkmann—Osborn closed his letter with an appeal for swift help from the Economics Ministry in staving off the imposition of an outsider as plant leader and in securing the appointment instead of one of the firm's German managers who had been proposed to the Gauleiter.

The same day he wrote to Funk, Osborn informed Sprenger by letter that since the Gauleiter had taken up with the Economics Ministry the matters pending between them, he, too, had done so. It would be quite acceptable to him, Osborn wrote, if the ministry ruled on the issue under dispute. In a reply a week later, Sprenger again insisted that Osborn must honor his version of the concessions made by Howard and accept his man Avieny as plant leader. The Gauleiter claimed, moreover, that he was acting on behalf of Economics Minister Funk.[21]

A fortuitously timed visit to Germany in August by Alfred P. Sloan enabled Osborn to drive a final wedge between Gauleiter Sprenger and the Economics Ministry. Among State Secretary Brinkmann's urgent concerns at the time was resistance on the part of the U.S. State Department to German proposals for a restrictive bilateral trade treaty that clashed with American insistence on the most-favored-nation principle. When the Opel dealer in Berlin, Eduard Winter, pointed out that Sloan enjoyed direct access to Secretary of State Cordell Hull, Brinkmann jumped at the suggestion of a meeting. After Sloan had completed his consultations at Rüsselsheim, Osborn accompanied him to Berlin where they dined with Brinkmann. The state secretary laid out his arguments in favor of the German government's trade proposals and obtained Sloan's agreement to present that viewpoint to Secretary Hull immediately upon his return to the United States. When the Americans then raised the problems Gauleiter Sprenger was causing them, Brinkmann assured them that the matter would be settled "within a few days to our entire satisfaction."[22]

Brinkmann quickly made good on his promise by helping Eduard Winter draft a letter to Gauleiter Sprenger for Osborn's signature. Incorporating much of the wording of Osborn's letter to Economics Minister Funk, Winter and Brinkmann produced a far more assertive document. In blunt language, it spelled out multiple reasons why appointment of an outsider as plant leader would have a "destructive influence" on Opel. New was the charge that such an appointment would interfere with "the great and responsible tasks" the firm had taken on for the German military. Among these, the gear plant for the Air Ministry received prominent mention, as did General von Blomberg's visit to the Rüsselsheim factory. The most significant departure from earlier communications lay, however, in wording which, in effect, denied that the Gauleiter enjoyed any authority whatever over the choice of a plant leader. Howard and Osborn had, the letter stated, "voluntarily" consulted with Sprenger about the matter out of "courtesy" and in hopes of fulfilling his "wishes." Absent was any reference to Howard's earlier agreement that the new plant leader must be acceptable to the Gauleiter or to his concession regarding GM's willingness to accept an outsider for that post. As for Osborn himself, the letter stated that if Sprenger had concluded he was in agreement with the Gauleiter's "suggestion" on the latter point, there must have been a misunderstanding. After Brinkmann had reviewed the final draft and informed Winter that he found it "most marvelous," it was sent by air mail to Osborn, who signed it in late August and dispatched it by messenger to the Gauleiter, with a request for confirmation of receipt.[23]

Sprenger's response revealed him to be both in retreat and angered by the letter. In his answer of early September he rejected as "fundamentally false" the American's claim that his insistence on a plant leader of his choice amounted to the first step toward a German takeover of Opel. His only concern, he wrote, was to make sure that all plant leaders of firms in his region were good National Socialists. He refrained from repeating his demand that GM accept his Nazi underling Avieny as Opel's plant leader. Moreover, presumably as a result of Brinkmann's exertion of influence on GM's behalf at the Economics Ministry, the Gauleiter omitted his earlier claims of support from Minister Funk. Instead, he accused Osborn of dishonesty and inveighed against the challenge to his authority implicit in Osborn's statement that the Americans had dealt with him merely as a courtesy. Nevertheless, he indicated a readiness to continue negotiations on the matter.[24]

By September Osborn had decided that it was hopeless to seek agreement with Sprenger, and his resolve was bolstered by the results of an unexpected meeting between GM's president, William S. Knudsen, and Air Minister Göring. Seeking ways to increase the output of a key airplane engine developed by Daimler-Benz, Göring had been urged by the chief executive officer of the Bavarian Motor Works to end GM's ownership of Opel and take over the firm for that purpose. Göring recognized, however, the value of Opel's access to American technology and operational methods, so he decided instead to seek GM's cooperation. When he learned that Knudsen was visiting Berlin he let it be known through Eduard Winter that he wanted to see GM's president immediately. Although this involved altering his travel plans, Knudsen complied and was driven to Karinhalle, Göring's lavish hunting lodge in the countryside near Berlin, accompanied by Winter. Knudsen was ceremoniously received by the solicitous air minister, who was full of praise for American production methods and for Opel's contributions to the German economy. After expressing great interest in a new airplane motor then under development by GM, Göring proposed that Opel, with GM's help, build a factory in Germany equipped with American machines that would be capable of producing 180 motors per shift. Knudsen protested that he could not immediately respond to such an unexpected proposal, but he did not rule out the possibility and requested detailed specifications. When Göring then inquired whether GM and Opel were finding German authorities cooperative, Winter seized the opportunity to lay out GM's difficulties with the Hessian Gauleiter. After hearing his account, Göring replied that he would summon Sprenger and "personally bring the matter to a close." Whether he actually did so remains unclear, but knowledge that the second most prominent figure in the Nazi regime was seeking a favor from GM could only strengthen Osborn's resolve by holding out the prospect of assistance from that potent quarter.[25]

In the third week of September, Osborn found himself in a position to cut the ground out from under the Gauleiter. In a letter to Sprenger he again specified that he and Howard had sought to reach agreement merely out of courtesy and once more set forth the reasons why an outsider as plant leader would be harmful to Opel and why the appointment of any one of the insiders he and Howard had proposed would benefit the firm. After mentioning Sprenger's threat to refer the matter to the Economics Ministry if his demands were not accepted, Osborn delivered what amounted to crushing news. The ministry had, he announced, now authorized Opel's Directorate to name one of its members as plant leader. As a result, the post had been unanimously bestowed on Hanns Grewenig, the manager of Opel's Brandenburg truck factory who was a member of the Nazi Party. Missing from the letter was any mention of need for the Gauleiter's approval of that step.[26]

Sprenger's response to this move revealed that he recognized he had been bested but was left deeply embittered. After a long silence, which he attributed to illness, he wrote to Osborn in November and accused him of failing to comply with the wishes of the Economics Ministry by not obtaining his approval for the appointment of a new plant leader. The absence of any expression of intent to contest Grewenig's installation amounted, however, to tacit acceptance of defeat in the face of the superior influences brought to bear against him. Most of Sprenger's letter was devoted to venting outrage at Osborn's claim that GM's men had consulted him merely as a courtesy, which he took as an expression of disrespect for the authority he wielded as Gauleiter and governor. Under the circumstances, he announced, he would engage in no further negotiations with Osborn. When Geheimrat von Opel met with Sprenger on another matter in late December, the Gauleiter again gave vent to his anger and denounced Osborn, whom he accused—not entirely without grounds—of reneging on points agreed to by Howard. In February 1939, while Osborn was visiting GM's headquarters in New York, his chief American aide at Opel reported to him that at a recent dinner in Frankfurt attended by some fifty automotive executives Sprenger had pointedly snubbed Opel's representatives.[27]

In mid-March 1939 the GM executives in charge of Opel were forcefully reminded of how dangerous it was to have enemies among the rulers of a totalitarian state. A German member of the Directorate, Karl Stief, was, upon returning from a visit to GM plants in the United States, arrested by the Gestapo and placed under indefinite detention without access to either legal counsel or a court of law. His office at the Rüsselsheim factory was searched, some of his papers were seized, and four of his staff were detained for several days. Held incommunicado by the Gestapo, Stief was accused of betraying state secrets to foreigners by taking with him to the United States technical specifications of the Volkswagen designed by Ferdinand Porsche. In view of the public availability of those specifications, however, that was a patently absurd charge.[28]

After Stief had been incarcerated for two weeks, GM's James Mooney, who arrived in Germany at the end of March, sought an intervention by Hitler through Otto Meissner, the state secretary of the presidential chancellery. The previous spring Mooney had, like several other American businessmen whose firms owned subsidiaries in Germany, received a civilian medal from the Reich government with a citation signed by Hitler and by the state secretary. Before meeting with Meissner, Mooney had a letter delivered to him, alluding to his medal and describing his cordial meeting with Hitler in 1934. On that earlier occasion, he wrote, the Führer had expressed the desire to have GM feel at home in Germany and asked Mooney to let him know if any serious difficulties should arise. He then laid out the Stief case and suggested that Hitler would wish to be informed about it. At their appointment, Meissner expressed sympathy but initially claimed that not even Hitler could interfere in police procedures. He became more responsive, however, when Mooney stressed that Stief's arrest could have a seriously adverse affect on GM's commitment to its operations in Germany. As Hitler was away, Meissner promised to convey Mooney's information to the dictator as soon as he returned to Berlin.[29]

Meissner apparently kept his word. Within days, Hitler's chief adviser on automotive matters, Jakob Werlin of Daimler-Benz, reported that the dictator was very upset by the matter, since he regarded GM's German operations as useful in numerous ways. When Stief nevertheless remained behind bars, Mooney appealed to the chargé d'affaires at the American Embassy, as well as to a high official of the Gestapo and to Foreign Minister Joachim von Ribbentrop. Whose influence proved decisive was never determined, but at the end of the first week of April Stief was finally freed. By then his detention by the dreaded Gestapo had further heightened the atmosphere of fear and suspicion that had been growing within Opel's upper ranks.

Because of the cloak of secrecy that shielded the Gestapo's operations from any scrutiny, the actual reasons for Stief's arrest were never determined. It is possible that he was denounced by one of the numerous Nazis who worked at Opel, as he had proved less than fully compliant with the imposition of party influence at the Rüsselsheim factory. He had also resisted efforts to recruit him for party membership and had refused to show favoritism to party members in assigning tasks and promotions. Another possibility, which Stief himself thought the most likely explanation, was that he had been targeted by Gauleiter Sprenger as part of his vendetta in the wake of the frustration of his designs on Opel. Stief's transfer, following his arrest in Hamburg, to a prison located in Darmstadt in the state of Hesse, where Sprenger held sway as governor, would appear consistent with that explanation.

In the contest of wills with Gauleiter Sprenger the GM executives had prevailed. Their mobilization of influential support in Berlin had succeeded in intimidating the Gauleiter. But that success had not come without cost. They had incurred the bitter enmity of a high official of a dictatorship capable, as Stief's arrest and detention demonstrated, of lawless acts against innocent persons. Even more important, in hopes of gaining support from the Luftwaffe and its powerful chief, Air Marshal Göring, in their efforts to thwart the Gauleiter, they had taken a first step toward entangling GM's German subsidiary in Hitler's preparations for war.

Chapter 6 Opel Is Conscripted for the German War Effort

The Stief affair took place in an atmosphere of rising tensions between the United States and Germany. In the wake of the anti-Semitic mayhem and murder carried out by Nazi storm troopers in the "crystal night" pogrom of November 1938, a wave of revulsion swept the United States. President Roosevelt at once condemned that outbreak of barbarism and recalled the American ambassador, a move swiftly reciprocated by Berlin. Although diplomatic relations were not formally broken, a war of words developed during the ensuing months. American officials, including the president, became increasingly outspoken in their condemnations of Nazi practices while hostility toward the United States mounted in the government-controlled German press.

In early February 1939 Cyrus Osborn's assistant, Elis Hoglund, took stock of the implications of these developments for Opel. Writing to Osborn, who was in New York, about to sail back to Germany after a visit to GM's headquarters, Hoglund described Opel's situation as "lousy." The strained relations between Germany and the United States had, he reported, accentuated the firm's American ownership, thereby emboldening its enemies in Berlin and weakening its position even among its friends. "The strength of the party is greater now than ever before in every field and on every level," he warned, noting that "whatever opposition or lukewarmness existed in the army is quashed." Gauleiter Sprenger remained unreconciled: "We are definitely on his black list." It was therefore essential, Hoglund concluded, to avoid offending those government officials with whom the firm enjoyed good relations. As the most important of these, he named Colonel Adolf von Schell, who had placed many truck orders with the firm as army vehicle procurement officer and who was now the plenipotentiary for motor vehicle questions in Göring's powerful four-year-plan organization. Also very important, he added, was State Secretary Brinkmann of the Economics Ministry, who had proved so helpful the previous summer in thwarting the Gauleiter. Brinkmann and von Schell, Hoglund observed, "occupy positions of dominant authority in the two agencies of the government where our fate is determined. Any actions which may harm these relationships may jeopardize our company's future."[1]

Shortly after Hoglund made these observations, Brinkmann became mentally incapacitated and was removed from his post, which greatly heightened Colonel von Schell's importance to Opel. He wielded sweeping authority over the automotive industry, even with regard to which models a firm would be allowed to produce and in what quantities. Upon assuming his new responsibilities, von Schell had made it clear that he intended to subject virtually all aspects of the industry to increasingly tight centralized control. "The automobile industry has," Hoglund informed Osborn, "definitely got a new boss in the full sense of the word, and with no ifs and ands." Thus far, Hoglund observed, Opel had stayed in von Schell's good graces, and he expressed the hope that friendly relations with him would serve to counter hostility toward the firm on the part of the industry's government-created advisory board, which was dominated by Opel's German competitors. Permission was therefore readily granted when von Schell's office approached Opel with a request for access to GM's automotive proving grounds in Michigan in order to gather ideas for a projected facility of the same sort that would be shared by the German industry. As a result, a delegation of government and military engineers, headed by an army lieutenant colonel and accompanied by a German manager from Opel's truck factory, visited the GM proving ground, as well as GM and Ford automotive factories, in April 1939.[2]

In mid-March 1939, the Policy Committee that stood atop GM's pyramidal managerial structure convened in New York, with board chairman Alfred P.

Sloan presiding and president William S. Knudsen participating, to render decisions on pending matters of importance in the corporation's worldwide operations. One item on the lengthy agenda was a general discussion of "the current political conditions in Germany, and the status of our operations in that country." What was said was not recorded, but the two resolutions adopted at the close of the discussion leave no doubt that the assessment was not positive. The first of these instructed the corporation's overseas operations division that "no commitment shall be made in respect to our German operations that will involve the investment of any additional dollars in Germany." The second resolution informed the same division "that the Corporation will not approve of the Opel Company's entering into any program looking toward the manufacture of airplane engines in Germany." The corporation's top policy-making body thus rendered its verdict on the proposal Air Minister Hermann Göring had made to Knudsen the previous September. Faced with the issue of whether to allow Opel to embark upon production of a clearly military nature for the government of the Third Reich, GM's top leadership firmly ruled out that possibility.[3]

At the time this resolution was adopted, a request incompatible with its spirit, if not its letter, was pending at a lower level in the corporation's complex decision-making structure. Submitted in early February by Cyrus Osborn, chairman of Opel's Directorate, it asked for GM's authorization to use marks from the German subsidiary's reserve funds to pay for constructing and equipping the gear plant Osborn and Graeme Howard had the previous year agreed to build at the request of the Air Ministry. As Osborn explained in an accompanying letter to Howard, who was back at his post as general manager of GM's overseas operations in New York, the gear plant was already under construction. He warned, however, that the financial arrangements with German authorities, which they had believed would make the use of Opel reserve funds unnecessary, seemed in danger of unraveling. To prepare for that eventuality, Osborn submitted a request to use almost five million of Opel's marks to cover the costs of the gear plant. Included in that figure, he explained, was a million marks necessitated by the Air Ministry's insistence on adding a department for experimental gear development.[4]

Osborn made clear in his request that the gear plant project was not a normal business venture, but rather that it had become necessary in order to protect GM's investment in Germany by cooperating with influential circles within the government. As Howard well knew, this was a reference to their efforts to cultivate ties to Hermann Göring's Air Ministry in hopes of gaining protection against Gauleiter Sprenger's designs on Opel. Although this was a highly un-usual justification for allocation of funds, GM president Knudsen approved the appropriation request in mid-May, thereby acquiescing in a project that was by then well under way. As a result, in spite of the Policy Committee's March pro-hibition on the manufacture of airplane engines, during the summer of 1939 Opel put into operation, with GM's approval, a plant designed, at the request of the German Air Ministry, to utilize American technology to develop ad-vanced components for aircraft engines in which the leaders of the Luftwaffe were particularly interested. Whether Opel funds were actually used to com-plete the plant remains unclear as does the nature of its eventual products, which were cloaked in military secrecy once the war began.[5]

By the time Knudsen agreed in May 1939 to allow Opel's gear plant project to proceed, the danger of war was high and rising. The hopes awakened by the Munich conference of the previous autumn, at which the British and French granted Hitler the German-inhabited regions of Czechoslovakia in return for promises that he had no further territorial demands, had been dashed. Hitler's brazen seizure in March of the rest of Czechoslovakia had revealed that his aims were not, as he had long proclaimed, limited to achieving national self-deter-mination for German minorities abroad. It seemed likely that his next target would be Poland, and the British and the French responded by pledging to de-fend that country should Germany attack. As a result, continuation of a project intended to enhance the performance of Luftwaffe warplanes entailed a strong possibility of implicating Opel in German preparations for armed conflict. The extent to which Knudsen and the other senior executives of GM took this into consideration cannot be ascertained on the basis of the surviving records. But even if they were concerned about this possibility, the alternative to allowing the already well advanced gear plant project to proceed must have seemed highly risky. If, after learning that the gear plant was under construction at Rüs-selsheim, GM's leadership had ordered the project halted, there would have been strong grounds to fear endangerment of the American corporation's con-trol over its German subsidiary. Cancellation of the project at that point would predictably have angered generals Milch and Udet, at whose request it had been launched. Such a step might well have also brought down upon the American management of Opel the wrath of the powerful Hermann Göring, who pre-sided over both the Air Ministry and the four-year-plan administration that exercised sweeping authority over the economy, including the automotive in-dustry. With State Secretary Brinkmann, Opel's protector at the Economics Ministry, removed by mental illness, and with Gauleiter Sprenger still embittered by his failure to gain leverage over Opel, the probable consequences of making additional enemies in high governmental circles apparently ruled out a decision to halt the gear plant project.

Despite the deteriorating international situation in 1939, Opel's peacetime operations initially proceeded at full throttle. Plans for further expansion and the introduction of new car models during 1940 were well advanced. Until shortly before the beginning of the war, Cyrus Osborn assured GM's executives in America that there was no reason why Opel should not expect to continue with business as usual. In mid-July, at a time when international tensions were rapidly mounting, he wrote to Graeme Howard in New York that war seemed unlikely. Omitting any mention of Hitler's escalating demands or the stiffening Western responses to them, Osborn concluded, on the basis of Opel's mounting difficulties in obtaining raw materials, that Germany would not wage war because it lacked the necessary resources. Similarly wishful were his confidence that the Nazi Party "could not remain in power for any great length of time under war conditions" and his belief "that the Party leaders must recognize this fact, which will act as a great deterrent to war." He assured Howard that in contrast to the previous year, when the crisis that led to the Munich conference had briefly raised the specter of war, "no one seems to be worrying particularly about the situation," which he described as "very quiet," with everyone "going along with their daily life and activities in a very normal way."[6]

Osborn's illusions were swiftly dispelled as signs of imminent war multiplied at Opel during the weeks that followed. Early in August, the German army placed urgent orders for spare parts for its Blitz trucks to be shipped to bases along the Polish border. Large-scale military requisitions of railway freight cars made it difficult for the firm to obtain raw materials or transport its products to dealers. Beginning in the third week of August, close to three thousand Opel employees were drafted, including some senior managerial personnel. On the advice of the American consul in Berlin, Osborn managed to arrange the evacuation of most American employees and their families to Holland before early September, when Hitler launched the invasion of Poland, which was swiftly followed by British and French declarations of war against Germany.[7]

The outbreak of war placed Opel in a precarious business position. New laws decreed by the Nazi regime obligated all private companies to produce and deliver whatever was needed for the war effort. Opel was put on notice that it would soon be prohibited from using steel to make cars and trucks for the domestic civilian market; production would be limited to replacement parts and vehicles for the military and for the few export markets that remained accessible. The company's Brandenburg factory, which made trucks for the army, seemed assured of continued operation. But Opel's main operation, the much larger automobile factory at Rüsselsheim, stood to lose the bulk of its prewar production. If that should happen, the factory would soon lack work for a large part of its workforce of some twenty thousand. In a labor market beset by a shortage of skilled manpower even before the war, workers unutilized at the Rüsselsheim factory would in all probability be assigned by the authorities to other companies making products destined for military use. In that event, GM would be left with a huge, largely idled, foreign-owned manufacturing facility that would predictably become an attractive target for a Nazi takeover in the name of wartime necessity.[8]

Aware of the opposition of his superiors in America to war production by Opel, GM oversees operations chief James Mooney met in Berlin with Osborn a few days after the invasion of Poland to consider ways to cope with German pressure in that direction. They agreed that the "integrity of our position could not be maintained if the Adam Opel A.G. as a company undertook the manufacture of new products such as war material." The best course lay, in their judgment, in continuing to produce Opel's regular products to the maximum degree possible in order to ensure a smooth resumption of peacetime operations after what they hoped would be a brief war. If Opel willingly undertook production for the military of the country responsible for launching the war, the German subsidiary's exports as well as sales of GM's own products in other countries would predictably suffer. Protests were to be expected at home from some GM shareholders, and adverse publicity in the American press might well have a damaging effect on sales of GM vehicles in the United States. As Osborn later reminded him, Mooney therefore "made the very strong point that we should under all circumstances avoid the manufacture of any parts or assemblies which in their use were peculiar to war purposes alone, such as for machine guns, hand grenades, ammunition etc." If the German government asked Opel to make war materials of any kind, the two Americans agreed, the firm should offer to loan its machines and workers to another company for such purposes with the proviso that they be returned once peace was restored.[9]

Mooney and Osborn sought to fend off demands by German officials for production of war materials at Rüsselsheim by taking the position that the Opel factory was designed solely for large-scale manufacture of cars and was unsuited for other uses. To justify keeping the main factory in full operation despite the pending prohibition on car production for the German civilian market, they proposed to shift to Rüsselsheim from Brandenburg the manufacture of a truck model on order for the army. They planned, in addition, to argue that production at Rüsselsheim of cars for the military and for export should be augmented by expanding the output of replacement parts for Opel vehicles sold earlier, which would presumably be subject to heavier wear and longer use in wartime. Also by way of dealing with the problem of keeping older vehicles in operation, they envisioned establishing a large-scale repair facility at the main factory. In the meantime, they sought to shield Opel's liquid assets from the regime by investing a sizable portion of the company's reserve funds in the stock of other German companies.[10]

During the two weeks following their meeting, Mooney and Osborn strove to gain the approval of the relevant authorities in Berlin for their plan to keep the Rüsselsheim factory functioning without agreeing to the manufacture of war materials there. General Thomas, the chief of military economic mobilization, expressed sympathy for their proposals, but he proved unwilling to commit himself. They received no encouragement at all, however, from General Hermann von Hanneken, who exercised life-and-death authority over German industrial firms through his control, as state secretary in the Economics Ministry, over allocations of iron and steel to the private sector. Brushing aside their concerns about the damaging effects of war production on Opel's future exports and its connection to GM, von Hanneken bridled at the Americans' unwillingness to produce war materials at Rüsselsheim. He found their proposal to lend part of the workforce and machines at Rüsselsheim to other companies unacceptable, objecting that dividing the factory in that fashion would disrupt its well-established operations and greatly diminish its productivity. Opel must, von Hanneken insisted, convert to war production all of the Rüsselsheim factory not needed for a minimal level of passenger vehicle output. Unless Opel complied with the needs of the German government, the general warned, he was prepared to appoint a Reich custodian to take over management of the firm.[11]

Mooney and Osborn encountered still further obstacles to their plans. In mid-September the army cancelled its order for the truck model whose production they had hoped to transfer to Rüsselsheim. It also became apparent that efforts to avoid war production would not go unchallenged even within Opel's own management. One of the senior German managers notified Osborn that, upon learning of the Americans' plans, he and four of his colleagues had met and "declared their willingness to accept any army orders that would be suitable for our shop." Otherwise, they would be "in great danger to be considered as of bad will which would classify all of us immediately into second-degree patriots." Faced with a possible revolt by indispensable members of the firm's management, Osborn and Mooney emphasized, in individual conferences with each of the German managers, the potentially irreparable damage to Opel's export markets and access to GM technology that would result from the manufacture of war materials for Germany. For the moment, they managed to quell the managers' patriotic fervor, but how long they would be able to hold their German colleagues in line under wartime conditions remained uncertain.[12]

Unbeknownst to Osborn and Mooney, the disposition of the Rüsselsheim factory was being determined by a chain of decisions set off well before the war began. In the spring of 1938 the Air Ministry had accorded priority to the production of a versatile new bomber, the Ju 88, designed by the Junkers aircraft firm. As Junkers lacked the capacity to mount the desired level of output, manufacture of many components for the plane was assigned to other firms. When Hitler ordered a sharp increase in Ju 88 production shortly before he launched the war, the attention of the Air Ministry focussed on Opel's Rüsselsheim factory. It had figured in the thinking of the Luftwaffe leadership since the previous autumn, as Göring's proposal to GM president Knudsen had revealed. Now, at a September 18 meeting in Berlin with Heinrich Koppenberg, the chief executive of Junkers, Generals Thomas, Milch, and Udet, and Colonel von Schell, Göring decided to use the main Opel factory to manufacture components for the Ju 88. The following day, Koppenberg and a colleague, accompanied by a major general and another officer, appeared in Rüsselsheim and carried out an inspection of the factory without the knowledge of Osborn or the other Americans there. They decided that the seven to nine thousand workers at the plant who would be freed up by the cessation of civilian production should be assigned to the production of Ju 88 components. Shortly after Osborn learned of these developments, Heinrich Wagner, the German production manager at Rüsselsheim, was summoned to the Air Ministry in Berlin. When Wagner returned, he reported to Osborn that he had been ordered to prepare to produce airplane parts and instructed to send more than a hundred Opel foremen to Junkers factories to study the manufacture of those parts.[13]

Faced with this turn of events, Osborn and Mooney considered two possible courses of action. One, which they quickly ruled out, involved withdrawing the Americans from Opel's Directorate and turning the company over to a wholly German management, which could then comply with demands for airplane-part manufacture without directly involving GM. They settled instead on a second option, which called for leasing part of the Rüsselsheim factory to

Junkers for the duration of the war. Junkers, or a new firm established by it, would take over much of the factory's personnel and provide the necessary financing for conversion to manufacture of Ju 88 components. Osborn and Mooney expected that it would be possible to segregate the floor space needed for such new production and limit it to a small portion of the factory. This arrangement would, they believed, free Opel from making war products but enable GM to retain ownership of the Rüsselsheim factory and use part of it to manufacture replacement auto parts and as many new cars as possible, especially for export. This would, they hoped, make it possible to retain a core automotive workforce that would provide the nucleus for swift expansion once resumption of peacetime production became possible. With the approval of those members of both the Directorate and the Supervisory Board who were then in Germany, the leasing option became the company's policy.[14]

When General von Hanneken was informed of the leasing plan, he reacted angrily. Like the earlier proposal to loan machines and workers to another company, it would, he objected, disrupt the operations of the factory and therefore diminish its productivity. Two companies could not, he insisted, function efficiently under one roof. The best way to shield GM from involvement in the production of war materials, he proposed, would be for Osborn to withdraw as chairman of the Directorate in favor of a German. That would, he maintained, relieve GM of direct involvement in war production while leaving it in a position to exercise ultimate control over the firm through the Supervisory Board. Von Hanneken specified that there could be no further discussion and demanded a written statement of Opel's plans to contribute to the war effort. Osborn responded with a letter in which he emphasized the injurious effects for Opel and GM of involvement in war production. He rejected the general's proposal to turn the company over to German management on the grounds that it would leave GM vulnerable to accusations of subterfuge. Defending the feasibility of dividing the Rüsselsheim factory, Osborn invited von Hanneken to send technical experts to join with Opel's managers in working out such an arrangement. Ominously, the general failed to respond to his letter. Instead, Osborn heard that von Hanneken had told Opel's plant leader, Hanns Grewenig, that he intended to ask Gauleiter Sprenger to "take action to bring Opel in harmony with the national necessities." Grewenig had, Osborn also learned, been summoned to the Gauleiter, who instructed him to see to it that the Rüsselsheim factory remained intact, that not a man or a machine was removed, and that every member of the firm's management did his duty as "as a good German."[15]

Hopes of keeping part of the Rüsselsheim factory in operation for vehicle production suffered a heavy setback at the end of September when Colonel von Schell informed Opel of the new production quotas it would be allowed. Whereas the Brandenburg truck factory was authorized to operate at full capacity to meet orders for the three-ton Blitz trucks, von Schell confirmed cancellation of the lighter military truck whose production Osborn and Mooney had hoped to transfer to Rüsselsheim. As for passenger vehicles, all production for the German civilian market must be terminated. Only as many cars as could be exported would be permitted. Since the outbreak of war had closed off most export markets, this was small consolation. As Osborn reported to Mooney, only 85 cars were on order for export during the entire month of October. That level of demand would scarcely justify operating a production line that had been turning out an average of 413 cars a day before the war.[16]

By early October the situation at Rüsselsheim was becoming increasingly precarious. On orders from the authorities, the whole factory was shut down for two weeks of inventory taking, and some five thousand workers were transferred to other companies in the vicinity. The loss of more labor was averted only by urgent pleas to the Air Ministry and the Labor Office. But the drain on the Rüsselsheim workforce continued: six hundred skilled workers had to be transferred to Brandenburg to meet the increased demand for army trucks and replace men who had been drafted. In reporting on these developments to Mooney, who was then in Switzerland, Osborn reckoned that after the inventory was completed, they must expect the Rüsselsheim workforce, which had been reduced from twenty to thirteen thousand, to dwindle to only approximately five thousand. Meanwhile, although no contractual agreement had been reached with Junkers, Opel was rapidly becoming entangled with the aircraft firm. The Rüsselsheim factory had been placed on notice by the Air Ministry to expect large orders for airplane parts any day. About a hundred foremen and workers had already been dispatched to Junkers factories for instruction in the manufacture of those parts. The questions of who would finance the purchase of the necessary raw materials and pay for the extensive retooling had, however, not been resolved. The same was true of who would manage the manufacture of the parts needed by Junkers.[17]

By mid-October, closer scrutiny of the difficulties involved in dividing the Rüsselsheim factory, along with emphatic opposition to such a step by both General von Hanneken and Gauleiter Sprenger, led Osborn and Mooney to abandon their plan to lease part of the factory and retain the rest for automotive operations. They therefore decided it would be best to lease all the production units to Junkers for the duration of the war and place orders with that company for cars and parts as needed. Under this revised plan, only those departments at Rüsselsheim not directly involved in manufacturing work—engineering, sales, and finance—would remain under Opel management. The company's production managers and workers would continue in place, but as employees of Junkers for the duration of the lease.[18]

When a lease of this sort was proposed to representatives of Junkers in the second half of October, the initial response was positive, and cordial preliminary discussions began. But when Junkers submitted a draft contract, the Americans found it "so far from what we considered to be a fair agreement that we felt it did not even provide a starting point for discussion." The terms set forth by Junkers led them to conclude that with Opel under orders from the authorities to make airplane parts, the aircraft firm had decided to exploit the situation and absorb the Rüsselsheim factory into its own organization. That impression was reinforced by news that representatives of Junkers had let it be known among the German managers at the factory that they would soon be working for the aircraft firm, which planned to transfer some of them to its own factories and shift Junkers managers to Rüsselsheim. News of this spread rapidly at the Opel factory, giving rise to fears that GM "was prepared to sell the organization down the river and that the fine Opel organization of the past would not continue to exist in the years of peace following the war." So great was the resulting unrest that Osborn felt it necessary to offer reassurances at a special meeting of the German managers and in individual conferences with the German members of the Supervisory Board.[19]

To stave off the danger of a takeover by Junkers, Osborn and Mooney dropped their plan for a leasing arrangement. Instead, they decided to keep the entire Rüsselsheim factory under Opel management and to make airplane components as a supplier for Junkers, an arrangement that would also avoid producing directly for the Luftwaffe. All the financing for the necessary retooling was to be provided by Junkers or by the government. Agreement along those lines was then worked out with the aircraft firm. Although Osborn was reluctant to relinquish his post as chairman of the Opel's Directorate, he gave way to Mooney's proposal to shield GM from direct involvement in the manufacture of airplane parts by turning management of the firm over to a wholly German Directorate. This was essentially the course of action proposed by General von Hanneken in September, but what had smacked of subterfuge to Osborn then was now embraced by the GM men in charge of Opel after all alternatives had proved unfeasible.[20]

The reorganization necessary to install a German management was carried out on November 15 at a special meeting of Opel's Supervisory Board hastily arranged by Osborn. Resignations from the Directorate were accepted from Osborn, Hoglund, and two other Americans who had already been evacuated to the United States. Heinrich Wagner, the German production manager, was appointed to succeed Osborn as chairman of a wholly German Directorate, which was augmented by two new members. Osborn and Hoglund were added to the Supervisory Board. So was Albin Madsen, a Danish citizen and chief executive of GM's subsidiary in Copenhagen, who was appointed in hopes of ensuring GM's representation at board meetings in the event that the war precluded the presence of Americans. As a result of these appointments, GM men now commanded a six-to-three majority on the Supervisory Board. These changes, it was stipulated, would remain in effect only for the duration of the war, after which peacetime arrangements would be re-established.[21]

The transition to German management was less sweeping than these personnel changes suggested. Unwilling to relinquish all control over Opel's operations, the Americans secured the creation, at the November Supervisory Board meeting, of an executive committee consisting of Osborn, Hoglund, and the three German board members—Wilhelm von Opel, Franz Belitz, and Carl Lüer. This new body was formally constituted as a committee of the Supervisory Board rather than a separate entity, with the consequence that its existence remained out of public view and went unmentioned in the legally required disclosures of the firm's organizational structure. The executive committee was accorded sweeping authority, however. As specified by the Supervisory Board, its consent would be required before the now all-German Directorate could alter any policies affecting the engineering, manufacture, sale, and export of vehicles produced by the firm. The same was the case with new projects involving expenditures in excess of the relatively low level of ten thousand marks of Opel funds. In addition, the executive committee was empowered to set general guidelines regarding "the manufacture, finance, and sale of any material other than cars, trucks and parts." The committee was also assigned particular responsibility for ensuring that the firm's financial interests were safeguarded in all new production undertakings. At the behest of the Americans, the German Supervisory Board members acquiesced in a proviso to the effect that rulings of the executive committee would be valid only if either Osborn or Hoglund consented. GM was thus assured veto power over a secret body designed to exercise tight control over the newly installed German management.[22]

With regard to the changes at Opel, GM's annual report for 1939, released in late April 1940, stated: "As a result of the declaration of war, and in line with the Corporation's operating policies, with full recognition of the responsibility that the manufacturing facilities of Adam Opel A.G. must now assume under a war regime, the Corporation has withdrawn the American personnel formerly in executive charge of this operation, and has turned the administrative responsibility over to German nationals. Its relationship is now limited to representation on the Board of Directors [Supervisory Board]." Three months later, however, Graeme Howard more accurately wrote in his semiannual internal report on GM's overseas operations that although "the Management of Adam Opel A.G. is in the hands of German nationals," General Motors was nevertheless "actively represented by two American executives on the Board of Directors."[23]

The minutes of the November 1939 Opel Supervisory Board meeting at which the changes in management were made contain no mention of war materials production or even of orders for airplane parts from Junkers. Instead, the euphemisms "new products" and "new materials" were employed. Moreover, at the insistence of Mooney, the board approved the following resolution: "it shall be the firm policy of the Adam Opel A.-G. that the Company shall under no circumstances become engaged in the manufacture of material peculiar to war alone and that Adam Opel A.-G. should not invest any money for this purpose." All those present must have been aware of the disingenuousness of the phrase "peculiar to war alone," as they well knew that the airplanes for which Rüsselsheim factory would soon be turning out components were designed solely for warfare use by the Luftwaffe. As early as mid-October, the term "war materials" was in use in internal Opel communications between Osborn and Wagner. The conclusion thus seems inescapable that Mooney wanted to avoid disclosing the unpleasant truth in documents he knew would reach GM's American management.[24]

Following the restructuring of Opel's management, the retooling necessary for production of the Ju 88 components commenced at the Rüsselsheim factory and continued throughout the first half of 1940. With car production drastically curtailed as a result of sharply reduced allocations of raw materials and with many idled workers kept on the payroll in anticipation of the orders from Junkers, the company lost more than a million and a half marks during the last quarter of 1939. In January 1940 the government advanced that amount to the firm to cover those losses. Osborn expressed misgivings about accepting the money, but he did so.[25]

During the lull of the "phony war" following the German conquest of

Poland, Osborn chafed under the frustrating interruption of his plans to launch production of innovative passenger car models at Rüsselsheim. He therefore set guidelines for Opel's German management that were designed to keep open the possibility of a rapid reconversion to peacetime business. Writing in late March 1940 from Switzerland in order to evade German government wartime decrees prohibiting the transmission of business data abroad, he lamented to Mooney, who was in New York, that "the war . . . entirely apart from its other tragic results, has been a serious blow to us." He held out the prospect, however, of a swift resumption of normal car production. By assigning the "new production" mainly to the plant's capacious storage areas, it had been held, he explained, to only 9.1 percent of the regular manufacturing floor space, none of which consisted of the automotive assembly lines. Permission had furthermore been obtained from the authorities to produce six thousand cars during the first three months of the year, making possible the retention of a nucleus of skilled autoworkers. Opel was on notice to cease car production for the German civilian market as of early April, but the company had been assured that it would be allowed a daily output even after that of twenty-five to thirty cars for export. If, as he hoped, the war should end soon, Osborn assured Mooney, full production of the planned new 1940 car models could be resumed within four months.[26]

These hopes collapsed when Hitler launched his Blitzkrieg against Western Europe in May 1940. The Rüsselsheim factory was forced to discontinue car production altogether early that month and shift production lines as well as increasing numbers of workers—ten thousand by the end of the year—to the manufacture of aircraft parts for Junkers. By September, the first of what would eventually become some four dozen Opel-made components for the Ju 88— including fuselage panels, cabin canopies, hydraulic devices, and landing gears—were being shipped to Junkers assembly plants. There they were combined with components manufactured by numerous other companies to produce the Ju 88, which was produced in greater numbers than was any other German bomber and has been characterized as the "backbone of the Luftwaffe." By the end of 1940 more than ten thousand employees at Opel's Rüsselsheim plant were engaged in producing parts for the Junkers bombers heavily used in raining death and destruction on London and other British cities during the air attacks of the Battle of Britain.[27]

The Rüsselsheim factory's enlistment in the Nazi war effort was not limited to components for the Ju 88. In December 1939 the firm's newly installed German management completed a feasibility study that resulted in a recommenda-

The German air force's heavily used fighter-bomber, Ju 88, was equipped with many components made at Opel's Rüsselsheim factory. U.S. National Archives.

tion to accept navy contracts for the manufacture of torpedo detonators, production of which began during the second half of 1940. Earlier that year the Rüsselsheim factory was also assigned contracts by the army for a variety of small, specialized ordinance items. By June, fifty workers had been assigned to these munitions projects, a number that grew to two hundred by the end of the year. By early 1941 the Rüsselsheim factory had been so thoroughly converted to war production that more than 98 percent of pending contracts were for military equipment. Eighty-six percent consisted of orders for Ju 88 components, 7 percent for torpedo detonators, 4 percent for aircraft motor gears, and 1 percent for army munitions. The remaining 2 percent of orders were for vehicle replacement parts, most of which were also destined for military use. At the Brandenburg factory, truck production was limited to military orders, which increasingly focused on the three-ton Blitz model.[28]

Osborn and Hoglund were not directly involved in these projects. After the war began, they moved their families to Switzerland and were frequently absent from Rüsselsheim. Because they were no longer members of the Directorate, they ceased to receive the detailed flow of operational information generated by the factory. Their names are absent from the lists of those who received internal memoranda about war material manufacture, which was accounted for by a special bookkeeping system separate from that for vehicles and parts. Military secrecy banned them from even entering those parts of the Rüsselsheim factory converted to war production. At the sessions of Opel's Supervisory Board they attended during 1940, discussion focused on plans for resumption of peacetime business, and the records contain only passing references to the new "special production." Osborn and Hoglund wielded, to be sure, extensive veto authority through the executive committee that had been established at the time of the 1939 reorganization. In practice, however, that committee limited its purview to financial and pricing policies and retention of the firm's remaining production of vehicles and replacement parts. Decisions about the manufacture of the wartime "special materials" were left to the German managers. There is no evidence, however, that the Americans ever raised any objections to the firm's increasing involvement in the German war effort.[29]

In spite of the withdrawal of the GM executives from the day-to-day operations of the Rüsselsheim factory, they knew a good deal about the new "special materials" being produced there. In March 1940 Osborn complained to Mooney that he lacked "a definite idea of the character of the new production." But when Osborn and Hoglund were questioned in the United States early in 1942 by the Office of Strategic Services—the precursor of the CIA—they were able to describe the major components produced for the Ju 88 and identify it as a bomber. They also provided estimates of the output levels of both those components and the reduction gears for Mercedes airplane engines. Although Osborn had known since May 1940 that an "ammunition program" was pending at Rüsselsheim, he and Hoglund expressed uncertainty in 1942 about whether it had been implemented. It is likely that both men had avoided looking closely into the details of such highly sensitive matters as munitions production. As they gave the American intelligence official who questioned them to understand, for foreigners in the wartime Third Reich it was "more comfortable *not* to know certain things."[30]

There remains the question of how much GM's executives in the United States knew about Opel's conscription for the Nazi war effort. To the extent that they relied on the written reports submitted by the men in charge of the corporation's German subsidiary, they had only minimal and contradictory information about what was happening at Rüsselsheim. In mid-January 1940, at a meeting of GM's Overseas Policy Group in New York, Graeme Howard spoke from notes to the effect that with car production rapidly winding down, the Rüsselsheim facilities were "being utilized to increasing degree for manufacture of various components of war supplies, principally aviation. . . . Up to now we have been able to avoid actual manufacture of shells, bombs and ammunition, but direction may turn increasingly with war." But two weeks later when Mooney submitted a formal, written report on overseas operations to the senior executives who sat on GM's Administration Committee, he disclosed only that "a plan has been worked out whereby Opel will produce non-automotive parts (mostly miscellaneous airplane parts) for whose manufacture the unused physical facilities and equipment at Rüsselsheim could lend themselves effectively." In early March GM president William Knudsen told an audience at the U.S. Army Industrial College: "I have to report with some regret that Mr. Hitler is the boss of our German factory. . . . [T]he war came along and they wanted us to make munitions and we didn't want to do it, so we resigned. We have a couple of men on the Board but the management is entirely German and what they are doing I don't know."[31]

Knudsen could have found little enlightenment in a report Mooney sent to him a few weeks after this speech, following a visit to Rüsselsheim. Employing the evasive wording he had inserted into the record of the Opel Supervisory Board meeting of the previous November, Mooney assured Knudsen that "None of this new manufacture consists of material peculiar to war." At a meeting of Opel's Supervisory Board in Germany just two weeks earlier, however, Mooney had revealed that he was well aware of the uses that would be made of the company's "new manufacture." In pleading for continuation of Opel's export sales on that occasion, he insisted that these were just as important for Germany as "the necessity to produce for military purposes." In short, the head of GM's overseas operations was considerably less than forthright with his superiors in the United States, presumably out of concern that they would object to the "new materials" he and Osborn had committed Opel to produce.[32]

This does not mean that the senior executives of GM necessarily remained completely in the dark about what was being made at Rüsselsheim. Upon returning from a trip to Germany at the end of March 1940, Mooney's chief aide, William B. Wachtler, was extensively questioned by GM chairman Alfred P. Sloan on the situation at Opel. In his memorandum on their meeting, Wachtler wrote that Sloan had asked him about "Opel's special product activities" as well as about its normal products. Wachtler's memorandum contains no mention of how much he knew about war production at Rüsselsheim or how much he divulged. It does suggest, however, that Sloan learned a good deal, for

Wachtler recorded that after hearing what he had to say on that subject, Sloan responded "that of course it would be ridiculous for anyone to attempt to offer any objection or interference to these activities."[33]

By June 1940 at the latest, GM's senior executives in America had access to first-hand information about war production at Rüsselsheim. Cyrus Osborn relocated to the New York headquarters that month on what proved to be an indefinite basis, so that his observations became available to the corporation's leaders if they wanted them. Also by June, GM executives could read in Opel's annual financial report for 1939 that "the change-over from peace to war production has been accomplished in a short time and without any incidents thanks to the excellent conduct and patriotism of our employees." Nevertheless, in a report of July 1940 Graeme Howard, who had the previous month succeeded Mooney at the head of overseas operations, again resorted to euphemisms. Opel's principal activity, he informed GM's Administration Committee, "has been as a supplier of specialized parts on governmental work." In a report to the same body in February 1941, Howard became less guarded. Both Opel and GM's British subsidiary, Vauxhall, were, he wrote, achieving "large volume sales in their domestic markets of trucks, spare parts, and certain armament materials." Obviously seeking to place these overseas operations in a favorable light despite the war's curtailment of the market for civilian vehicles, Howard assessed such sales by the two subsidiaries in purely commercial terms, predicting that they "will continue to permit quite satisfactory returns which, however, will be subject to the burden of extremely high war taxes."[34]

Clearly, the executives in charge of GM's overseas operations initially believed their superiors in the United States would object to production of war materials by Opel. They therefore withheld the harsh facts in euphemism-laden reports to GM in which the words "bomber" and "ammunition" did not appear. Mooney's assurances that nothing being made at Russelsheim was "peculiar to war" may have deceived GM's leaders for a time. But from all indications, by mid-1940 at the latest enough information had become available to them to reveal the basic facts about their German subsidiary's growing contributions to Hitler's war effort. What they may have thought about this remains unclear. In all likelihood, they resigned themselves to what was happening because they realized they had little or no choice in the matter. They had the authority, of course, to order Opel to cease making war materials. That would, however, have predictably resulted in confiscation of the firm by the German government and its continued use for war production. The only important change would have been the loss by GM of a major investment. The daunting prospect of attempting to justify such a self-inflicted financial wound to share-holders presumably ruled out any serious consideration of such a step. Instead, GM's leadership responded as most people do when confronted with in-tractable situations: they did nothing and hoped that Opel's main factory would somehow soon be able to resume making and selling cars.

Chapter 7 Mr. Mooney Tries to
Stop the Second World War

In mid-October 1939, while GM's James Mooney was in Rüsselsheim overseeing the negotiations with Junkers that led to Opel's production of warplane components for that company, he received a phone call from Berlin that unexpectedly swept him into the highest realms of international politics. The caller was Heinrich Richter, Opel's legal counsel in the German capital. He had just learned from Louis Lochner, Berlin bureau chief of the Associated Press, that Hitler's press aide, Otto Dietrich, had that day indicated the desirability of finding an unofficial American emissary—preferably a "broadminded businessman"—willing to explore the possibility of mediation by Washington on behalf of a negotiated end to the war. Richter quickly suggested that the best possible man for that undertaking would be Mooney. Ruggedly handsome, dapper, and affable, the outspoken head of GM's overseas operations was something of a celebrity in the United States. Because of the striking successes of the overseas division despite the Depression, he was portrayed in newspapers and popular magazines as the ideal pragmatic, problem-solving American businessman. His flamboyant style made him a popular after-dinner speaker, and his views on world affairs were headline news. Knowing that Mooney was in Germany, Richter proposed him, via Lochner, to Dietrich, who quickly gave his approval. After hearing the reason for Richter's call, Mooney left at once for Berlin and embarked upon what was to become a quixotic, year-long, one-man crusade to end the war.[1]

Dietrich's initiative reflected the deviousness of Hitler's policies following his lightning conquest of Poland. Although the British and the French had declared war when, despite their warnings, he had launched his armies eastward six weeks earlier, they made no effort to come to the aid of the Poles militarily. After Poland succumbed in late September, what became known as the "phony war" set in. Aside from occasional artillery exchanges across the French-German border and some German naval attacks on British ships, no combat took place. In an effort to weaken his opponents by driving a wedge between London and Paris, Hitler sought to cultivate antiwar sentiment in Britain by appealing for a negotiated settlement in widely publicized speeches. Even as he secretly laid plans for massive aggression against Western Europe, he protested that Germany had no quarrel with Britain and France and no interest in pursuing a war they, not Germany, had declared. Despite repeated British rejection of negotiations, hope remained alive in Berlin that pressure might be brought to bear on London by the United States, where antiwar isolationism was still ascendant. Lackeys of Hitler like Dietrich therefore sought to enlist possible American message-bearers.[2]

Mooney proved ideal for such purposes. Although he was later sometimes depicted as a pro-German, Irish-American Anglophobe, such was not the case. He had fought against the Germans in the First World War as a captain in an American artillery unit, and he never wavered from the view that if the United States should be drawn into another European war it would fight "on the side of our old allies, the English and the French." He enjoyed cordial relations with the staff of GM's British subsidiary, Vauxhall Motors, whose operations, like those of Opel, he supervised for the American corporation. He preferred to spend time in Britain rather than in Germany, a country whose language he never mastered and whose culture remained alien to him despite his frequent visits to Opel's Rüsselsheim headquarters.[3]

Mooney was also not, as sometimes charged, an isolationist. Having made a highly successful career in international trade, he opposed a U.S. withdrawal from the world market or overseas affairs. He believed, however, that American foreign policy should be restricted to the furtherance of the material interests of the United States. In no sense a pacifist, he publicly advocated vigorous Amer-

James D. Mooney, president of General Motors Overseas Operations. Courtesy of GM Media Archive.

ican preparations for the possibility of war as the crisis mounted in Europe, even as he cautioned against involvement in a new war. Armed neutrality was, in his view, the proper posture for the United States. A new war would, he predicted, be a disaster for all involved. "If the last war very nearly ruined the warring nations," he warned in a speech to the American Academy of Political and Social Science in 1937, "the next war may do so utterly. Such a debacle could only result in a gigantic and universal social upheaval, with bloody class war and revolution the only possible outcome." He himself, of course, had abundant personal cause for dreading a major European conflict, which would have a ruinous effect on the overseas operations of General Motors. Economic self-interest was therefore very much a factor in his fear of a new war.[4]

Like many influential persons in the United States and Britain, Mooney believed that Germany had been unjustly dealt with in the Versailles Treaty. But unlike his subordinate, Graeme Howard, who as late as May 1939 publicly defended Hitler's right "to regain for his people the things they lost" at Versailles, Mooney took no stand on the territorial demands of the Third Reich. In numerous speeches to American audiences during the 1930s, he maintained that frictions between nations "arise principally out of economic causes." With reference to the situation in Europe, he reduced that view to the most elemental level. "Germany will not be taken off the warpath," he warned the Rochester Chamber of Commerce in 1937, "until some means are provided for removing the threat of starvation that imposes itself upon sixty million German people. It is one of the axioms of history that hungry bellies cause wars and revolutions. Germany's hungry belly is the cause of the ugly face with which Germany confronts her European neighbors. Germany's belligerence is only a symptom: it is the result of hunger in Germany and of a desperate fear of hunger. . . . When this great war will come, whether it will come at all, I do not even pretend to be able to say. But I do know that the Germans will not starve. They will be on the march again before they starve." This dire warning was, however, not accompanied by any explanation of how the generally well-fed Germans of the day might be in peril of starvation.[5]

In Mooney's simplistic view of international affairs, ideological factors played little or no part. His education as a technical engineer at Cleveland's Case School of Applied Science had not equipped him for dealing with such matters, and his career in business had left him disdainful of governments in general. The ideologies then rampant in Europe seemed to him nothing more than smoke screens "used principally as a means of grasping and consolidating power." Injustices committed by fanatical regimes were of no interest to him so long as they did not interfere with the transaction of business. After a trip to the Soviet Union in 1930 that left him hopeful of a large market there for GM products, he described that country in glowing terms to an audience at the Council on Foreign Relations in New York despite the terror and mass privation then being imposed by the Stalinist regime. Like other businessmen, he feared a spread of Communism elsewhere, but he remained indifferent to the hardships experienced by the people of the Soviet Union. In explaining his position with regard to Russia to GM president Alfred P. Sloan, he summarized his view of political considerations: "The questions which I asked myself in this connection involved only one which touched upon the political aspect of things in any way, and that was the question that we have to ask ourselves in any market—including the United States—where we contemplate doing business; the question, simply as to whether or not the Government is stable. . . . I think that as business men we cease to be interested in whether that government is autocratic or democratic or bolshevik, or whatever it happens to be in the hands of Methodists or Catholics or Mohammadans or Atheists."[6]

Nazi tyranny left Mooney similarly unmoved. An American diplomat who in 1934 questioned his endorsement of the bilateral barter trade terms favored by the Third Reich found that he saw "no reason why we should let our moral indignation over what happens in a country stand in the way. He says that we make arrangements with other countries where conditions are practically as bad." When the diplomat warned that the Nazis could not be trusted, Mooney replied that "he felt as much confidence could be placed in an agreement made with them as with anyone else, that he had had enough experience to know that recently one could place little confidence in any agreements." In his 1937 speech to the American Academy of Political and Social Science, he scornfully dismissed "moralists and internationally minded politicians who would have us defend some political principle or ideology abroad."[7]

These views led Mooney into the ranks of the economic appeasers of the 1930s. Like many others in the upper echelons of government and business in both the United States and Britain, he advocated adoption of financial and trade policies that would assure Germany of an abundant supply of food and access to raw materials sufficient to supply its peacetime industries. Once such measures were in effect, he was confident that the Nazi regime would curtail its military preparations. "If Germany is not to move east politically," he was quoted in October 1938 as saying, "she must move west economically." Blinkered by his subordination of politics to economics, Mooney was incapable of registering the mounting evidence that Hitler was a megalomanic outlaw who could never be deterred from his pursuit of sweeping conquests by mere adjustments in the terms of international trade. Like many others, he also saw Germany as a bulwark against the spread of Communism.[8]

Mooney clung to economic appeasement even after Hitler seized the remainder of Czechoslovakia in March 1939 in brazen violation of the Munich Agreement. In April he went to Berlin with the aim of seeking a way to free GM from the necessity of expending more dollars to pay for imported rubber needed to outfit Opel vehicles with tires. In hopes of ending the currency controls that prohibited the use of Opel's German marks for that purpose, he proposed to German finance officials a large Anglo-American gold loan in return for abandonment of those controls and other trade restrictions. When those officials responded encouragingly, he saw an opportunity to pacify Europe through economic appeasement by arranging such a loan. He therefore headed to Britain to promote his idea. Upon hearing Mooney's proposal, the American ambassador in London, Joseph P. Kennedy, expressed interest and agreed to travel to Paris to confer with one of the German financial officials. To the ambassador's chagrin, however, the State Department vetoed such a trip. Undeterred, Mooney made arrangements for one of the German officials, Hellmuth Wohlthat, Göring's deputy in the four-year-plan economic administration, to travel to England and meet secretly with him and Ambassador Kennedy at Mooney's London hotel early in May. He later recalled that Kennedy had gotten on well with Wohlthat, a non-Nazi who spoke fluent English as a result of having spent considerable time in the United States. A London newspaper quickly learned, however, of Wohlthat's mysterious visit and published a report attributing sinister motives to him. As a result, the ambassador had to drop the matter, and Mooney's effort petered out. After returning to the United States in late May 1939, he nevertheless continued to speak out publicly in favor of American initiatives for economic appeasement of Germany.[9]

Not even Hitler's invasion of Poland shook Mooney's belief in economic appeasement. In an interview with a prominent American journalist in early October 1939, after the fall of Poland, he said he saw no obstacles to "a permanent settlement on an amicable basis" if the British and French would make extensive economic concessions to Germany and restore to the Reich the overseas colonies stripped from it after the First World War. The article based on that interview appeared in numerous American newspapers, and it is likely that it did not escape the notice of Nazi agents in the United States. This may explain the alacrity with which Hitler's press aide Dietrich gave his approval when Louis Lochner proposed Mooney as a mediator with Washington.[10]

Upon arriving in Berlin in mid-October 1939 in response to attorney Richter's telephone call, Mooney consulted with him and with Louis Lochner. At their suggestion, he telephoned Göring's aide Hellmuth Wohlthat and arranged to dine with him the following evening. When Mooney disclosed his intention to promote a negotiated peace, Wohlthat offered his encouragement and arranged an appointment for him with Göring. When he consulted with Wohlthat again, the evening before meeting with Göring, Mooney thought he heard the German make a startling disclosure in veiled language: "Dr. Wohlthat was trying," he later wrote, "to tell me that the British would not be required to reverse their previous expressed refusal to deal with the existing German government. He gave me the unmistakable impression that the Germans could, if necessary, shift the line-up of their team, as it were, and retire Herr Hitler to a kind of Valhalla or, as we might say in America, make him Chairman of the Board." Coming from an aide of the second most prominent Nazi, this message seemed of the utmost importance to Mooney.[11]

On October 19, Mooney met with Göring for several hours, with Wohlthat translating. Göring adhered to the Nazi propaganda line by holding out a vague prospect of autonomy for Poland and Czechoslovakia under German hegemony. Questioned about the British Empire, Göring reiterated Hitler's offers of a guarantee for its integrity. When Mooney inquired whether Germany would be willing to abandon its ties with Japan and the Soviet Union if a deal could be arranged with London that was acceptable to Paris and Washington, Göring's answer was, as Mooney later recalled, "immediate, spontaneous, and emphatic. What he said in German was the equivalent of the American expression, 'Hell, yes!'" According to Mooney, Göring then added: "If we could make a deal with the British, we'd throw the Japs and Russians overboard the next day." As he rose to leave, Mooney later recalled, Göring "came around from his side of the huge desk, took hold of my arm and, shaking his finger in my face, said: 'Now Mooney, don't get me wrong about this situation. I am asking you, for our government, to go over to see the British and find out what this war is all about. We have read [Prime Minister] Chamberlain's recent speeches and can't figure out whether he really wants to fight or not. . . . Whatever answer you bring back will be satisfactory to me, so long as the matter is made perfectly clear.'" For his part, Mooney agreed to find out on what terms the British would be willing to end the war and to suggest to them that representatives of the two governments meet incognito in a neutral country "for a confidential chat as a preliminary to a peace proposal." As they parted, Göring indicated his readiness to represent Germany personally at such talks if the British wished. After their meeting, it occurred to Mooney that this final remark by Göring seemed to confirm what he had the previous evening taken as Wohlthat's suggestion that Hitler could, if necessary, be pushed aside in order to end the war.[12]

Unaware that the Nazis had assigned the same mission to several citizens of neutral countries, including other American businessmen, Mooney assumed that he alone had been chosen to bear a message of momentous significance. Since there was no American ambassador in Berlin, he left for Paris the day after his meeting with Göring to explain his mission to the ambassador to France, William C. Bullitt, by way of courtesy to the U.S. government. A seasoned diplomat, the ambassador was aware of the duplicitous game the Nazis were playing. He received Mooney cordially, but upon hearing of his mission grew concerned that his amateurish intervention might damage American relations with the British and the French. In the course of a conversation at the embassy and later over tea at his residence, Bullitt sought, in what Mooney later described as "his charming and genial fashion," to prevail upon him to drop the matter. When Mooney nevertheless asked him to urge Ambassador Kennedy to persuade the British government to take up Göring's proposal of a meeting, Bullitt refused. The ambassador also declined to commend Mooney's message to the French authorities, a decision promptly confirmed by Secretary of State Cordell Hull.[13]

Mooney later bitterly wrote: "I am quite certain that William C. Bullitt did everything he could to spike my mission." That was true, but Bullitt was far from alone. The top echelon of the State Department also set out to thwart Mooney. The ambassador's telegram informing Secretary of State Hull about what Mooney had told him set off alarms in Washington. Lord Lothian, the British ambassador to the United States, telegraphed the Foreign Office that the State Department "warns us to beware of Mr. James Mooney, Vice-President of General Motors, who is now in Europe and has been completely got at by the Germans." Mooney was, Lothian's telegram continued, "propagating the tale of the Hitler-Göring split" earlier borne to London by another American businessman enlisted as a messenger by Berlin. Mooney was, the British ambassador noted, "formerly quite an important and responsible man, but is believed by his friends to have gone quite off his head." General Motors was, Lothian added, "much embarrassed by his behavior, of which they strongly disapprove."[14]

Undeterred by Bullitt's rebuff, Mooney proceeded to London, determined to convey Göring's proposal to the British government. There he received a decidedly chilly reception from Ambassador Kennedy, who had been briefed by Bullitt. "While still shaking my hand in greeting," Mooney later recalled, "he exclaimed loudly that he refused to have any part in the 'damned affair.'" The ambassador, who was pessimistic about Britain's chances of surviving a German onslaught, began to display interest, however, upon hearing that Göring had held out the possibility of a peaceful end to the war. He therefore urged Mooney to put the matter to the British foreign secretary, Lord Halifax. Kennedy also advised Mooney to speak with Halifax's senior adviser, Sir Robert Vansittart, whose brother Nicholas was a manager in the European division of Mooney's GM overseas organization. Informed immediately by Mooney of his mission, Nicholas Vansittart arranged for him to see Sir Robert that afternoon at the Foreign Office.[15]

Robert Vansittart, who had met Mooney earlier through his brother, heard him out and promptly reported at length to Halifax. Referring to the warning from Washington in Lord Lothian's telegram, Vansittart wrote: "I do not think that Mr. Mooney is off his head, but I think it is quite likely that he may have been got at by the Germans. After all, a great number of 'important and responsible' English people have, up to the verge of war and even beyond it, been got at by German propaganda without being in the least off their heads." Mooney was not to be confused with shady American businessmen who were proposing to mediate with Berlin. He was instead "presumably a man of complete personal integrity" who had "held a high position in a great American company for a long while." Mooney, he pointed out, "evidently has free access to Messrs. Bullitt and Kennedy, who have apparently not treated him as a lunatic."[16]

Although he vouched for Mooney's character, Robert Vansittart expressed grave reservations about his mission. He dismissed as naïve Mooney's belief in Göring's sincerity and a possible split in the Nazi leadership ranks. He also doubted that anything more than "wedge-driving between us and the French" was behind Göring's mention of German concessions in the event of peace negotiations. Nevertheless, Vansittart was "in favour of playing this hand out" by encouraging Mooney to report to Göring that there was interest in London in his proposals. If "adroitly played," he explained, this could "have one of two results." The optimal outcome, which he thought unlikely, could "lead to within sight of a solid peace." Even if that failed to be the case, he saw "considerable advantage" in "gaining time" and thereby possibly staving off a German attack to the west until the British and the French were better prepared to fight. Since no official British involvement would be necessary, Mooney's effort could at any point be disavowed without any damage to London, he pointed out.[17]

Sir Robert's recommendation prevailed, despite delays apparently resulting from the Foreign Office's need to assess other peace initiatives. At his urging, Mooney sent two encouraging messages to Berlin via businessmen traveling to the Continent from London in late October and early November. The day before he was to depart for Berlin, he was received by Halifax himself. In the course of a brief conversation, the foreign secretary warned Mooney that Britain could not engage in peace discussions with the Germans at that time. As a result of past disappointments, he explained, Prime Minister Chamberlain and he could place no trust in Hitler and his foreign minister, Joachim von Ribbentrop. Moreover, any such move on Britain's part would be regarded as another "Munich" and result in a loss of face politically. Nevertheless, Halifax raised no objections to Mooney's returning to Berlin and instructed him that Robert Vansittart would the following day give him an answer to take with him.[18]

When Mooney, accompanied by Nicholas Vansittart, arrived at the Foreign Office the next morning, the message the British wanted him to take to Göring lay before Sir Robert on his desk. Mooney was not permitted to see it, however. Instead, Sir Robert repeatedly read the text to him until he had committed it to memory. As Mooney later recalled, the message reiterated Britain's refusal to negotiate until the Nazi regime had been replaced by a government in which London could place confidence. Mooney also recalled that in the course of repeating this message in order to memorize it, he at one point mistakenly said "a form of government" instead of "a government." At that point, Sir Robert "corrected me briskly. The message, he pointed out emphatically, did not say 'a form of government,' but 'a government.'" From this, Mooney concluded that the British might be willing to negotiate even with a Nazi regime if—as he believed Wohlthat had suggested to him—Hitler could be shoved aside. After the meeting with Sir Robert, Mooney and Nicholas Vansittart proceeded to GM's London office, where they checked each other's memory and wrote the British message down. The next day, Mooney later recalled, he carried the text with him in the bottom of one of his shoes. After reading it through again to check his memory on the boat train to Dover on his way to Germany, he tore it into pieces and committed these to a toilet. Disappointed that the British message failed to respond positively to Göring's overture, Mooney nevertheless remained hopeful of serving as "a sort of catalytic agent" to bring representatives of the two warring countries to the peace table.[19]

Reaching Berlin in mid-November, Mooney at once sought to contact Hellmuth Wohlthat. Believing that Wohlthat had a month earlier held out the possibility of replacing Hitler—presumably with Göring—Mooney hoped he would respond positively to the British message. Concerned that the message would displease, if not anger, Göring, he was willing to deliver it only after obtaining Wohlthat's support and only if the latter accompanied him and again served as translator. To his disappointment, however, he found that Wohlthat was absent from the capital. Declining an offer by Wohlthat's aide to arrange an appointment with Göring, Mooney proceeded to a hotel in Rome, where he had been led to believe that Wohlthat would soon arrive. After waiting there in vain for two weeks, he finally established contact with Wohlthat, who was in Madrid, and arranged to meet with him there. To Mooney's disappointment, however, Wohlthat responded negatively to the British message when they finally met. In contrast to what Mooney believed to have been earlier hints on his part about a change of leadership in the Nazi government, the German now dismissed that idea as impossible. Left without any encouragement from Wohlthat, Mooney decided against delivering the British message to Göring and flew to New York in mid-December.[20]

Upon his return to the United States, Mooney set out to take his case for peace negotiations directly to President Roosevelt. Although he, like most American businessmen, objected to many New Deal economic policies, he was a registered Democrat in good personal standing with the president. The two had met on several occasions, and Roosevelt had consulted him on commercial matters. Through one of his GM staff, Edward Riley, Mooney gained access to Basil O'Connor, a New York attorney and personal friend of the president since their days as young partners in the same law firm. Impressed with Mooney's account of his trip, O'Connor arranged an off-the-record appointment for him with Roosevelt at the White House a few days before Christmas.[21]

As Mooney later recalled, he was cordially received by the president. With obvious pride, he noted that the president insisted at the outset on lighting his cigarette as a gesture of welcome. What he had expected would be a brief meeting stretched, at Roosevelt's insistence, into an hour-and-a-half conversation. After hearing a detailed account of his European trip, the president began sharing thoughts of his own. Immediately after leaving the White House, Mooney recorded some of Roosevelt's observations as follows: "I am not interested in saying to the Germans what they shall do about Hitler. That is their own affair. . . . I wish you would remind the Germans that I went to school in Germany, that I became very familiar with the country in my younger days, and have a great many German personal friends. . . . But I wish Germany would pipe down about dominating the world." According to Mooney, Roosevelt added that he would be no more favorably inclined to "a scheme for world domination on the part of the British or the French than I am on the part of the Germans." He recalled that the president then launched into an explanation of his administration's aims for trade liberalization but expressed understanding that it would take time for a country like Germany to abandon restrictive controls and prepare for acceptance of the most-favored-nation principle favored by the United States.[22]

When Roosevelt turned to the war in Europe, Mooney wrote after their meeting, he expressed the view that it ought to be "reasonably simple to get around a table with the proper will and settle problems like Silesia, Poland, Czechoslovakia, and the general attitude toward Russia." He also held out the possibility of a role for himself: "I would much prefer to present myself as a possible moderator in the situation and offer my services in this capacity than to offer them as an arbitrator." At the close of the conversation, Mooney noted, Roosevelt agreed with him that the "problem is to take his general peace approach and dovetail in practical suggestions satisfactory to Berlin, London and Paris." Mooney came away from the meeting with the impression that the president had suggested that he should undertake informal talks with the belligerents in order to encourage preliminary steps toward formal peace negotiations. "I would appreciate being informed on what they really and actually have on their minds," he recorded the president's saying as they parted.

Upon returning to New York in January 1940 from a Florida vacation, Mooney heard from Basil O'Connor that another appointment had been made for him at the White House. Roosevelt wanted him, O'Connor confided, to return to Europe and sound out the leaders of the warring states about their aims and the terms on which they would discuss a peaceful settlement. When he entered the president's office on the appointed day, Mooney later recalled, Roosevelt's first words were, "Well, when are you leaving?" Having made advance steamer reservations, he was able to reply that he would be sailing for Naples the following week. In discussing the practicalities of his new mission, the president asked that Mooney make his trip "on my own steam," avoiding official channels and traveling on an ordinary passport. As he was about to leave, Roosevelt offered to provide him with a letter as a "kind of informal credential" and dictated the following words to an aide:

> Dear Jim:
>   I enjoyed our little chat this morning very much. Just a line to wish you good luck and I shall expect you to drop in to see me when you return to America.
>   Very sincerely yours,

Two days later, the note, on White House stationery and bearing the signature of the president, arrived at Mooney's New York office.[23]

In the course of his conversation with Roosevelt, Mooney suggested, and the president agreed, that it would be advisable for him to inform Secretary of State Cordell Hull of his trip. But when he arrived at the State Department later that day he was informed that Hull was confined to his home by illness. He was referred to George S. Messersmith, a veteran diplomat with whom he had long been on friendly terms. Upon hearing of his plans, Messersmith objected strongly that such a venture would be ill-advised. He vehemently sought to dissuade Mooney, pointing out that the State Department had looked with great disfavor on his actions the previous autumn. But when Mooney announced that the president had approved his plans, the "flabbergasted" Messersmith reluctantly granted his request for an expedited passport renewal. On a subsequent trip to Washington, Mooney similarly received no encouragement from Assistant Secretary of State Adolf Berle.[24]

Mooney soon had reason for added concern about lack of support from the State Department. While at sea on his way to Europe, he learned that Undersecretary of State Sumner Welles had been dispatched to Europe by Roosevelt. Pausing in Rome, Mooney found that, despite the assurances he had received from the State Department, the American ambassador there had not been informed of his mission but was instead preoccupied with preparations for Welles' arrival. Upon reaching Berlin, Mooney addressed a letter to Welles in care of the Rome embassy, expressing hope that they could meet. It went unanswered, as did a similar letter that Mooney left with the American chargé d'affaires on the eve of Welles' arrival in Berlin on March 1. A calling card he sent to the undersecretary's hotel also brought no response. When Mooney requested to see Welles the chargé d'affaires responded evasively and provided no information about his schedule. This snub was in keeping with other efforts by his critics in the State Department to discredit him. Soon after his arrival in Berlin, the secrecy of his trip was dispelled by an article in a London newspaper based on information that could only have come from insiders in Washington. Its report that he was carrying a peace feeler to Germany on behalf of Roosevelt once again set off alarms among British diplomats, leading one to comment: "US businessmen are capable of anything."[25]

Learning that many Americans in Berlin had been invited to an embassy cocktail party in honor of Welles on March 2 following the latter's meeting with Hitler, Mooney saw an opportunity for an exchange of information with the diplomat. Although he had not received the usual printed invitation, he waited in his hotel room that afternoon in hopes of receiving one by telephone. When none came, he nevertheless went to the embassy in the company of Lochner, who had been invited as a prominent member of the press corps. When Mooney arrived, the unpleasantly surprised chargé d'affaires declined to introduce him to Welles. By the time he finally located the diplomat in the throng of guests, Welles was quickly whisked away to meet someone else before they had exchanged more than what Mooney later described as two minutes' worth of "commonplace remarks." He later complained that for "the typical stuffed shirt diplomat" Sumner Welles, he was "just a dumb businessman."[26]

Attributing the State Department's cold-shoulder treatment to resentment of an outsider on the part of professional diplomats, Mooney set out to convey Roosevelt's views personally to Adolf Hitler. Upon his arrival in Berlin in mid-February he had sent a letter to the dictator requesting a meeting. "The people of my own country," he wrote, "feel that the war can only end in disaster for Europe and that the war will eventually have very serious consequences in America. I know that the welfare of the people and their inner feelings have always lain close to your heart, and I believe that it would serve a useful purpose if I were given the opportunity to discuss this problem generally with you. I also know that you . . . belong to the group of men in Europe who believe that the present war is a poor and disastrous way to dispose of the many international political and economic mistakes that have been made since 1914, and it is on this common ground that I should like to discuss the entire problem with you."[27]

Since Mooney refrained from claiming to be Roosevelt's emissary, he would presumably have failed to gain access to Hitler had it not been for the brief note to him that bore the president's signature. When he showed it to Göring's aide Wohlthat and to Hans Heinrich Dieckhoff, the German ambassador to the United States who had been recalled from Washington two years earlier, they attached greater significance to his request to see Hitler than would otherwise have been the case. In view of Welles' pending official visit, Dieckhoff asked Lochner whether the unofficial Mooney could have anything important to say to Hitler. Lochner, who was supportive of Mooney's mission, replied that President Woodrow Wilson's highly influential foreign policy adviser, Colonel Edward House, had also operated in unofficial fashion. Soon thereafter, Mooney was granted an appointment with Foreign Minister von Ribbentrop. After being shown Roosevelt's note, Ribbentrop pressed Mooney to disclose what the president had told him. Maintaining that he was obligated to convey Roosevelt's message first to Hitler, Mooney promised to share it with the foreign minister, but only after he had personally disclosed it to the dictator. Shortly thereafter, he was notified that Hitler would receive him.[28]

At midday on March 4, two Foreign Ministry officials called for Mooney at his hotel and accompanied him in a government limousine to Hitler's grandiose new Chancellery on the Wilhelmstrasse. As he emerged from the car, uniformed guards presented arms, and at the entrance he was received with elaborate formality by State Secretary Otto Meissner, whose help he had sought in the Stief affair a year earlier. Inside, he was marched along the same route described by Sumner Welles in a report to Washington two days earlier, down the length of "a tremendously long red marble hall, of which the walls and floor are both of marble; then up a flight of excessively slippery red marble steps into a gallery . . . also of red marble." After a brief wait in an antechamber off the gallery, Mooney was admitted to Hitler's huge office, where he soon found himself seated at an outsized hearth, alone with the dictator of Germany except for an interpreter and a uniformed guard in the background.[29]

After an exchange of polite remarks, in the course of which Hitler recalled their meeting of 1934, Mooney showed him the note he had received from Roosevelt, along with a German translation. When Hitler indicated his readiness to hear him out, he spoke from a lengthy memorandum he had prepared with the help of the journalist Lochner. From it, Mooney quoted Roosevelt's remarks to him about his youthful experiences in Germany, his German friends, and his unwillingness to tell the Germans who should head their government. Leaving unmentioned Roosevelt's wish that the Germans would "pipe down about dominating the world," Mooney quoted only his more general rejection of world domination by any country. He also spelled out the president's desire for trade liberalization and free access to raw materials, placing added emphasis on Roosevelt's observation that countries like Germany would require time before they could abandon their restrictive policies. Finally, Mooney quoted the president's expression of interest in serving as a moderator in peace negotiations. By way of clarification, he handed Hitler an analysis, in German, of the meaning attached to the term "moderator" by American Protestants. That statement, which Hitler read after donning the eyeglasses he never wore in public, explained that whereas arbitrators joined in negotiations and proposed settlements, moderators were limited to clarifying points of disagreement among contesting parties and helping them resolve their differences themselves.[30]

When Mooney had finished his presentation, Hitler launched into one of his lengthy monologues. In contrast to his sarcastic ridicule of Roosevelt as a naïve busybody in a much-publicized speech a year earlier, he began by expressing admiration for the president's accomplishments. The rumor to the effect that he had had urged German-Americans to vote against Roosevelt when he stood for re-election in 1936 was, he indignantly claimed, a lie. Turning to the current situation in Europe, Hitler denied any responsibility for the war. Britain and France, not Germany, had declared war. He had no further war aims other than to thwart the intention of the British and French to destroy and partition the Reich. In eliminating the Czechoslovak state and occupying Poland, Germany had merely acted to remove the Western powers' hostile dominance over eastern Europe and halt persecution of the German minority in Poland. The only way to end the war, Hitler insisted, was for the British and French to abandon their aim of destroying Germany, end discrimination against German trade in their colonial empires, and return the colonies they had taken from Germany after the First World War. In return for their recognition of Germany as a world power, the Reich stood ready to respect the integrity of Britain and France. He was confident, Hitler said, that he and Roosevelt would quickly reach agreement on these points if they could speak directly with each other. Germany had no quarrel with America. It was essential, however, that the United States not encourage the British and the French to continue a futile war they were bound to lose against a militarily superior Germany that now enjoyed the sympathy of three powers that had helped defeat the Reich in the First World War: Italy, Japan, and Russia.

Mooney left the Chancellery believing he had achieved significant progress toward ending the war. Dazzled, like so many others, at being accorded a private audience in such an awe-inspiring setting with the most powerful man in Europe and lulled by the moderate tone Hitler could adopt on such occasions, he failed to recognize that the dictator had expressed no readiness to make significant concessions and no willingness to accept Roosevelt as a moderator. Mooney himself had made no attempt to challenge Hitler's self-serving version of the war's origin and the aims of Germany and its adversaries. Instead, he had responded to the dictator's recitation of German grievances ingratiatingly, assuring him that far more Americans, including the president, were sympathetic to the German viewpoint than was revealed by the country's media. Hitler's assessment of Mooney's message is not recorded. But after hearing much the same "rather verbose statements" from Mooney later that day, Ambassador Dieckhoff informed the Foreign Ministry: "I do not believe that the Mooney initiative has any great importance, particularly since he proceeds from an erroneous, though doubtless sincere, conception" regarding Roosevelt's attitude toward Germany.[31]

Unaware that Hitler had, three days before their meeting, embarked upon open conflict with the Western powers by ordering the invasion of Denmark and Norway to begin in April, Mooney pressed on, assuming that peace was within reach. Before leaving Berlin he met again with Göring, who assured him that Germany was prepared to deal generously with the Czechs and Poles. Still seeking to divide the British from the French, Göring again insisted that London must take the first step toward peace. After a stop in Munich for a meeting of Opel's Supervisory Board, Mooney proceeded to neutral Rome. There he composed five lengthy letters to Roosevelt, encompassing nearly thirty single-spaced typed pages, which he arranged, as an officer in the Naval reserve, for the Naval attaché at the American embassy to encode and dispatch by cable in mid-March.[32]

In his voluminous letters to Roosevelt Mooney provided an exhaustive account of his visit to Berlin and his meeting with Hitler, accompanied by appeals for intervention by the president. He characterized the attitude of the German officials as "one of warm response to your personal, informal, unofficial interest in the whole problem. They seem eager to work with you to resolve the present difficulties in the direction of a more orderly political and economic world." Germany was ready for peace and "willing to make such concessions for Poland and Czechoslovakia as could please world opinion in relation to the religious, cultural and political autonomy of these nations." Roosevelt was, Mooney assured him, the only person who could stop the war. The peoples of Europe, he repeatedly asserted, longed for peace and looked to the president for a way out of the war. Although the president had made clear his unwillingness to involve himself in negotiations as an arbitrator, Mooney appealed to him to "set forth before the belligerents an attractive framework for an orderly political and economic world, which you would invite the belligerents to join."[33]

When no reply came from Roosevelt, Mooney dispatched his aide William Wachtler to the United States with copies of his five messages while he himself continued to wait in Rome. Arriving by plane in New York in late March, Wachtler contacted Roosevelt's friend Basil O'Connor, who agreed to pursue the matter with the president. By that time, Sumner Welles' bleak report on the defiant stance of the German government had dampened Roosevelt's interest in exploring the possibilities for peace negotiations. After acknowledging receipt of Mooney's messages in a brief telegram at the end of March, the president addressed a letter to him in Rome at the beginning of April. Although he wrote that Mooney's messages had "been of real value to me," Roosevelt did not respond to the appeals for intervention on his part. He also avoided mention of any further role for Mooney, writing only: "I hope from time to time you will give me further news." A week later, prospects for a peaceful settlement of the war were greatly diminished when German forces invaded Denmark and Norway, a move that brought them into combat with British and French units there.[34]

Entrusted to the navy, the president's noncommittal letter would not reach

Mooney in Rome until four weeks after it was sent. In mid-April, however, Mooney was informed via trans-Atlantic telephone by his GM subordinate Edward Riley that Basil O'Connor had spoken to Roosevelt by phone in Riley's presence and relayed the president's wish that Mooney remain in Rome for another week and then return to Berlin. Late in April, after awaiting in vain further instructions from Washington, Mooney received instead the president's delayed letter as well as a report from his colleague Osborn to the effect that in the wake of the successful German invasion of Denmark and Norway, Wohlthat no longer showed any interest in peace talks. Upon hearing from Riley at the end of the month that O'Connor saw no reason for him to remain in Europe, Mooney abandoned his mission and sailed from Naples for New York. Failing to recognize that the president's letter revealed that he had no further use for him, Mooney composed still another lengthy letter to Roosevelt during his voyage. Expressing confidence that that the German invasions would not preclude a negotiated settlement he again offered his services in pursuit of a "peaceful way out." The same day this letter was posted in New York to the White House, the Third Reich launched its massive offensive against the Low Countries and France.[35]

While at sea, Mooney also drafted a speech that he delivered at the beginning of June to an alumni gathering at his alma mater, the Case School in Cleveland, after clearing the text with Basil O'Connor. In it, he predicted dire consequences if the war continued and proposed "that we consider the possibility of using America's enormous economic and potential military strength to compel a discussion of peace." The speech, which was broadcast by a national radio network, printed in pamphlet form, and entered into the *Congressional Register*, attracted such widespread attention that the editor of a popular weekly magazine, the *Saturday Evening Post*, offered to publish an expanded version of Mooney's views. In the article that resulted, Mooney attributed the war to economic grievances on the part of Germany and fear of German power on the part of the French and British. "Our sympathies have been and are with England and French," he wrote. But although America had "moved step by step, always closer to actual participation in the war on the side of England," he warned that the United States could not be fully armed for another two or three years. Rather than "encouraging the British to make a last stand," America should therefore step in as a "referee" and "stop this fight" in order to "save England from further misery." The United States should serve notice that unless the belligerents agreed to a peaceful settlement, America would eventually enter the war. The British should be told, "If you won't talk peace now, but insist on continuing the struggle, we will not enter the war in a military way to help you." The Germans should be told, "If you won't talk peace now, and talk reasonably, we will arm to the teeth and make war by ourselves, if need be, against you."[36]

When an advance copy of Mooney's article reached Roosevelt via O'Connor in late June, the president was not pleased with what he read. Mooney's claim that the United States was drifting toward war must have been particularly annoying, since Roosevelt was striving to reassure the still largely isolationist public of his opposition to any American involvement in the conflict as he approached a bid for an unprecedented third term as president. In his response to O'Connor about Mooney's article the president wrote: "I wish very much that he would run down to talk to me about it because there are a good many statements in it which are contrary to fact, and I am sure he does not want to go on record in regard to certain matters about which he has little, if any, personal knowledge. Incidentally, this article, in its present form, would receive enormous quotation in the Hitler-controlled German press. . . . You might tell Jim, in addition, that the principal premise of the article is, in the judgement of the President of the United States, dangerously false. The premise is that we are about to enter the war." Nevertheless, the president informed O'Connor, "I should be glad to see Jim, here on Monday, Tuesday or Wednesday of next week."[37]

A telegram was promptly sent to Mooney, inviting him to meet with Roosevelt the following week, but he was not to see the president again. A day after the invitation was extended, Secretary of Commerce Harry Hopkins wrote to Roosevelt that he had informed Basil O'Connor that Mooney's article "expressed the very antithesis of your viewpoint." Later that day, Mooney was notified by telegram that a change in the president's travel plans necessitated cancellation of his appointment. He responded with yet another letter to Roosevelt, expressing the view "that under the present conditions of a lull in the actual warfare and in view of the fact that England is now faced with confronting her enemy alone, it would be very useful, from the standpoint of the mutual interest of the United States and the British Empire, if the hostilities could be called off. . . . I still hope that I may be able to interest you in taking a position for peace." There is no record of any response from the White House.[38]

After Mooney's *Saturday Evening Post* article appeared in early August he found himself under attack in the press. A New York tabloid, *PM,* accused him, along others, including Colonel Charles Lindbergh, of belonging to a "League of Benedict Arnolds" that was conducting a "treasonable undeclared war against the United States" on behalf of Hitler. By selectively quoting from Mooney's article and claiming that the German medal he had received two years earlier had just been bestowed on him by Hitler, the paper portrayed him as a tool of the Nazi dictator. Misleadingly identified by *PM* as a "chum" of a German foreign trade official stationed in New York, he was falsely accused of having been one of that official's guests at banquet at the Waldorf-Astoria Hotel to celebrate the fall of France. A labor weekly, *New Leader,* branded Mooney as a "supporter of Nazi Germany" and "leader of an American Cliveden set," a reference to upper-class British advocates of appeasing Hitler. Deeply wounded by these aspersions on his patriotism, Mooney had an attorney draft a letter demanding a retraction on the part of the publisher of *PM* under threat of a libel suit, but he was persuaded by GM colleagues to drop the matter.[39]

Transferred within GM in June of 1940 from its largely immobilized overseas division to a new staff in charge of conversion to American war production, Mooney persisted in exploring possibilities for a negotiated peace during the rest of the year. In mid-July he informed a German trade emissary in New York that his efforts had, for the time being, failed, but, like Henry Ford, he expressed the view that Berlin could still exert influence on American public opinion by reiterating what he took to be Hitler's standpoint before any attack on England. Beginning in September 1940, Mooney found encouragement for his efforts on the part of Sir William Wiseman, a London financier in the employ of a New York investment bank who had headed British intelligence operations in the United States during the First World War. With Britain and Germany at an apparent stalemate, Wiseman thought a settlement might be possible if an initiative came from Berlin and encouraged Mooney to consider another mission to the capitals of the two belligerents. Mooney's efforts also found encouragement from Cardinal Spellman of New York and Roosevelt's friend Basil O'Connor. But in the absence of any official support from Washington, nothing came of his discussions with these men. Nevertheless, in February 1941 Mooney drafted still another appeal to Roosevelt for an American peace initiative. In it, he proposed that in return for German guarantees of the British Empire and respect for the Monroe Doctrine, the United States express its willingness to "recognize Germany's claim to a sphere of influence" in "Central and in certain parts of Western Europe." The United States, he further proposed, should pledge not to "support or encourage Great Britain in the further maintenance of a balance of power policy in Continental Europe, so long as Germany can substantiate her ability to exercise that influence benevolently and constructively" and "assure political autonomy for the small democracies of Western Europe." From all indications, this letter did not reach the president and may never have been sent.[40]

Mooney's efforts earned him mounting hostility on the part of the State Department. In February 1941 the American consul in Zurich relayed to Washington a false rumor from an exiled French journalist to the effect that Mooney maintained covert communications with high German officials in occupied Paris. Apprized of this, his erstwhile friend George Messersmith, then ambassador to Cuba, denounced him in letters to colleagues. Mooney was, he wrote, "fundamentally Fascist in his sympathies" as well as "quite unbalanced in the sense that he has not only one screw, but a number of screws, loose." He was "completely obsessed by this strange notion that a few business men, including himself, could take care of the war and the peace." Messersmith was sure that Mooney was maintaining contact with the Germans "because he believes, or at least still hopes, that they will win the war, and he thinks if they do that he will be our Quisling"—a reference to the collaborator installed by the Nazis at the head of a puppet regime in occupied Norway. Although Messersmith's views were dismissed by others in the State Department, Assistant Secretary Adolf Berle requested Federal Bureau of Investigation chief J. Edgar Hoover at the end of May 1941 to conduct "a most discrete investigation" of Mooney, Howard, and Sloan. When the investigation was concluded in September, the FBI had collected numerous unsubstantiated allegations from informants, including a charge that Mooney was a "strong Communist Party supporter." Nothing was found, however, that incriminated any of the three. In Mooney's case, the FBI concluded that he "has made 'appeasement' speeches but direct pro-Nazi sympathy is not reflected."[41]

In April 1942, with the United States at war and Mooney on active service as a lieutenant commander in the navy, he again came under fire from the New York newspaper *PM*, which denounced him as an "apologist for Hitler" unfit to serve in the armed forces. That accusation, which rested on the inaccurate allegations made earlier in that publication, was unfounded. Mooney was neither pro-Nazi nor pro-German. He was, however, blind to the criminal nature of Hitler's regime and the barbarous tyranny it imposed on countries over which it gained control. Moreover, like other prominent Americans, including Ambassador Kennedy and Roosevelt's friend Basil O'Connor, he assumed in 1939 and 1940 that the combined might of Germany and its then ally, the Soviet Union, hopelessly outweighed that of the European democracies. After the fall of France, he, like they, concluded that Britain would have to accept German dominance of the Continent or suffer a crushing defeat itself. Like so many others, he underestimated the defiant resoluteness of the British and feared American involvement in what seemed a hopeless war.[42]

Mooney was, to be sure, misled and used by Roosevelt. Rather than reining in his unrealistic hopes, the president led him on when they met in December 1939. Seeing an opportunity to augment what he heard about the Nazi regime's intentions through official channels with additional information, Roosevelt encouraged Mooney's illusions. His mention of possibly assuming the role of a moderator among the belligerents led Mooney to assume erroneously that the president wanted him to offer America's services as a peace broker. Although Roosevelt confided to Sumner Welles in early January that he rated the odds against America's altering the course of events in Europe at a thousand to one, Roosevelt's send-off of Mooney shortly thereafter left the impression of optimism. Once Roosevelt saw from Mooney's messages that his trip had yielded nothing new, he lost interest in him. When Mooney publicly proclaimed increasingly unrealistic views incompatible with the president's political stance, Roosevelt dropped him completely.[43]

The Germans also sought to use Mooney. The hints he received from Wohlthat and Göring that Hitler might be pushed aside in the interests of a peaceful conclusion of the war were part of a calculated effort to lure the British into negotiations and thereby drive a wedge between them and the French. So were the mendacious assurances of Hitler and Göring regarding Germany's alleged readiness to agree to generous peace terms and respect the rights of countries they had conquered. Desperately anxious for a return to peace and business as usual and impervious to the inherent aggressiveness of Nazism, Mooney naïvely mistook their lies for honest expressions of an interest in peace. For them, he was nothing more than a potentially useful dupe.

There remains the question of GM's role in Mooney's quest for peace. In 1947, after Mooney had left the corporation, several former colleagues successfully dissuaded him from publishing a memoir he had, with the assistance of Louis Lochner, written about those events on the grounds that GM would be harmed. His longtime assistant William Wachtler protested that readers of his account "would not realize that General Motors as such actually was not involved in any way." That was, however, not entirely accurate. Throughout what he referred to in his memoirs as his "strange odyssey," Mooney continued to draw his salary and presumably drew on GM funds to cover his expenses. He relied on his GM subordinates to make arrangements and relay messages and information for him. Moreover, neither Chairman Sloan nor President Knudsen objected when he informed them of his intentions before his departure for

Berlin in 1940. Their acquiescence in his pursuit of a mission personally approved by the president of the United States scarcely amounted, however, to corporate initiation or endorsement. Still, in view of the loss of overseas business that GM had to fear from a war, they could hardly have foreclosed even the faint possibility of a negotiated end to the conflict. Once Mooney's mission was under way, his superiors at GM neither exercised any control over his actions nor received from him reports about his ventures in diplomacy. He had long since become accustomed to acting on his own, sometimes without informing GM where he was. In April 1940 one of the corporation's senior executives grew concerned that his activities in Germany might be construed as pro-Nazi and briefly considered proposing that he take a leave of absence. But Mooney's stature within GM was such that nothing came of that idea.[44]

Sloan, still GM's dominant figure, was from the outset profoundly skeptical about Mooney's efforts at peacemaking. In late March 1940 he told Wachtler, who had just returned after accompanying Mooney to Berlin, that he did not believe anything could be accomplished by dealing with the Nazi regime. "Jim sat right there in the chair you're in and told me about what he was trying to do, and I didn't have the heart to tell him that he was wasting his time dealing with that crowd, although that's what I felt." It would be wonderful if the war could be ended without further bloodshed, Sloan added, but his own view was that peace could not be restored until "about twenty-five of the ringleaders over there in Germany had been lined up against a wall and shot." In August 1940 Sloan wrote to Mooney: "I . . . from the very beginning have not agreed with your thinking—not that I would not like to see it come about, but to my mind it is thoroughly impossible. A racketeer is an outlaw. He will never recognize anything but force. The only way to meet the issue is through more force."[45]

Chapter 8 GM Loses Control
but Takes Wartime Profits

After the fall of France in June 1940, the United States increasingly extended aid and encouragement to a beleaguered Great Britain with the result that GM's presence at Opel became untenable well before American involvement in the war. In a July report to Gauleiter Sprenger's headquarters, a local Nazi official denounced the Rüsselsheim plant as an "American plutocratic complex" and counted Opel among the "un-German forces" in the region. The place reeked of treason and foreign espionage, he wrote. Convinced that Stief was guilty of betraying plans for the Volkswagen, he lamented his release, which he attributed to American intervention. Apparently on the basis of reports by Nazi informants within the Rüsselsheim plant, he charged that the Americans there were spying for the British. His suspicions focused on Cyrus Osborn, who had been in ill favor with Sprenger ever since he had thwarted the Gauleiter's attempt to impose his will on Opel two years earlier. Among the German employees of Opel, fear of sabotage led to mounting mistrust and hostility toward the remaining Americans at the firm. By late summer, Nazi animosity toward Osborn had become so intense that Graeme Howard decided

not to send him back to Germany following what had been intended as a temporary stay in the United States. This left as GM's sole executive at Rüsselsheim
Osborn's aide Elis Hoglund, who was there only intermittently, having moved
his family from Germany to the town where GM's Swiss subsidiary was located.[1]

Excluded by strict German security regulations from access to information
about the war-materials production that had become the bulk of the Rüsselsheim plant's output, Hoglund found himself increasingly becalmed. He occupied himself as best he could with planning for postwar reconversion of the
factory to civilian car production, but in early October 1940 he indicated in a
telephone conversation with a colleague in New York that he was "not quite as
happy as he might be because naturally he has considerable time on his hands."
When German hostility toward the United States grew more intense as a result
of President Roosevelt's transfer of fifty American destroyers to the Royal Navy
in September 1940, Hoglund began preparations for his own departure. In November he signed over to GM's Berlin attorney, Heinrich Richter, the proxy he
had received from GM earlier in the year, thereby authorizing Richter to control Opel shareholder meetings by voting all the stock. That month, Hoglund
took part in what would be the last Supervisory Board meeting attended by an
American. In February 1941, with anti-American sentiment rampant in Germany as a consequence of Roosevelt's support of lend-lease legislation authorizing American credits for British purchases of war materials in the United
States, Hoglund departed for home via Switzerland after entrusting Richter
with oversight over Opel and defense of GM's interests.[2]

With the last American gone, the question of who would control Opel if the
United States entered the war against Germany hung over the firm. A decree issued with the force of law in early 1940 empowered the government to appoint
a custodian to administer enemy properties in wartime if that became necessary
to ensure their usefulness to the German economy. Although the decree failed
to specify what would trigger that step, the prospect of a transfer of control
over Opel to someone appointed by the Nazi government alarmed the GM executives responsible for the firm. To prepare for that eventuality, they sought to
influence the choice of a custodian. Before Hoglund left, he and attorney
Richter agreed that the interests of Opel would best be served with Supervisory
Board member Carl Lüer in that capacity. Despite his duplicitous behavior at
the time of the confrontation with Gauleiter Sprenger three years earlier, Lüer
had subsequently cooperated with GM's men and was now regarded as prefer-
able to someone from outside the firm. The golden Nazi membership button

he wore in his lapel commanded the deference due to an "old fighter" and offered hope that he would be in a strong position to defend the firm.[3]

Lüer's candidacy was called into question when Heinrich Wagner, the chairman of Opel's Directorate, reported to attorney Richter in March 1941 that Gauleiter Sprenger was promoting as custodian former Opel treasurer Rudolf Fleischer, who had headed the Henschel aircraft firm since late 1938. In view of the acrimony occasioned by Fleischer's role three years earlier and his forced departure from Opel, the prospect of his return as an all-powerful custodian, possibly bent on retribution, was alarming. By April, rumors of the impending appointment of Fleischer were circulating at the Rüsselsheim factory, giving rise to fears among the German managers who had earlier sided with the Americans against him. Richter therefore asked Lüer to seek the Gauleiter's support for his own candidacy. The attorney's apprehension was heightened, however, by news that Lüer had been unable to gain such a commitment from Sprenger, even though he had originally been the Gauleiter's protégé.[4]

The custodial question assumed added urgency in the second week of April, when Nazi storm troopers invaded the Rüsselsheim factory and briefly took up positions outside the firm's managerial offices. This lawless display of force, which followed the American government's seizure of German ships interned in United States ports, served as a potent manifestation of growing Nazi animosity toward GM's ownership of Opel. Badly shaken, the German managers appealed to Richter for help. Accompanied by Lüer and Directorate chairman Wagner, the attorney set out to marshal support for Lüer's candidacy among the officials in Berlin who were expected to have a voice in the selection of a custodian. They soon learned, however, that one of the most important of these, Adolf von Schell, plenipotentiary for the automotive industry in Hermann Göring's powerful four-year-plan administration, was opposed to Lüer. Von Schell, who had recently been promoted to the rank of general, made it clear that his candidate, and also Göring's, was a man all too well known at Opel: Eduard Winter.[5]

Once a valued colleague, Winter had by 1941 become anathema for GM. The cordial relations he had developed with important government and military officials as proprietor of the large Opel dealership in Berlin had served the Americans well at the time of Gauleiter Sprenger's bid for control over the firm in 1938. But when Winter sought appointment to Opel's Supervisory Board as a reward for his services, Graeme Howard grew mistrustful of his ambitions. At considerable cost, Opel bought out Winter's dealership and severed all ties with him. Following the German conquests of 1940, however, Winter used his contacts with high army circles to secure his installation as administrator of GM's branches in Belgium and France. In that capacity he initially claimed to be solicitous of the American corporation's interests, and GM instructed its representatives to cooperate with him. But by 1941 it had become apparent that Winter was pocketing profits for himself and seemed bent upon establishing permanent control over GM's properties in the two occupied countries. The prospect of his becoming custodian of Opel therefore alarmed attorney Richter in his capacity as the guardian of GM's interests. Richter's apprehensions were further heightened by a report from General von Hanneken of the Economics Ministry to the effect that plans were afoot for Winter to restore Opel to German ownership by purchasing its shares. Under the circumstances, such a transaction would amount to a forced sale on terms that could only be highly disadvantageous for GM.[6]

Rebuffing Winter, who called on him in Berlin in an effort to ingratiate himself, Richter turned for help, at the urging of Lüer, a bitter enemy of Winter, to GM's old adversary, Gauleiter Sprenger. After consulting with Graeme Howard by trans-Atlantic telephone, the attorney went with Lüer to Frankfurt in late April 1941 to seek Sprenger's support for Lüer's candidacy as Opel's custodian. After angrily giving vent to resentment about what he regarded as Osborn's disrespectful treatment of him three years earlier, the Gauleiter became more conciliatory. His support could be had, he indicated, but only at the price of major changes in Opel's management that would give him potentially great leverage over the firm. Why, Sprenger asked, since everyone at Opel regarded Lüer as a suitable custodian, would it not be best to position him optimally for eventual appointment to that post by immediately making him chairman of the Directorate and plant leader? The current Directorate chairman, Heinrich Wagner, might be a competent production man, the Gauleiter maintained, but he lacked the stature appropriate for the head of a major firm's management. Without mentioning his indignation at the appointment of Hanns Grewenig to replace Fleischer as plant leader in 1938, Sprenger also insisted that it made no sense to separate that post from the chairmanship of the Directorate. Both Grewenig and Wagner must give way to Lüer, he made clear, if his support for the latter's candidacy as custodian was to be had.[7]

To gain the Gauleiter's support, Richter decided to push aside Wagner, the experienced engineer chosen by GM in 1939 to head Opel, in favor of Lüer, despite misgivings about the latter's qualifications. Keeping Hoglund apprised by trans-Atlantic telephone, the attorney arranged the necessary changes during May 1941. He prevailed upon Wagner to accept demotion to deputy chairman of the Directorate and brought the German members of the Supervisory Board behind Lüer as his successor. To protect GM's interests, he insisted that Lüer sign a letter pledging loyalty to the American corporation and cooperation with Richter as its representative. The attorney then read the text of that letter over the telephone to Hoglund, who gave his approval. Pleading a loss of income as a result of resigning as a director of the Dresdner Bank in order to avoid a conflict of interests, Lüer secured a contract that assured him a salary for five years far in excess of what Wagner had been paid. In contravention of the company's by-laws, his appointment was not effected at a meeting of the Supervisory Board, since none of the American members could be expected to attend. Instead, Hoglund's approval by telephone was regarded as sufficient. Lüer's installation as plant leader took longer because of the Nazi Party connections of Grewenig, who was finally persuaded to resign in July after extracting a sizable financial settlement from Opel.[8]

Concurrently with these steps, Richter sought to persuade General von Schell to drop his support for Winter's candidacy as custodian. To that end, he worked closely with the Gauleiter, now referred to as "our friend in Frankfurt" in the attorney's communications with GM. Their collaboration became so close that Richter began preparing for Sprenger drafts of letters to von Schell that spelled out arguments in favor of Lüer and against Winter. But despite personal visits by Richter as well as by the Gauleiter himself, the general remained firm in his backing of Winter. By late May, however, Sprenger was able to inform von Schell that Economics Minister Funk as well as Göring's chief aide Paul Körner had approved Lüer's installation as chairman of Opel's Directorate. Although embittered by this setback, the general acquiesced and agreed not to oppose Lüer's eventual appointment as custodian. In an effort to preempt that decision, Gauleiter Sprenger informed the administrator in charge of enemy property in no uncertain terms that Lüer was his candidate for the post of custodian and that he regarded Winter as out of the question. Aware of the dispute, the administrator at first avoided committing himself on the grounds that the matter remained hypothetical since Opel had not been sequestered. But in September 1941 he informed Sprenger that he was ready to comply with his wishes and appoint Lüer as custodian if one was needed for Opel.[9]

During the months following Hoglund's departure from Germany, Richter sought to counter what he described as "the general tendency to forget that the company is owned by an American concern." The question of ownership became an issue during the preparations for a ceremonial celebration of Geheimrat Wilhelm von Opel's seventy-fifth birthday in mid-May 1941, to which

Gauleiter Sprenger, General von Schell, and other government officials were invited. As Richter informed Hoglund in advance by telephone, he planned to use his speech on that occasion to assert publicly that "General Motors' ownership of the company is not a thing shamefully to be concealed." But when Hanns Grewenig, the Nazi who was still plant leader, learned of Richter's plan, he alarmed the Geheimrat by protesting that, should GM be even mentioned, the Gauleiter would disrupt the ceremony by ostentatiously walking out. Approached through intermediaries, Sprenger, who had been mollified by GM's acceptance of Lüer as the head of Opel's management, at first proposed that Richter refer merely to "the owner" in his speech. But after the attorney pointed out that he had cleared the text of his remarks with the Foreign Ministry, the Gauleiter gave way. To Richter's relief, Sprenger joined in the applause for his remarks, in which he conveyed birthday greetings from GM to the Geheimrat and announced, on behalf of the American corporation, a gift by Opel of a quarter million marks in his honor toward construction of a hospital in Rüsselsheim.[10]

Despite Richter's efforts, it soon proved impossible to uphold GM's banner at Opel in face of the mounting tensions between Germany and the United States. In June 1941, Washington froze German assets in the United States, and Berlin retaliated by freezing American assets. At a ceremonial introduction of Lüer as the new plant leader to an assembly of the workforce at Rüsselsheim in July, none of the speakers—among whom Richter was not included—mentioned Opel's American ownership. From atop a high podium adorned with a large swastika Gauleiter Sprenger delivered a speech replete with belligerent Nazi propaganda in which he denounced an unspecified former manager of the company—obviously a reference to Osborn—for having failed to keep his word. Proclaiming Opel a German company, Sprenger included the United States among Germany's enemies in boasting that Hitler was destined to triumph over the hostile forces of bolshevism, plutocracy, and Judaism headed by the triumvirate of Stalin, Churchill, and Roosevelt.[11]

In his own speech on the same occasion, Lüer avoided mention of GM but stated that although Germany's current relationship to the United States closely resembled a state of war, there was no reason to be ashamed about Opel's past because of its American ownership. The company was, he emphasized, now a German firm and would remain one for all future times, thus implying that GM's role belonged to the past. When Lüer addressed a similar assembly at the Brandenburg truck factory early in the fall, he dismissed the issue of foreign ownership by assuring the workforce that Opel's ties to the American corporation had become a mere "matter of form" that would in no way limit its full par-

Opel workers assembled at the Rüsselsheim factory for a ceremony introducing the Nazi Carl Lüer as plant leader in July 1941. Courtesy of Adam Opel AG.

ticipation in a victorious war effort as a German firm. Thereafter, no further references to GM's ownership appeared in management's communications to Opel's workforce. Mention of the American corporation had vanished even earlier from the pages of the company's in-house magazine, *Der Opel-Kamerad,* which from the beginning of the war conformed to the strident Nazi propaganda line.[12]

As relations between Germany and the United States deteriorated during 1941, Richter's contact with GM became ever more tenuous. Transmission abroad of financial data of a German firm had been outlawed soon after the war began, and a dire fate awaited violators. The vital flow of information required for knowledgeable control of Opel by the American corporation thus ceased to function. Richter managed to secure Hoglund's approval by trans-Atlantic telephone for the measures he took during the spring to promote Lüer as custodian, but he could convey only minimal information that way for fear of the Gestapo's well-known use of wiretaps. Untrammeled communication by mail was altogether out of the question, since there was no postal privacy in Nazi Germany. Regular mail service between Germany and the United States had in any case become so disrupted by the war that routine business letters from Opel to GM were sent, at great delay, through Russia via trans-Siberian rail. In June 1941, Hitler's invasion of the Soviet Union closed off even that communication link.[13]

Richter's last recorded conversation with an executive of GM took place on July 28, 1941, when he obtained by trans-Atlantic telephone Howard's approval to use his proxy to remove from Opel's Supervisory Board Osborn and another American who had offended the Nazis. In preparation for that step, the attorney successfully blocked candidates for the board favored by its German members by asserting his authority, as holder of GM's proxy, to determine its composition. After consulting with friendly officials at the Economics Ministry and obtaining resignations from the two Americans by telegram, Richter voted the stock at a shareholder meeting on August 20 to reconfirm Hoglund, Howard, Mooney, and Sloan as Supervisory Board members. His intention had been to restore German-American parity on the board by replacing the two departing Americans with Germans of his choice. But when he failed to obtain Howard's approval for that step he merely reconfirmed the two German members, Geheimrat von Opel and Munich banker Franz Belitz, as well as Albin Madsen, the Danish manager of GM's subsidiary in Copenhagen. GM thus continued to command a nominal majority, although wartime conditions made it unlikely that the American members would be able to attend meetings. At a Supervisory Board session held the same day as the shareholder meeting, the executive committee established in November 1939, which had long since ceased to function, was dissolved and replaced with one consisting of the Geheimrat, Belitz and Madsen.[14]

During the summer of 1941, Richter resorted to relying on American State Department officials to convey written reports to GM's New York headquarters via diplomatic pouches that were immune from German inspection. But even in those communications the attorney felt constrained by the dire consequences of violating Nazi censorship. In a report to Howard of early September he lamented: "It is unfortunate, but it cannot be helped, that such developments as would interest you most cannot be disclosed to you." The information he did convey was, moreover, badly out of date by the time it reached the United States. Two reports he sent in June and July did not reach New York until late August, and one he dispatched in early September arrived six weeks later. Richter's last report, accompanied by a few documents that included Opel's 1940 financial balance sheet but no figures on 1941, was communicated orally to GM in New York in late October by an American diplomat who had just returned from Germany by ship.[15]

Richter received no responses from GM to any of these reports. Requests on his part for information that would help discredit the custodial candidacy of Eduard Winter went unanswered. So did his pleas for power of attorney or at least written authorization to act on behalf of GM beyond merely using the proxy that entitled him to vote its Opel stock at the German company's shareholder meetings. In light of the events of the second half of 1941, GM's silence is understandable. By the summer, German submarine attacks on ships conveying American war materials to Britain were drawing the United States ever closer to open hostility with the Reich. In early September, American naval vessels in the Atlantic were authorized by President Roosevelt to shoot on sight when encountering hostile submarines. In October, two American destroyers were sunk by German U-boats. A month later, the previously isolationist Congress revised the Neutrality Act to allow the arming of American merchant vessels. At home, GM was rapidly converting its factories to American military production under Roosevelt's Victory Program, in which GM president William Knudsen, on furlough to the government since the fall of 1940, played a prominent administrative role. Under these circumstances, GM's management apparently decided that it would be inadvisable to involve itself any further in the affairs of a subsidiary that was producing war materials for a country with which the United States seemed increasingly likely to be openly at war.[16]

Immediately after Hitler's declaration of war on the United States on December 11, 1941, the Gestapo unleashed its pent-up resentment at the foreign ownership of Opel. During the preceding months, the Nazi regime had forbidden anti-American measures in order to deprive Washington of grounds for entering the war alongside the British, but that constraint was now removed. The Gestapo could not, however, target the two top executives at Opel. Directorate chairman Lüer's golden Nazi Party badge rendered him immune to attack, and the party membership that his deputy Heinrich Wagner had belatedly acquired in 1940 shielded him as well, even though his commitment to Nazism was regarded in party circles as dubious. The Gestapo therefore directed its wrath at two behind-the-scenes managerial figures, Opel treasurer Hermann Hansen and Karl Schäffer, head of the firm's managerial staff. Hansen had the year before defied a military intelligence officer by denying him access to Opel's financial records on the grounds that these were American property. Hansen had threatened, moreover, to have Mooney use his connections in Berlin to block any attempt at coerced access. Schäffer, although a Nazi Party member since 1933, had angered the Gauleiter Sprenger by working closely with Osborn to thwart his designs on Opel in 1938. Both men were summarily arrested on unspecified charges on December 12 and held in what was called preventive detainment for two weeks. Following their release, they were dismissed by Opel on orders from the Gestapo. After the war, Schäffer reported that he was then drafted into the army and assigned to one of the "penal battalions" that were used for especially hazardous missions on the Russian front.[17]

After Hitler's declaration of war made the United States an enemy country, efforts to influence the choice of a custodian for Opel intensified. That post was especially alluring in light of the possibility that it might lead to permanent control over one of Germany's largest and most profitable manufacturing enterprises in the event of a victorious conclusion to a war that was still going very much the Reich's way. The government official authorized to name a custodian, Johannes Krohn, a non-Nazi career bureaucrat who had recently been appointed commissar for the administration of enemy property, soon found himself facing conflicting pressures. At the insistence of Gauleiter Sprenger, Krohn's predecessor had committed himself to Lüer's candidacy. But soon after Krohn took office General von Schell let him know that Göring wanted Eduard Winter appointed custodian. After learning this, Krohn reconciled himself to accepting Winter, but he declined to act without a written order from Göring. Unwilling to offend the Gauleiter, Göring put the matter off. Krohn therefore postponed a decision on the grounds that American holdings in Germany had not yet been officially classified as enemy property.[18]

There ensued months of behind-the-scenes machinations, with advocates of Lüer and Winter seeking to sway Commissar Krohn. General von Schell accused Lüer of failing to maximize Opel's production of war materials, and Lüer defended himself by circulating statistics indicating sharply rising output, along with a commendation of the firm's contribution to the war effort by Göring's deputy at the Air Ministry, Field Marshal Erhard Milch. For his part, Winter assured Krohn that his long association with GM and Opel made him best qualified for the post of custodian and reminded the commissar that Göring stood firmly behind him. Seeking to discredit attorney Richter, Winter accused him of a Jewish connection through his earlier association with Manfred Wronker-Flatow, the Opel executive who had been transferred to GM's New York office soon after the Nazi takeover. Lüer also gained a potent backer in Jakob Werlin, Hitler's general inspector for motor vehicles, who wrote to the commissar on behalf of his candidacy, stressing his good standing as a veteran member of the Nazi Party. But Krohn, despite entreaties on his part, received no written order from Göring, and so the custodial issue remained stalemated even after American holdings were officially designated as enemy property in April 1942.[19]

With Opel's fate hanging in the balance, Richter strove vigorously to shield GM's subsidiary from hostile control. Rather than see the firm placed under a custodian such as Winter, he sought to convince Commissar Krohn that there was no need to appoint anyone. GM had, he contended, relinquished control over Opel to a purely German management that was serving the German war effort in exemplary fashion. By portraying Mooney's efforts at diplomacy during 1939–40 as evidence that GM was pro-German, he sought to awaken sympathy on Krohn's part for Opel's foreign owner. The attorney also set out to remove the remaining American members from the firm's Supervisory Board, a step that could be taken only by a shareholder meeting. He considered a number of possible replacements, including Commissar Krohn, and received proposals for others from the German board members. Gauleiter Sprenger put forward the name of Wilhelm Avieny, the Nazi he had unsuccessfully promoted as Opel plant leader in 1938. Rejecting all of these possible candidates, Richter acted on his own at the end of March 1942. Appearing before a judge at a court in Berlin, he convened a shareholder meeting consisting of one person. Using the proxy he had received from Hoglund to vote all the Opel stock, he installed a four-man Supervisory Board that consisted of Geheimrat von Opel, the Munich banker Belitz, the Dane Madsen, and himself. Madsen was, however, a less than full member. As a foreigner, he was required to step out of the boardroom whenever the war production that made up virtually all of the firm's business was discussed. In May the board resolved no longer to send him the minutes of the Directorate, which were indispensable for assessing the firm's affairs. Those minutes were, in any case, now written only in German, a language Madsen did not command. In order to follow what was being said at board meetings he required help from a secretary who knew English. Madsen would remain a peripheral figure at Opel until the Supervisory Board ceased to function later in the year.[20]

None of these developments were known to GM at the time. The last eyewitness news from Opel to reach the New York headquarters cast no light on such matters. The bearer was a naturalized American of German birth who had continued working at the Rüsselsheim plant until he and his family were allowed to return to the United States by sea in May 1942, along with American diplomatic personnel stranded in Germany. But as he had worked in the cost accounting department, he was able to provide no information about the custodial issue or other high-level matters. In the absence of any information to the contrary, the men in charge of GM's overseas operations continued to rely on Richter's final message, conveyed orally in New York in late October 1941 by a returning American diplomat. The attorney had told him, the diplomat reported, that the German authorities had given informal assurances that Lüer would be named custodian in the event of war with the United States.[21]

Although Richter had also sent word in his final message that Lüer was doing "a really outstanding job" as chairman of the Directorate, such was no longer the prevailing view at Opel by the spring of 1942. By then Lüer had alienated Heinrich Wagner, his deputy and predecessor, by employing what Wagner regarded as autocratic methods and by failing to check the activities of the Gestapo's network of informers at the Rüsselsheim plant. On these and other grounds, Lüer had also offended Supervisory Board members Geheimrat von Opel and Franz Belitz, who complained about not being informed by him about important developments.[22]

Richter, too, had come to oppose Lüer. In June he complained to Commissar Krohn that Lüer had indulged in reckless behavior, potentially to the great detriment of Opel. The previous month, Lüer had pledged the firm's full cooperation when Jakob Werlin summoned him to the Reich Chancellery and presented him with a plan—which Werlin said Hitler had personally approved—for solving the army's acute shortage of trucks. The plan called for greatly expanding Opel's Brandenburg plant so as to triple its output in short order. Opel production managers at the truck factory had, however, already warned that no large-scale expansion was feasible because of shortages of building materials and labor. Because the proposal put forth by Werlin was based on overly optimistic data supplied by Lüer, Richter feared that Hitler would conclude he had been misled by Opel once the expansion proposal proved unworkable—a development that could have the most dire consequences for the firm. That peril had been averted, but only because concern about Brandenburg's vulnerability to Allied bombers led to a subsequent order by Hitler for an even greater increase in Opel truck production elsewhere, at a new plant to be established in Riga, the capital of occupied Latvia—an idea that quickly proved impractical.[23]

Richter was also concerned about Lüer's willingness to cooperate with Werlin because of the latter's close ties to SS chieftain Heinrich Himmler. As the overlord of an expanding network of concentration camps, Himmler had at his disposal a rapidly growing reservoir of slave workers at a time when a chronic labor shortage was the major constraint on war production. In the spring of 1942 Himmler was busily exploiting that advantage to construct, with Hitler's acquiescence, an SS economic empire by taking over a wide variety of enterprises both at home and in occupied territories. In pressing for adoption of the truck factory expansion plan, Werlin had invoked his link to Himmler by hold-ing out to Lüer the prospect of help from the SS, presumably in the form of slave labor. Richter's disapproval of Lüer was reinforced when a rumor reached the attorney that the SS was already far advanced with plans to take over Opel. The rumor proved inaccurate, but it was not entirely unfounded. Soon there-after, in early July, Himmler informed a member of Armament Minister Albert Speer's staff that he intended to create a new truck factory for Opel in occupied Poland that would be constructed and operated by the SS—an arrangement that would give him a major role in the firm's operations.[24]

In Opel's case, Himmler's grasp for once exceeded his reach. After the plan to establish a factory for the firm in Riga proved unfeasible, Hitler decided to re-solve the truck shortage by having the three-ton Blitz truck produced by Daim-ler-Benz as well as by Opel. Lüer's response to that decision added to Richter's objections to his management of the firm. The attorney charged that because of negligence on Lüer's part during the subsequent negotiations, Daimler-Benz had been able to secure the designs for the truck on terms disadvantageous to Opel. As a result, Richter reported to Commissar Krohn, the production staff at the Brandenburg factory was demoralized, and its seasoned manager had re-signed to take a post with another firm. His disillusionment with Lüer became so intense that he dropped his earlier objections and urged Krohn to appoint Eduard Winter as custodian. Winter's fortunes were, however, on the wane, in part as a result of his having come to the attention of the Gestapo, whose chief looked upon his freewheeling financial practices with distaste and regarded him as a "completely americanized businessman."[25]

News of the mounting dissatisfaction with Lüer quickly reached Hermann Göring. At a meeting with Speer and Field Marshal Milch at the end of June 1942, he decided to remove Lüer as chairman of the Directorate and reinstall production manager Heinrich Wagner in that post. In an attempt to assuage Gauleiter Sprenger, who had vigorously promoted Lüer's custodial candidacy, Göring informed him that he saw no need for a custodian. In hopes of concili-ating Lüer, Göring asked that he continue to serve the firm as a member of the Supervisory Board. Viewing Göring's decision as a governmental order even though it lacked any legal basis and violated Opel's by-laws, the members of the board informally approved it in early July and planned to implement the nec-essary changes officially at a regular meeting later in the month. Meanwhile, Wagner began functioning as head of the Directorate.[26]

Göring's peremptory intervention left Richter and the other members of the Supervisory Board with a problem that would perplex them as well as Göring for several months. The difficulty arose from the injured feelings of Lüer, who complained that his removal from the top managerial post at Opel would stigmatize him in business circles and cost him his prestigious posts on Nazi economic advisory bodies. Relegation to the Supervisory Board, as proposed by Göring, struck him as an unacceptable arrangement that would be perceived by knowledgeable onlookers as a clumsy means of camouflaging his loss of managerial authority. Since Lüer was a Nazi "old fighter" whose demotion would offend not only him but also his patron, Gauleiter Sprenger, the matter could not be ignored even by the mighty Göring. Apprised of Lüer's grievance, the Reich marshal instructed the Supervisory Board to put off formal enactment of the changes he had ordered and withhold any public announcements. This resulted in a period of uncertainty during the summer and early autumn of 1942, with Wagner exercising de facto control but with Lüer still chairman of the Directorate so far as persons outside the firm, or even most of the workforce, knew.[27]

Göring's eventual solution was to console Lüer for his demotion by appointing him custodian of Opel, but on terms so restrictive that all real authority would reside with Wagner as head of the Directorate. Lüer acquiesced in this but insisted in retaining the post of plant leader. In early September the Supervisory Board met to accept his resignation as Directorate chairman and formally appoint Wagner as his replacement. After still more delays, Göring instructed Commissar Krohn in writing at the end of October to appoint Lüer custodian of Opel but with the proviso that this in no way diminish the authority of the Directorate or Wagner as its chairman. The formal actions were effected in November. As everyone involved understood, this was a purely facesaving arrangement designed to appease Lüer and his patron Sprenger while removing managerial control of Opel from a well-connected Nazi who had demonstrated his incompetence and assigning it to a veteran production manager.[28]

In taking these measures, the second most prominent official of the Third Reich in effect ratified the key personnel choices made earlier by GM's men at Opel. He reinstalled at the head of the firm's Directorate the German engineer they had chosen in 1939 to shepherd the firm through the war, and he bestowed the post of custodian on the man they had favored for that post a year earlier, although attorney Richter had in the meantime turned against him. Göring acted, however, not out of any solicitude for the American corporation's wishes or interests but in order to maximize Opel's effectiveness for the German war effort. That became abundantly apparent soon thereafter, when his four-year-plan administration, which increasingly exercised control over the country's economy, joined with other agencies to advocate outright confiscation of enemy property, including Opel. Efforts in that direction nevertheless repeatedly foundered. The German law of 1940 governing enemy property was the work of career officials resolved to prevent a repetition of the confiscations of enemy properties by the imperial regime during the First World War, measures that had afterward resulted in costly losses of German foreign holdings. The law therefore called for confiscation only in retaliation for enemy seizure of German property, which in the case of the United States had not occurred. A scrupulous bureaucrat, Commissar Krohn tenaciously adhered to the law's terms. With the backing of the Foreign Ministry, he succeeded in blocking all demands for confiscation from Göring's staff, from other government agencies, and even from Hitler's right-hand man, Martin Bormann. Although it was an agency of one of the most lawless regimes in modern history, the Commissariat for Administration of Enemy Property held punctiliously to the letter of the law throughout the war.[29]

Unaware of these developments, GM wrote off Opel for tax purposes in the United States. Making use of an act of Congress signed by President Roosevelt in October 1942, GM declared Opel a total war loss later that year. That did not necessitate divestment of the corporation's Opel stock, however, the value of which was set at one dollar on GM's books. As a result of the stand adopted by Commissar Krohn, the firm's physical assets and funds were throughout the rest of the war merely under sequestration in Germany, so that the American corporation's ownership of its stock remained in effect there as well.[30]

The German enemy property law required that the economic interests of sequestered firms be safeguarded, and Commissar Krohn conscientiously adhered to that principle. As by far the largest American enterprise in the Reich, Opel received sustained attention from the commissar and his staff. Since the authority of both the Supervisory Board and the shareholder meeting nominally passed to Lüer upon his appointment as custodian, attorney Richter grew concerned. He pressed upon Krohn the desirability of a body that would scrutinize Lüer's actions and review the Directorate's conduct of the firm's business. The result was the creation by the commissar in early 1943 of an advisory council consisting of Geheimrat von Opel, banker Belitz, Richter, a spokesman each from the armament and air ministries, and a prominent executive of the IG Farben chemical firm. As a sop to Gauleiter Sprenger, who had been angered by Lüer's demotion, his protégé Wilhelm Avieny was installed as chairman of the new body. As custodian, Lüer had to report regularly to this advisory council,

whose approval of his conduct in that post was required. Ultimately, he was responsible to Commissar Krohn, who retained authority to resolve differences
between Lüer and the advisory council and whose prior consent was required
in all important matters. The custodian's already tightly circumscribed authority was further diminished in the spring of 1943, when he resigned as plant
leader to accept reappointment as a director of the Dresdner Bank.[31]

With Lüer devoting his attention increasingly to his other responsibilities,
his role at Opel was essentially reduced to reviewing and signing quarterly reports to Commissar Krohn, which were prepared by the managerial staff. Effective control over the operations of the firm remained in the hands of Directorate chairman Wagner, who became plant leader after Lüer resigned from
that post. Richter, who was appointed by Krohn as custodian of GM's other
properties in Germany, was regarded by the commissar as the spokesman for
the American owner of Opel's stock, even though he lacked power of attorney
and his proxy had lost its validity upon Lüer's appointment as the firm's custodian. Following developments at Opel as best he could from his Berlin office,
Richter kept Krohn and his staff closely informed. Down to the fall of the German capital to the Red Army, when he disappeared, apparently to die in Soviet
captivity, Richter assiduously sought to protect the interests of both Opel and
GM. As a result of his vigilance, Wagner's management skills, and Commissar
Krohn's scruples, orderly procedures prevailed in the upper reaches of Opel's
authority structures until they were disrupted by the chaos of the final months
of the war.[32]

Under the supervision of Krohn, Opel also complied fully with the enemy
property law's requirement that sequestered firms operate in the interests of
Germany. In 1943 both company factories were designated "model war plants"
by the Armaments Ministry. The main plant at Rüsselsheim served as a vital
link of the Luftwaffe's supply system, providing Junkers with large quantities of
components for the Ju 88, a plane that was increasingly outfitted as a fighter after air war setbacks restricted the Luftwaffe to a defensive role against Allied
bombing attacks. Beginning in 1942, following personal intercession on the
part of Field Marshal Milch with Directorate chairman Wagner, components
for Messerschmitt warplanes, including early jet-propelled models, were produced at Rüsselsheim. Gears were also supplied for aircraft engines made by
Daimler-Benz. After the Allied convoy system and underwater detection devices curtailed the effectiveness of German submarines in the latter stages of the
war, munitions production at Rüsselsheim shifted from torpedo detonators to
landmines designed to fend off advancing Allied armies.[33]

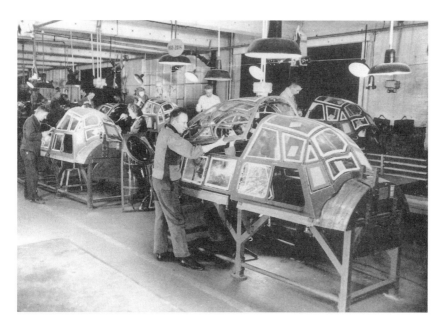

Work on components for the Ju 88 warplane at Opel's Rüsselsheim factory. Courtesy of Adam Opel AG.

Throughout the war, Opel's Brandenburg factory was the prime supplier of heavy-duty trucks to the German army. Under a vigorous manager, Heinz Nordhoff—who would later play a major role in making the Volkswagen a postwar success—production focused on the three-ton Blitz model favored by the military. To cope with the poor roads in Russia, many of the trucks were equipped with four-wheel drive or outfitted as halftracks on which the rear wheels were replaced by running treads similar to those of tanks. The factory also supplied the army with buses and ambulances. Average monthly production of vehicles at Brandenburg rose from 1,572 in 1942 to 1,936 in 1943 and peaked at 2,600 in July 1944, after which heavy bombing damage sharply curtailed the factory's operations. The three-ton Blitz truck continued to be produced, however, by Daimler-Benz under the terms of the arrangement imposed by the Armaments Ministry in 1942. For the maintenance of vehicles already in military use, both Opel factories turned out large quantities of replacement parts, and repair shops for military cars and trucks were established in occupied Poland and Latvia.[34]

Opel's high levels of productivity were made possible only by the harsh wartime exploitation of labor practiced by German industries under pressure

Work on motors for German warplanes at Rüsselsheim. Courtesy of Adam Opel AG.

from Nazi authorities. Night and day shifts kept the Rüsselsheim factory in operation around the clock seven days a week. Sixty hours became the minimum workweek, which in some cases extended to sixty-nine hours. Hourly wages were replaced by a piece-work system that reduced workers' take-home pay. After the departure of GM's men, disciplinary authority over the workers was increasingly exercised by henchmen of Gauleiter Sprenger who were placed on the company payroll at his insistence. Through a network of informers and a squad of strong-arm enforcers, they imposed Nazi-style order on the workforce. Responding to denunciations, these ideological watchdogs zealously meted out punishment for what they regarded as insubordination or expressions of political dissent or defeatism. Their actions were rubber-stamped by the council that purportedly represented the employees but actually consisted of handpicked party members. Workers who had been Social Democrats or Communists before the Third Reich were particularly singled out for harassment. The victims were in some cases turned over to the Gestapo without access to a trial or even a hearing. Other offenders were prosecuted and received long sentences. One worker who ran afoul of Nazi surveillance at Rüsselsheim was placed on trial before the notorious "People's Court" in Berlin, which convicted him of treasonous activities for spreading demoralizing war news and imposed a death sentence that was carried out in December 1942.[35]

Demands by Nazi activists at Opel for thoroughgoing conformity with the regime's racist ideology became increasingly insistent during the war. Intent upon purging all employees whom they regarded as racially tainted, they sought to have such individuals dismissed or relegated to menial jobs. The members of the party-dominated employee council were particularly zealous in their pursuit of racial purity. At a meeting in November 1941 they objected to the heads of the firm's legal, statistical, and tax sections on the grounds that they or their wives were of partially Jewish parentage. But although the council instructed Lüer, who presided over the meeting in his capacity as plant leader, to deal with the matter, the three section heads remained in their jobs throughout the war despite recurrent racist denunciations. Afterwards, one of them attributed his retention of his post to protection by Heinrich Wagner. Another reported being protected by Geheimrat Wilhelm von Opel. Several less prominent employees deemed racially tainted by the Nazis were, however, demoted or dismissed.[36]

Like other German firms, wartime Opel became increasingly dependent on foreign labor, much of it involuntary. Even before the war, there had been a shortage of skilled workers, and ongoing military conscription kept that problem acute. To compensate for the loss of drafted workers, sizable numbers of French prisoners of war were assigned to Opel, beginning in 1941. Civilians from occupied countries in Western Europe were recruited by the army with economic incentives, but many soon returned home. When these measures and the employment of German women failed to satisfy the need for labor, the Nazis resorted, beginning in 1942, to impressing civilians from the Soviet Union and other occupied territories in the east. By the end of that year, 18 percent of the 18,500 workers at Opel's Rüsselsheim plant and 44 percent of the 4,000 at Brandenburg were foreigners. In 1943, Italian prisoners of war were added to Opel's workforce following the collapse of Mussolini's regime, and the number of other foreigners at both factories continue to increase as well. In all, more than 7,000 foreigners worked at the Rüsselsheim factory in the course of the war. Behavior by any foreign worker regarded as laggard or disrespectful by the Nazis who oversaw the workforce could lead to beatings and summary consignment to dreaded Gestapo penal camps.[37]

By the fall of 1944, nearly a quarter of those working at Rüsselsheim were foreigners, about the same level as in German industry as a whole. Close to a tenth were forced laborers from the east, many of them women. Some had initially come voluntarily, having been led to expect normal employment at a time when little or no work was available at home. They soon found that they were not free. When not at work, they were restricted to a barracks compound adjacent to the factories except for brief periods when they were permitted access to the immediate vicinity. Like the Soviet prisoners of war, the eastern workers were paid meager wages, from which the cost of their food, clothing, and shelter was deducted, along with special taxes. Denied access to underground air raid shelters and confined to their barracks at night, the foreign workers at Rüsselsheim, including the prisoners of war, became the prime victims of nocturnal Allied bombing raids. In August 1944 a raid took the lives of 115 foreign workers and left another 260 severely wounded, whereas there were no casualties among the German workforce. Two years earlier, twenty French prisoners of war died and twenty others were severely wounded during another air raid, which also took no lives among the German employees.[38]

Opel also made use of Jewish slave labor. There is no indication that any concentration camp inmates worked at either of the firm's factories in Germany. But matters were different at the vehicle repair shops established at the behest of the army in the capitals of occupied Latvia and Poland. Like other private businesses, the Opel shops in Riga and Warsaw made use of Jews confined by the Nazis to large ghettos in those cities. The pay for their work went not to the Jews themselves but to the ghetto authorities. This practice, which began soon after the creation of the repair shops in the spring of 1942, continued until the second half of 1943, when the ghettos emptied as the Nazis shipped their victims to death camps. Before that, the written reports submitted to Rüsselsheim by the managers of the repair shops routinely recorded the number of Jews working there and the cost of their labor, which was lower than that paid to Poles, Latvians, and Russian prisoners of war.[39]

By supplementing its workforce with foreign and forced labor as well as increasing numbers of German women, Opel's management maintained production at full tilt until the final year of the war. By 1944, heavy damage from bombing attacks—facilitated by information supplied by GM executives formerly assigned to Opel—had sharply curtailed output at both Rüsselsheim and Brandenburg. Until then, lucrative contracts for military products yielded a mounting flow of profits. Like other enemy-owned firms, Opel was forbidden, with rare exceptions, to invest in plant expansion, and shortages of raw materials precluded even the normal replacement of equipment. Only a small fraction of the profits could be declared as dividends, which had been limited by law as of 1940 to 6 percent of the firm's capitalization. A law of 1941 made it possible to increase the dividends by raising Opel's capitalization from sixty

Opel's Rüsselsheim factory after Allied bombing attacks. Courtesy of Adam Opel AG.

million marks to eighty million through the issuance of additional shares, but dividends continued to account for a decreasing portion of profits. The result was ballooning liquidity, which exceeded a quarter of a billion marks by the end of 1942. Some of those funds had to be used to repair bombing damage, but the cash reserves continued to mount. This attracted hostile attention from Nazi officials, who objected to an enemy-owned firm's benefiting from the German war effort. Urged on by attorney Richter, however, Commissar Krohn successfully resisted Nazi pressure for confiscatory taxation of Opel's wartime profits. Through the efforts of those two and the manager of the Brandenburg truck factory, the firm also obtained, shortly before the end of the war, access to Armament Ministry funds for the repair of bombing damages at that plant, despite official resistance to extending that benefit to an enemy-owned firm. Attempts to gain compensation funds for the Rüsselsheim plant failed, however, because its management incurred the ministry's disfavor by failing to submit a detailed accounting of damages. Under the watchful eye of Richter, the maximum permissible dividends derived from Opel's mounting profits—more than four million marks after taxes—were each year declared and credited to GM until the disruptive conditions of 1945 ruled out an orderly conclusion to the business of the previous year.[40]

Opel's Rüsselsheim factory after Allied bombing attacks. Courtesy of Adam Opel AG.

The management of GM knew nothing of these developments and had no way of influencing them, as all contact with Opel and Richter had long since been lost. This becomes clear from the content of an internal report on Opel prepared for the Overseas Policy Group in early 1944 as part of a global survey of postwar prospects for the American corporation's subsidiaries abroad. At a time when it would have been vital to include everything known about what was going on at Opel, the report contained no solid information on that score. Twenty-five of its twenty-seven pages consisted of data on the prewar years and speculation about the overall prospects for business in postwar Europe. The two pages devoted to Opel's current situation contained no information beyond what had been known before the United States entered the war, aside from an observation that the Rüsselsheim plant had not been expanded as of May 1942, which suggests reliance on the minimal news brought by the belatedly returning German-American employee who had left Rüsselsheim in mid-May of that year. Regarding Opel's management, the report assumed that the firm was being administered by a custodian and that "to the best of our knowledge" Lüer had been appointed to that position. "Despite the fact that Opel has been charged off the books as a war loss," the report pointed out that under American law "General Motors is still owner of the Opel shares." On the basis of an analysis of the German enemy property law of 1940, the report concluded that it was "in all probability" unlikely that the company had been confiscated. If the American government did not provoke retaliation by confiscating German-owned property in the United States, the report predicted, "the Opel properties will be maintained during the war corporately intact."[41]

In the last week of March 1945 American troops took possession of the heavily damaged Opel factory in Rüsselsheim, and a month later the Red Army occupied Brandenburg and seized the truck factory there. Later in the spring, the Russians began dismantling the entire Brandenburg factory for shipment to the Soviet Union. At Rüsselsheim the American occupation authorities quickly set in motion the repair of war damages. Initially that task was assigned to the wartime plant management headed by Heinrich Wagner, but in October the Americans dismissed him, along with other German managers they regarded as implicated in Nazism. To replace them, the occupation authorities installed a new management headed by a custodian of their choice. In accordance with wartime Allied agreements, some of the machines and tools at Rüsselsheim, including the entire production line for the Kadett sedan, were dismantled and shipped to the Russians in 1946 as reparations for the Nazi devastation of the Soviet Union. When the factory began operating again, it was initially used by the American authorities to produce spare parts for the Opel vehicles in use by the occupation forces. By mid-1946 trucks were being produced and sold for civilian purposes, and in late 1947 a small number of passenger cars began to be turned out.[42]

At the urging of General Lucius D. Clay, military governor of the U.S. occupation zone, GM resumed control over Opel in the fall of 1948, after considerable hesitation because of the unsettled conditions in Germany and the heavy war damages to the Rüsselsheim plant. A new management that initially included no Germans took over. Three years later, GM laid claim to the Opel dividend account. Added to the prewar dividends that had been frozen in Germany by currency controls, those of the wartime years brought the GM dividend account to nearly 22.4 million marks by the end of the conflict. Devalued in line with the West German currency reform and sold for dollars, this yielded GM $261,061 in 1951.[43]

Chapter 9 Circumstances and Options—Responsibility and Guilt

At first sight, General Motors' ownership of Adam Opel A.G. throughout the Third Reich appears dubious or even reprehensible, particularly in light of the German firm's role in war production for Hitler's regime and its extensive exploitation of involuntary labor. This has given rise to charges that GM collaborated with the Nazis in pursuit of profit, willingly contributed to the German war effort, and continued to exercise control over Opel's management even after the Third Reich was at war with the United States. In light of the extensive evidence now available, those charges have proved groundless. This book has, however, revealed several hitherto unnoticed aspects of GM's relationship with Opel that raise serious questions about actions by the American corporation or executives acting on its behalf.

An assessment of how GM dealt with Opel during the Third Reich has to avoid an anachronistic application of attitudes that became widely held among Americans only later. The United States was in many ways a very different country in the 1930s from what it has since become. The failure of American intervention in the First World War to resolve the conflicts among Europeans had given rise to deep disillusionment. The Versailles Treaty was widely regarded as an unjust peace settlement. Isolationist sentiment prevailed. For most Americans, the rest of the world seemed remote and the behavior of foreign countries incomprehensible as well as incorrigible. Only a small minority felt called upon to concern themselves with what went on elsewhere, even when grave violations of human rights were known to be occurring. GM was only one of dozens of U.S. companies doing business in Germany and other countries ruled by dictatorships, and for most Americans no stigma attached to the conduct of international business without regard to political conditions. So many recently established democracies had failed that the Third Reich initially seemed nothing extraordinary. In the context of those times, the responses of GM executives to the problems arising from ownership of a major firm in Nazi-ruled Germany did not deviate significantly from either the practices of the business community or from prevalent American public opinion.

Implicit in much of the criticism of GM's role at Opel is the assumption that the American corporation did business in the Third Reich by choice. Such was not the case. When GM purchased Opel, Germany was a democratic republic and the Nazis a fringe phenomenon. Well before Hitler gained power, the corporation's large investment had been locked in by German currency controls that drastically restricted the conversion of marks into dollars. Recouping GM's investment by selling Opel was not a viable option because the currency controls greatly reduced its dollar value, while a sale for nonconvertible marks would have resulted in a host of daunting problems. Nor did GM have the option of simply abandoning ownership of Opel. After years of heavy losses during the Depression, the German firm prospered handsomely from Hitler's promotion of the automobile and from the remarkable recovery of the German economy. A failing subsidiary can be written off, but dropping one that was generating rising profits was simply not feasible for an American corporation answerable to its shareholders and subject to stock-market forces at home during a period of lingering depression in the United States. Even though German currency controls prevented GM from converting more than a limited part of Opel's profits into dollars, the subsidiary could be carried on the corporation's books as a sizable asset. Like other American companies with operations in Germany, GM therefore opted under the circumstances to hold on to what amounted to a hostage of the Third Reich in hopes of better times.

Some of the GM executives charged with responsibility for Opel have been unjustly branded as pro-Nazi. But with the exception of Graeme Howard, none had any particular interest in Germany or its politics. Howard, who was well disposed toward that country by his youthful experiences there, initially admired the peacetime successes of Hitler's regime, as did many other foreigners. Personal exposure to Nazi methods soon dispelled his illusions, although he continued to believe that Germany had legitimate territorial grievances as a result of Versailles. Howard's chief, James Mooney, refused to take seriously ideological politics of any kind, including Nazism. For him, Hitler was just another of the foreign potentates he had to cope with in running GM's far-flung overseas operations. Scorning ideology and regarding war as the result of failure by governments to resolve their differences in businesslike fashion, Mooney was unable to recognize the Nazis' aggressive intentions. His political naïveté was amply demonstrated by his gullible responses to the bogus peace offers of Göring and Hitler. The senior figure at GM, Alfred P. Sloan, despised the Nazis as outlaws but set the tone in the corporation with his insistence that business in a foreign country should be conducted without regard to its government's political orientation. For Cyrus Osborn and Elis Hoglund, the GM executives directly in charge at Opel, their jobs were merely temporary assignments from a worldwide employer whose practice it was to shift them from one country to another every few years. Like Mooney, they had little or no knowledge of Germany's language or culture and made no attempt to fathom the nature of Nazism. Hitler's minions became for them predators who had to be fended off in order to protect the interests of the corporation they served. As far as the GM executives involved are concerned, this may be a story without heroes, but it also lacks villains.

Far from enjoying allegedly cordial relations with Hitler's regime, the GM men in charge of Opel regarded Germany's new xenophobic rulers with apprehension from the outset. Nazi resentment of the subsidiary's foreign ownership led the Americans to withdraw into the background during the early years of the regime and turn over representational roles to German colleagues. The nazification of plant life at Opel was not a matter of choice on their part but rather acquiescence in the face of militant local Nazis and a workers' factory council dominated by Hitler's followers. The addition of a well-connected Nazi Party member to the firm's Supervisory Board resulted from an effort to gain political insulation, not from any sympathy for his politics. The unsuccessful pursuit of the Volkswagen project that brought the GM executives in charge of Opel briefly into direct contact with Hitler was motivated by commercial considerations, not from any desire to serve the purposes of his regime. Subjected to Nazi pressure to remove the few "non-Aryans" from its payroll, Opel complied, but the GM executives in charge of the firm did not share the regime's anti-Semitism and, where they could, arranged jobs at corporation operations in other countries for employees let go on those grounds. Some highly placed members of Opel's German administrative staff deemed racially tainted by Nazi standards remained at their posts throughout the duration of the Third Reich.

The vulnerability of GM's control over Opel to Nazi ambitions was amply demonstrated by the persistent efforts of Hessian Gauleiter Jakob Sprenger to gain a foothold in the firm's management. Had he been successful in 1938, GM's ownership would have been seriously undermined. In countering his schemes, the Americans in charge of Opel demonstrated considerable adeptness at politics as practiced in the Third Reich by mobilizing more potent forces against him. Invoking the Economics Ministry's interest in maintaining the sizable influx of foreign exchange generated by Opel export sales through GM's global marketing system, they were able to frustrate Sprenger with backing from that quarter. Air Minister Hermann Göring's interest in obtaining access for the Luftwaffe to GM technology via Opel made it possible to gain a pledge of additional aid against the Gauleiter from the second most prominent figure in the Third Reich.

Much of the criticism of GM's ownership of Opel has focused on the uses made of that firm's products by Hitler's armed forces during the Second World War. Without question, just as GM served as one of America's major wartime arsenals and its Vauxhall plant played a similar role in Great Britain, its German subsidiary became an important source of war materials used against the United States and its allies. From the outset of the war, Wehrmacht troops and supplies were transported to all theaters of the conflict in Blitz trucks made at the Opel factory in Brandenburg an der Havel. Ju 88 bombers made by the Junkers aircraft company and equipped with components manufactured by Opel's main factory at Rüsselsheim showered destruction and death on other countries during the early stages of the war. When the Luftwaffe shifted to a defensive role, the Ju 88, reconfigured as a fighter, was used to attack American and British bombers. Some of the many allied ships sunk on the Atlantic by German U-boats were presumably struck by torpedoes with detonators produced by Opel at Rüsselsheim. Landmines made there during the latter stages of the war were deployed with the aim of killing or maiming American and other Allied ground troops. In short, the potent productive capacities of GM's German subsidiary became a significant military asset for the Third Reich and a liability for the United States and the other countries that joined at great cost—human and material—in defeating Hitler's outlaw regime. As the record reveals, however, war production by Opel for the Third Reich was neither sought nor desired by GM or its executives and met with rejection from the corporation's top leadership.

Sales to the German army of large numbers of trucks made at the Opel factory built at Brandenburg in 1935 have been construed as evidence of collusion by GM in Nazi preparations for war. Plans for the new factory were well under way, however, before Hitler set in motion his rearmament program by renouncing the disarmament clauses of the Versailles Treaty. The truck factory was a byproduct of GM's bid for the Volkswagen project and was initially conceived for mass production of an inexpensive civilian car. Its location was chosen in response to a government stipulation that it be situated in the central part of the country in line with the regime's efforts to reduce the vulnerability of German industry to air attacks from the west. General Motors' subsequent decision to use the new factory to make trucks rather than cars arose from hopes of accelerating the potentially lucrative Volkswagen project by freeing up space for it at the main factory by moving the assembly line for trucks to Brandenburg. The well-established facilities and seasoned workforce at Rüsselsheim held out the promise of swifter progress toward realization of a Volkswagen than would be possible at a new factory built from the ground up at a location distant from the firm's headquarters. The option for truck production at Brandenburg may well have been subsequently reinforced by the prospect of eventual sales to the army held out by military procurement officers. But the switch from car to truck production—which very possibly cost Opel the Volkswagen project—was motivated by practical manufacturing considerations, not by pursuit of military contracts. When orders for trucks began to be received from the army, no war was in sight, and profitable sales were willingly made on commercial grounds, just as GM subsidiaries in other countries sold vehicles to their armies. There was in any event no choice. If a foreign-owned firm as large and conspicuous as Opel had refused to sell its regular products to the army during the Third Reich, dire consequences would have predictably followed in an economy subject to tight governmental controls. Under the circumstances, that was simply not a realistic option.

Far from willingly agreeing to full war production once Hitler unleashed his armies in the fall of 1939, the GM executives in charge Opel strove to evade Nazi demands to convert the firm's main factory for such uses. Left to their own devices, they sought as best they could to keep Opel from becoming involved. Only after being confronted with a credible threat of expropriation did they give way under duress. Resisting direct involvement in war production, they agreed to allow the firm to produce components for a warplane as a supplier for the Junkers company. Concerned about disapproval on the part of their superiors in America, they were less than candid in reporting this, resorting to euphemisms and employing a narrowly restrictive definition of what constituted war production. It is unlikely, however, that GM's leadership remained ignorant very long about the uses being made of the Rüsselsheim factory. But rather than risk losing the ownership of Opel by objecting, GM's leaders took refuge, as did the Americans in charge of the German subsidiary, in hopes that the war would be brief and that car production for the civilian market could soon be resumed. Among the available options, inaction seemed, under the circumstances, the least hazardous course.

Once the conflict was under way in Europe, the foreign ownership of Opel increasingly became a liability in a hyperxenophobic, chauvinistic wartime Third Reich. The GM executives withdrew from active management roles but sought to exercise control behind the scenes. This proved unfeasible, however, in the face of mounting German antagonism toward the United States and wartime security measures that barred the Americans from entering areas of the main factory used to manufacture war materials. Regarded with suspicion, they were increasingly shut out of that fast-growing sector of the plant's operations. Acting on their own, the German managers placed in charge of production by the GM executives soon began accepting contracts from the armed forces to manufacture additional items destined for military use. Recognizing the futility of attempting to resist the uses being made of the firm under wartime conditions, the remaining American executives at Opel averted their eyes, spent increasing time in neutral Switzerland, and eventually withdrew from Germany altogether.

Allegations that GM continued to exercise control over Opel even after Hitler declared war on the United States in December 1941 are unfounded. Well before then, all direct contact with the Rüsselsheim headquarters of Opel had been lost. The last American had departed many months earlier, leaving the subsidiary's German lawyer in Berlin as the sole remaining channel of communication. Trans-Atlantic telephone contact with him ceased during the summer of 1941. After that, a few written reports of his, in which he felt constrained to omit sensitive information, were covertly conveyed to GM with considerable delay by American diplomats. General Motors chose not to respond, despite repeated entreaties from the lawyer for a grant of power of attorney. Once the United States was in the war, he had to act on his own, without instruction or assent from GM, in seeking to defend its interests. His actions cannot therefore be attributed to the American corporation. As for the preservation of GM's ownership of its Opel stock under German law, that was determined by a scrupulous bureaucrat in Berlin whose existence was unknown to GM's management.

After the Americans' departure, and even after the sequestration of Opel by the government in 1942, the top executive posts at the firm were occupied throughout the rest of the war by Germans previously placed in high positions by GM. This does not, however, confirm allegations that the American corporation somehow continued to exercise control over personnel at the firm. As the managerial shakeup carried out by Göring in 1942 left no doubt, authority over who would head Opel had been usurped by the Nazi regime. For Göring, all that mattered was the firm's efficient operation in the interests of the German war effort. He therefore shunted aside the ill-qualified man installed at the head of Opel's management with GM's concurrence a year before and replaced him with the man demoted to make way for him, the experienced production manager chosen for that post by GM after the onset of the war. The American corporation neither had any voice in that change nor received any notification of it.

Whereas the instances cited by critics of GM's management of Opel as evidence of willing complicity in the German war effort fail to support that indictment, the agreement in 1938 to construct a gear plant at the request of the Air Ministry—which has hitherto escaped notice—raises troubling questions. Since that project was designed to draw, via GM, on advanced American technology, it had the potential to contribute importantly to the enhancement of engines destined for warplanes of Hitler's Luftwaffe. It thus ranks as the most dubious aspect of GM's management of Opel during the Third Reich and therefore merits close examination.

The decision to build a plant to develop advanced gears for aircraft engines was not the result of an option by GM's leadership for the production of war materials for Germany. That decision was made in the spring of 1938 on the spur of the moment by the Americans in charge of the German subsidiary, without the approval of GM's top leadership in the United States. Urgently seeking influential protection against the increasingly threatening designs on Opel of Gauleiter Sprenger, they turned to the only governmental sector that enjoyed a measure of independence from the Nazis, the military. Especially important in that regard was the Air Ministry headed by the powerful Göring. When the top Luftwaffe generals at the ministry responded to their overtures by requesting that Opel build a gear plant, the Americans readily agreed. Bent upon a quick defensive ploy against a predatory Nazi threat to GM's ownership, they acted on their own in granting the generals' request rather than invoking the time-consuming decision-making procedures of GM. Since they were led by the generals to expect that no Opel funds would be needed for construction of the new plant, they proceeded in accord with the corporation's decentralized managerial practices, which assigned executives wide discretionary decision-making authority except where significant amounts of company capital were involved. Preoccupied with the pressing problem of fending off the Gauleiter, they apparently gave no thought to the possible long-term implications of making advanced American technology available to the Luftwaffe. In light of the German military buildup at the time, theirs was, at the minimum, a rash and irresponsible decision with potentially grave implications. Although they were motivated by an urgent quest for protection against the Gauleiter, their decision involved Opel in the military-industrial complex that was preparing Germany for war.

The belated approval of the gear plant project by GM's American leadership amounted, in light of the circumstances, to acquiescence rather than endorsement. No authorization was sought by the chief GM executive at Opel until more than half a year after the agreement with the Air Ministry, when funding problems led him to request permission to use Opel funds for the project. By the time that request reached the attention of GM's president, the American corporation's top policy-making body had firmly rejected the possibility of Opel's producing airplanes for the Luftwaffe in response to an earlier proposal to GM's president by Air Minister Göring. Nevertheless, the president several months later approved continuation of the gear plant project by authorizing the use of Opel funds. Construction of the plant was then already far advanced, so that canceling it would have predictably antagonized the Luftwaffe generals and, very possibly, Göring himself. With the angry, resentful Gauleiter still a threat to the American corporation's control over Opel, allowing the gear project to proceed in order to avoid alienating those potential sources of political protection scarcely amounted, under the circumstances, to a freely chosen option by GM for war production in Germany.

No evidence could be found in the surviving records of Opel or those of the Air Ministry about the military significance of the gear plant's output. Whether the application of GM's American technology resulted in enhanced performance of planes destined for use by the Luftwaffe therefore remains unclear. That possibility was, however, inherent in the project from the outset. And any improvements in German air power that may have resulted from the project would have had damaging wartime consequences for the Allies. Whatever the gear plant's contributions to the German war effort may have been, ultimate responsibility must be assigned to GM. The American executives in charge of Opel were, in effect, acting on behalf of the corporation when they acceded to the request of the Luftwaffe generals in hopes of gaining protection against the Gauleiter. As their action demonstrates, GM's decentralized managerial structure left it open to commitments with potentially far-reaching consequences made by subaltern executives acting without authorization from the corporation's policy-making ranks. And as the case of the gear plant project indicates, under the circumstances of the Third Reich, reversal of such a commitment could come to seem prohibitively perilous.

The exploitation by Opel of victims of involuntary labor during the war is a shameful chapter of that firm's history. Like other German companies, it complied with Nazi practices in utilizing the toil of thousands of men and women from occupied countries, hundreds of whom were killed or maimed in Allied bombing attacks as a result of being denied adequate protection against air raids. General Motors cannot, however, be held responsible for the fate of those victims at that time. When the use of forced labor began in 1942, the American corporation had lost all control over its subsidiary and was cut off from information about what was happening there. It is an elementary principle of all equitable systems of law that owners of property cannot be held liable for uses made of it when, in their enforced absence, it is controlled by others, as was Opel during the time of forced labor.

General Motors bears full responsibility, however, for laying claim in 1951 to the Opel dividends put aside for it during the war, another aspect of the corporation's relationship to its German subsidiary that has hitherto escaped notice. That decision appears not to have been made by the top ranks of GM, possibly because the money involved, which amounted to only a twentieth of one percent of GM's net income for that year, seemed too paltry to merit attention at the highest level of management. But regardless of who decided to claim that tainted money, its receipt rendered GM guilty, after the fact, of deriving profit from war production for the Third Reich made possible in part by the toil of unfree workers. A half century later, Opel, still a GM subsidiary, agreed to contribute thirty million marks, the equivalent of about fifteen million dollars, to a German fund established—in the face of class action suits in the United States—to provide a measure of compensation to surviving victims of involuntary labor in the Third Reich.[1]

Appendix: GM and German Tetraethyl Lead Production

It has been alleged that during 1935–36 "at the urgent request of Nazi officials who realized that Germany's scarce petroleum reserves would not satisfy war demands," GM and Standard Oil "joined with German chemical interests" to build plants to produce tetraethyl lead that "contributed substantially to the German war effort."[1] Such plants were in fact established and did indeed become militarily important although they did not increase Germany's petroleum reserves. The circumstances of their origins were, however, quite different from those implied by this allegation.

Since the mid-1920s the Ethyl Gasoline Corporation (EGC), which was jointly owned by GM and Standard Oil of New Jersey, had produced and sold internationally tetraethyl lead (TEL), an additive that increased the octane level of gasoline and significantly reduced engine knocking or "pinging." To retain control over this product, EGC secured patents in numerous other countries but refrained from utilizing those patents or issuing licenses for their use. In 1934, however, the Italian government overrode the EGC patent in that country and assigned production of TEL to a state-financed company. This led EGC to fear a similar move on the part of Germany, where the government was empowered by law to grant a license to a patent if the holder failed to do so. In 1935 EGC therefore responded positively to a proposal from the German chemical firm IG Farben to form a new company, Ethyl G.m.b.H., that would be licensed to build plants to produce TEL in Germany. Quarter shares in the new company were assumed by a German subsidiary of Standard Oil and by Opel on behalf of GM; the other half was held by IG Farben. The Ethyl Gasoline Corporation entered into this arrangement, however, only after making a full disclosure to American military authorities and alerting them to the possible use of TEL to enhance the octane content of German coal-derived gasoline in order to make it usable in aircraft engines. As EGC pointed out in a submission to the chief of the U.S. Army Air Corps, there was no way to prevent unauthorized German development of TEL production, since the essential technical information was available in EGC's foreign patents and in the published literature on the subject. To guard against the disclosure to Germans of any new American technical information that might be of military use, EGC inserted, on its own initiative, a clause into the contract with IG Farben specifying that any such information would be conveyed only after approval by the proper U.S. military authorities.[2]

An internal IG Farben wartime communication indicates that the agreement with EGC facilitated and expedited the production in Germany of TEL, which became an essential additive to the fuels that powered Luftwaffe warplanes. That was, however, not the aim of EGC, which had entered into that agreement in defense of its commercial interests and in response to "the urgent requests" not of Nazi officials, but of IG Farben. The Farben communication also noted that "the War Department in Washington gave its permission only after long deliberation." As for GM, it was from all indications a passive partner in EGC, which in May 1939 sold its holding in Ethyl G.m.b.H. to a British firm, Associated Ethyl Co., Ltd., of which GM held a quarter share. When the U.S. government later instituted civil antitrust proceedings against Standard Oil for dealings with IG Farben, GM was not included in the suit.[3]

Abbreviations

BAB	Bundesarchiv, Berlin-Lichterfelde
BA/MA	Bundesarchiv/Militärarchiv, Freiburg im Breisgau
BLHAP	Brandenburgisches Landeshauptarchiv, Potsdam
BR	Business Research Library, General Motors, Detroit (GM-Opel Collection, Yale University Library)
CR	Central Records, General Motors, Detroit (GM-Opel Collection, Yale University Library)
GM	Legal Staff, General Motors, Detroit (GM-Opel Collection, Yale University Library). This prefix, used in the notes for the Bates-stamped pages of this collection, does not appear on the documents preserved on the CD-Roms of the GM-Opel Collection.
GSA	Geheimes Staatsarchiv, Berlin
HHStAW	Hessisches Hauptstaatsarchiv, Wiesbaden
HWAD	Hessisches Wirtschaftsarchiv, Darmstadt
HP	Franklin D. Roosevelt Presidential Library, Hyde Park, N.Y.

MA	Media Archive, General Motors, Detroit (GM-Opel Collection, Yale University Library)
MBAG	Mercedes-Benz AG, Historisches Archiv, Stuttgart
NARA	National Archives and Records Administration, College Park, Md.
OPR	Adam Opel AG, Rüsselsheim (GM-Opel Collection, Yale University Library)
OR	Adam Opel AG, Rüsselsheim (GM-Opel Collection, Yale University Library)
PR	Public Relations Office, General Motors, Detroit (GM-Opel Collection, Yale University Library)
PRO/FO	Public Records Office, Foreign Office Records, London
SHStAC	Sächsisches Hauptstaatsarchiv, Chemnitz
SMR	Stadtmuseum, Rüsselsheim
TX	Tax Staff, General Motors, Detroit (GM-Opel Collection, Yale University Library)
VX	Vauxhall Motors Limited, Luton, England (GM-Opel Collection, Yale University Library)

Notes

PREFACE

1. See Reinhold Billstein, Karola Fings, Anita Kugler, and Nicholas Levis, *Working for the Enemy: Ford, General Motors and Forced Labor in Germany during the Second World War* (New York, 2000); Bernd Heyl and Andrea Neugebauer, eds., *". . . ohne Rücksicht auf die Verhältnisse": Opel zwischen Weltwirtschaftskrise und Wiederaufbau* (Frankfurt a.M., 1997); Ludolf Herbst, "Der Krieg und die Unternehmensstrategie deutscher Industrie-Konzerne in der Zwischenkriegszeit," in *Die deutschen Eliten und der Weg in den zweiten Weltkrieg,* ed. Martin Broszat and Klaus Schwabe (Munich, 1989); Charles Higham, *Trading with the Enemy: An Exposé of the Nazi-American Money Plot, 1933–1949* (New York, 1983); Charles Levinson, *Vodka Cola* (New York, 1978); Morton Mintz and Jerry S. Cohen, *Power, Inc.* (New York, 1976). The source of many of the gravest allegations against GM is a paper by Bradford C. Snell, "American Ground Transport," appendix to pt. 4 of *The Industrial Reorganization Act: Hearings before the Subcommittee on Antitrust and Monopoly of the Committee on the Judiciary, on S. 1167,* United States Senate, 93rd Cong. 2nd sess. (Washington, D.C., 1974). The allegations have appeared in numerous magazines and newspapers; see, for examples, "Gut für Nazis," *Der Spiegel,* Mar. 25, 1974; Bradford C. Snell, "GM and the Nazis," *Ramparts,* June 1974; Joseph DeBaggio, "The Unholy Alliance," *Penthouse,* May 1976; Michael Dobbs, "Ford and GM Scrutinized for Alleged Nazi Collaboration," *Washington Post,* Nov. 30, 1998.

CHAPTER 1. GM'S COSTLY SUBSIDIARY SAGS WITH THE SLUMP,
THEN SOARS UNDER THE SWASTIKA

1. On this and the following, see Alfred P. Sloan, Jr., *My Years With General Motors* (New York, 1963), pp. 321–28. On Sloan's career, see David R. Farber, *Sloan Rules: Alfred P. Sloan and the Triumph of General Motors* (Chicago, 2002); Carl H. A. Dassbach, *Global Enterprises and the World Economy* (New York, 1989), pp. 206–57; Paul F. Douglass, *Six upon the World* (Boston, 1954), pp. 129–97. On the ratio of cars to populations, see *Wirtschaft und Statistik,* vol. 9 (Berlin, 1929), p. 786.

2. Sloan's memoirs (note 1, above) considerably exaggerate Opel's share of the German market prior to its purchase. For Opel's 1928 production see Hans-Jürgen Schneider, *Autos und Technik: 125 Jahre Opel* (Weilerswist, 1987), p. 471; for that of German industry as a whole, see *Automotive Industries* (Philadelphia), Feb. 28, 1931. On Opel's operations, see "Opel verkauft," *Frankfurter Zeitung,* Mar. 18, 1929 (#206); Heinrich Hauser, *Opel: Ein deutsches Tor zur Welt* (Frankfurt a.M., 1937), pp. 163–86; Jürgen Lewandowski, *Opel* (Bielefeld, 2000), pp. 47–60.

3. For the early history of the firm, see Hauser, *Opel;* Lewandowski, *Opel;* and Schneider, *Autos und Technik.* On its incorporation, see *Frankfurter Zeitung,* Dec. 4, 1928, erstes Morgenblatt.

4. "General Motors Gets Opel as Ally," *New York Times,* Mar. 18, 1929; "J. D. Mooney Back after Opel Deal," ibid., Apr. 6, 1929; Opel annual financial reports, 1929–32, OR 053318–49.

5. On the first manager, see Sloan, *My Years,* p. 327; on "co-ordinated decentralization," ibid., pp. 429ff. For the membership of the *Aufsichtsrat* and *Vorstand,* see the Opel annual financial reports for 1933–34 (OPR 032509–54), 1935–36 (BR 075583–615), and 1937–40 (BR 004795–835).

6. See "General Motors Investment in Germany," report to GM's Finance Committee by Albert Bradley, Jan. 5, 1937, GM 000817–60. On the 1929 shutdown, see *"Morgen kommst du nach Amerika": Erinnerungen an die Arbeit bei Opel 1917–1987,* ed. Peter Schirmbeck (Bonn, 1988), p. 210. On other shutdowns and curtailments, see Schneider, *Autos und Technik,* p. 177. On Opel's performance relative to the rest of the German auto industry, see Heidrun Edelmann, *Vom Luxusgut zum Gebrauchsgegenstand* (Frankfurt a.M, 1989), p. 139.

7. On Nazi attitudes toward Opel and other American-owned automotive firms, see "Quarterly Automotive Report for Germany," Mar. 27, 1933, by Douglas Miller, assistant American commercial attaché in Berlin, RG 151, box 259, NARA. on the racing track incident, see the letter of Adam Bangert to Wilhelm von Opel, Aug. 20, 1946, and the latter's statement quoted by his attorney in a submission at his denazification trial, Sept. 9, 1946, both in the records of the trial, Abt. 520, Wiesbaden Neuablage, Nr. 167, HHStAW; also the testimony of Walter Behrens at the denazification trial of Rudolf Fleischer, Aug. 19, 1946, Abt. 520, KS-Z, Nr. 3297, HHStAW.

8. For Göring's threat, see Douglas Miller's report of Mar. 27, 1933 (note 7, above) and his book, *You Can't Do Business with Hitler* (Boston, 1941), pp. 196f. For the journalist's account, see Hubert R. Knickerbocker, *The German Crisis* (New York, 1932), p. 239.

9. On the rumors and reactions to them, see "Monthly Automotive Report for Germany,

March 1933," Mar. 24, 1933, pt. 2, by Douglas Miller, assistant American commercial attaché in Berlin, RG 151, box 259, NARA.

10. See Edelmann, *Luxusgut,* pp. 157ff.; Hansjoachim Henning, "Kraftfahrzeugindustrie und Autobahnbau in der Wirtschaftspolitik des Nationalsozialismus 1933 bis 1936," in *Vierteljahrschrift für Sozial- und Wirtschaftsgeschichte* 65 (1978). On Hitler's appearance at the Opel display, see the company magazines *Der Opel Geist,* Mar. 28, 1933, and *General Motors World,* Apr. 1933.

11. Edelmann, *Luxusgut,* pp. 157ff. R. J. Overy, *War and Economy in the Third Reich* (Oxford, 1994), pp. 68–89; Overy, "Transportation and Rearmament in the Third Reich," *Historical Journal* 16 (1973).

12. See "General Motors Investment in Germany" (note 6, above).

13. See "Adam Opel A.G. Dividend Declarations and Remittances Covering Period 1929–1948," compiled by GM Overseas Operations Tax Section, Mar. 19, 1974, GM 000554–555; for sales statistics, see "History of Opel Operation," appendix C of a report to GM's Executive Committee by C. R. Osborn, Mar. 18, 1960, CR 075649.

14. On the currency controls, see Ludwig Hamburger, *How Nazi Germany Has Controlled Business* (Washington, 1943); Howard S. Ellis, *Exchange Control in Central Europe* (Cambridge, Mass., 1941).

15. See the Opel correspondence with GM and the Economics Ministry about the rubber problem, 1936–40, OPR 031602–4, OR 047425–521. For a summary of the payments and yields, see the report by Albert Bradley to GM's Policy Committee, "General Motors Cash Position in Germany," May 1, 1940, schedule VI, PR 008144.

16. On the indirect profits from Opel exports, see "History of Opel Operation" (note 13, above), CRO 075651. The estimate of $20 million for these profits in the anonymous report of 1940, "Opel under General Motors Management" (GM 002680ff.) seems greatly exaggerated and reflects that report's vigorous promotion of the corporation's retention of its German subsidiary, GM 002681.

17. See "Adam Opel A.G. Dividend Declarations and Remittances" (note 13, above); also "General Motors Investment in Germany" (note 6, above). The quotation is from "Opel under General Motors Management" (note 16, above), GM 002680.

18. "Adam Opel A.G. Dividend Declarations and Remittances" (note 13, above); "Opel under General Motors Management" (note 16, above), GM 002693f. and 002707f.; "Comparison of the Big Five Automobile Manufacturers in Germany," submitted to GM by Opel, July 31, 1938, OR 059333–60.

CHAPTER 2. OPEL AND GM ADAPT TO THE THIRD REICH

1. See Arnold Busch, *Widerstand im Kreis Gross-Gerau 1933–1945* (Gross-Gerau, 1988), p. 110; Axel Ulrich, "Betrieblicher Widerstand gegen die NS-Gewaltherrschaft am Beispiel der Opel-Werke in Rüsselsheim," in " . . . *ohne Rücksicht auf die Verhältnisse": Opel zwischen Weltwirtschaftskrise und Wiederaufbau,* ed. Bernd Heyl and Andrea Neugebauer (Frankfurt a.M., 1997), p. 111; *"Morgen kommst Du nach Amerika": Erinnerungen an die Arbeit bei Opel, 1917–1987,* ed. Peter Schirmbeck (Bonn, 1988), p. 264.

2. See "Adam Opel Observes Tag der Arbeit on May First," *General Motors World,* June 1933,

p. 14; also the issues of the company magazine, *Der Opel Geist,* for June, July, Oct., Nov., and Dec. See also, the management "Mitteilungen" to employees, 1933–34, in Abt. 112, file 578, HWAD.

3. On the lecture series and the library, see *Der Opel Geist,* Nov. 2, 1933; Hanns Schäcker, "Historischer Rückblick auf die Entwicklung der Personalabteilung der Adam Opel AG," manuscript of 1961, OR 066940f. On the company magazine, see the monthly issues of *Der Opel Geist* for 1933–34; also the report to American military intelligence in 1942 by former GM executives at Opel, RG 169, box 1232, #137252, NARA. On Nazi surveillance of company publications, see Alexander Michel, *Von der Fabrikzeitung zum Führungsmittel: Werkszeitschriften industrieller Grossunternehmen von 1890 bis 1945* (Stuttgart, 1997).

4. See *Der Opel Geist,* Sept. 4 and Dec. 1, 1933; also the denazification trial records of former sales manager Adam Bangert, Abt. 520, Gross-Gerau, Nr. 3673/46, HHStAW.

5. On the strategy of camouflage and false facade, see Graeme Howard's report of June 12, 1938, to J. D. Mooney, GM 001879; also R. A. Fleischer to Mooney, Mar. 3, 1937, OPR 032823–25. On Fleischer's role, see chap. 4. On the personnel changes of 1934, see Opel's "Report and Financial Statement for the Business Year 1934," OPR 032511. On the undated hostile speech by Kreisleiter Wellenkamp, see the letter of Cyrus Osborn to General William H. Draper, July 12, 1946, and the testimony of Karl Schäffer, Aug. 19, 1946, both in the records of Rudolf Fleischer's denazification trial, Abt. 520, KS-Z, Nr. 3297, HHStAW.

6. See the records of von Opel's denazification trial, Abt. 520, Wiesbaden Neuablage, Nr. 167, HHStAW. He was one of two dozen industrialists invited by Hermann Göring to a Feb. 20, 1933, meeting where Hitler spoke and Hjalmar Schacht solicited contributions to support the campaigns of the parties backing Hitler's newly installed cabinet in the March Reichstag election, with the bulk of the resulting three million marks going to the Nazi Party: H. A. Turner, Jr., *German Big Business and the Rise of Hitler* (New York, 1985), pp. 329–32. Three days later the trade association of the automotive industry (*Reichsverband der Automobilindustrie*) contributed 100,000 marks from a bank account of the annual Berlin auto show, NARA, RG 238, NI-391. Von Opel was rumored to have made a sizable personal contribution to Nazi Party afterward; see Robert Allmers to Nationalsozialistische Deutsche Arbeiterpartei, Abteilung zur Wahrung der Berufsmoral, Oct. 9, 1934, in "Anlagen zum Gutachten in der Schiedsgerichtsache Rasmussen gegen Auto Union A.G.," Auto-Union 1092, SHStAC.

7. See the testimony of von Opel at his denazification trial (note 6, above). On the Gauleiter's career, see Stephanie Zibell, *Jakob Sprenger* (Darmstadt, 1999).

8. On Lüer's career, see Zibell, *Jakob Sprenger,* pp. 319–21; also *Das Deutsche Reich von 1918 bis heute,* ed. Cuno Horkenbach (Berlin, 1935), pp. 253, 290, 542, 872, 875, 877, 981f.; see also the records of his denazification trial, Abt. 520, Frankfurt-Zentral, Nr. 646, HHStAW.

9. See the interrogation of Lüer on Nov. 26, 1947, NARA Publication M1019, roll 44; the quotation is from C. R. Osborn to J. D. Mooney, Nov. 22, 1939, GM 000733.

10. See Fleischer's memorandum on his meeting with the Gauleiter on Sept. 30, 1935, OPR 017434f.; also, Fleischer's letter to the Frankfurt Industrie und Handelskammer, Mar. 13, 1937, OPR 017379.

11. See, e.g., Fleischer's responses in early 1937 to an appeal from the Opel dealer in Schweinfurt for help in the face of local Nazi demands not to buy from or sell to Jews, OPR 017374–79. See also "Allg. Verkaufsargumente für Opel," enclosure in DKW-Kundendienst 326A, Dec. 21, 1936, Auto-Union 5600, SHStAC.

12. See Gauamtsleiter Feickert, Hesse-Nassau, to Gauwirtschaftsberater, June 13, 1935, Abt. 483, Nr. 10959, HHStAW; Fleischer to Staatsrat Rainer, July 1, 1936, OPR 017437.

13. See the written statement of Hass, July 14, 1947, in the records of Bangert's denazification trial (note 4, above); also the correspondence in which Fleischer sought in 1937 to counter Nazi accusations that the Opel dealer in Belgrade, Yugoslavia, was Jewish, OPR 017302–4.

14. According to *Der Opel Geist,* July 1, 1933, Wronker-Flatow made the introductory remarks, but in a letter to the Landrat of Gross-Gerau, Oct. 18, 1945, Wilhelm von Opel claimed that he had at the last minute substituted for Wronker-Flatow to appease the Gauleiter: records of von Opel's denazification trial (note 6, above). On Wronker-Flatow's rise under GM, see "Announcement of Future Plans for Adam Opel A/G and of the New Members of Its Staff," *General Motors World,* Oct. 1930; on his reassignment, see *Der Opel Geist,* Dec. 1, 1933, and *General Motors World,* July 1934. On the other staff members affected by Nazi racial laws, see the statements of Walter G. Behrens, Karl Mees, and Hanns Schäcker in the records of Wilhelm von Opel's denazification trial (note 6, above); the testimony of Schäcker at Heinrich Wagner's denazification trial, Abt. 520, Gross-Gerau, Nr. 3125/46, HHStAW; and the affidavit and testimony by Behrens for Fleischer's trial (note 5, above). For the 1936 questionnaire, see OPR 019295–7, 019208–10.

15. This is based on the extensive correspondence with and about Hofmann in the records of Vauxhall Motors, VX 006466–850.

16. See "Betriebs-Ordnung der Adam Opel A.G," Sept. 21, 1934, Sgl. Opel I, 2.2, SMR. On Nazi labor legislation, see T. W. Mason, *Arbeiterklasse und Volksgemeinschaft* (Opladen, 1975). There is testimony on Opel's lax enforcement in the records of the denazification trials of Rudolf Fleischer (note 5, above) and Heinrich Wagner (note 14, above).

17. This account is based on a report of Aug. 24, 1936, by Opel treasurer R. A. Fleischer to an aide of Wilhelm Keppler, Hitler's economics commissioner, and a lengthy Gestapo report of Aug. 28 to Keppler, both in the file of Wilhelm von Opel, Berlin Document Center, #08842, BAB. See also the versions in Günter Neliba, *Die Opel-Werke im Konzern von General Motors (1929–1948) in Rüsselsheim und Brandenburg* (Frankfurt a.M., 2000), pp. 56–62; Ulrich, "Betrieblicher Widerstand" (see note 1, above), pp. 117f., 146–53; Busch, *Widerstand,* pp. 113–19; Schneider, *Autos und Technik,* p. 198.

18. See Fleischer's report of Aug. 24, 1936 (note 17, above); also Neliba, *Die Opel-Werke,* p. 62; Busch, *Widerstand,* p. 119.

19. Busch, *Widerstand,* pp. 102f. On Riller, see Schäcker, "Historischer Rückblick" (note 3, above), OR 066944; Riller to Fleischer, July 16, 1937, OPR 017731; also the manuscripts "Mein Verhältnis zu Partei und Wehrmacht" and "Meine Einstellung zur NSDAP," submitted by Opel manager Karl Stief at his denazification trial, Abt. 520, Gross-Gerau, Nr. 2745/46, HHStAW. Opel's German treasurer Rudolf Fleischer was accused at his denazification trial of installing Riller at Opel, but his defense attorney produced a letter from

the postwar American custodian of Opel stating that Riller's certificate of appointment (*Einstellungsbescheinigung*) had been signed by both Fleischer and the senior GM executive, C. R. Osborn: E. U. Neumann, American custodian of Opel, to Artur Borgmann, Sept. 23, 1946, in the records of Fleischer's denazification trial (note 5, above).

20. See the letter by Koretzky's sister, S. Zimmer, Jan. 29, 1947, in the records of Fleischer's denazification trial (note 5, above).

21. On the fund, see Klaus Drobisch, "Hindenburg-, Hitler-, Adenauerspende," *Zeitschrift für Geschichtswissenschaft* 15 (1967), and Arthur Schweitzer, "Business Power under the Nazi Regime," *Zeitschrift für Nationalökonomie* 20 (1960). For a record of Opel's payments, 1938–44, see the chart "Spenden der Firma Opel A.G.," dated Sept. 26, 1945, in the records of Heinrich Wagner's denazification trial (note 14, above).

22. On the payments to the Winter Help, see "Spenden der Firma Opel A.G." (note 21, above). On the contribution for the Gauleiter's headquarters, see the minutes of the Supervisory Board meeting of July 3, 1939, GM 002436. There is information on Wilhelm von Opel's contributions to various Nazi organizations, including the SA and SS, in the records of his denazification trial (note 6, above).

23. On the gift to Hitler, see chap. 4. Correspondence on the loan of cars for guests at the 1937 party congress, OPR 017336f. The figure on sales to the party is from Graeme Howard's manuscript, "Notes for Discussion with Prof. Dr. Karl Lüer and Dr. Franz Belitz, May 1938," GM 003815. On Daimler-Benz and the Nazis, see Neil Gregor, *Daimler-Benz in the Third Reich* (New Haven, 1998); *Das Daimler-Benz Buch*, ed. the Hamburger Stiftung für Sozialgeschichte des 20. Jahrhunderts (Nördlingen, 1987); and *Die Daimler-Benz AG in den Jahren 1933 bis 1945*, ed. Hans Pohl et al. (Stuttgart, 1986).

24. See the anonymous 1940 report, "Opel under General Motors Management," GM 002707f.; also C. R. Osborn to J. D. Mooney, Mar. 26, 1940, GM 002650.

25. Letter to Mrs. Helen Lewis, Apr. 6, 1939, RG 59, 862.20211, Mooney, James D., confidential file, box C 296 (pp. 20–23 of FBI report of Aug. 8, 1941), NARA.

26. See Steven Casey, *Cautious Crusade: Franklin D. Roosevelt, American Public Opinion, and the War Against Nazi Germany* (New York, 2001); Patrick J. Hearden, *Roosevelt Confronts Hitler: America's Entry into World War II* (DeKalb, Ill., 1987); Arnold A. Offner, *American Appeasement: United States Foreign Policy and Germany, 1933–1938* (Cambridge, Mass., 1969); Offner, "Appeasement Revisited: The United States, Great Britain and Germany, 1933–1940," *Journal of American History* 64 (1977): 373–93; Offner, "The United States and National Socialist Germany," in *The Fascist Challenge and the Policy of Appeasement*, ed. Wolfgang J. Mommsen and Lothar Kettenacker (London, 1983), pp. 413–27.

27. See Hans-Jürgen Schröder, *Deutschland und die Vereinigten Staaten, 1933–1939* (Wiesbaden, 1970). On Mooney, see ibid., pp. 153ff. See also the report of George Messersmith, American consul general in Berlin, on his misgivings after a conversation with Mooney, in Messersmith's letter to Undersecretary of State William Phillips, Nov. 16, 1934, item 442, Messersmith Papers, University of Delaware Library. (I am indebted to Iris Snyder of the Library for a copy of this document.) On Opel's involvement in German war production, see chaps. 6 and 8, below.

28. Quoted from Howard's memorandum of Apr. 6, 1936, to J. D. Mooney, forwarded by the latter to A. P. Sloan, who submitted it to GM's Finance Committee on May 27 at the

recommendation of Donaldson Brown, vice chairman of the board of directors, GM 001608ff.

29. See Howard's report to J. D. Mooney, June 12, 1938, GM 001719 and 001834.

CHAPTER 3. GM FUMBLES THE VOLKSWAGEN, GAINS A TRUCK FACTORY, IDENTIFIES FOES AND FRIENDS

1. On Hitler's speech and the origins of the VW project, see Hans Mommsen and Manfred Grieger, *Das Volkswagenwerk und seine Arbeiter im Dritten Reich* (Düsseldorf, 1996), pp. 56ff.; Paul Kluke, "Hitler und das Volkswagenprojekt," *Vierteljahrshefte für Zeitgeschichte* 8 (1960).

2. Hans-Jürgen Schneider, *Autos und Technik: 125 Jahre Opel* (Weilerswist, 1987), p. 174. A clipping of the *Völkischer Beobachter* article of Mar. 10, 1934, "Das deutsche Volksauto," with photograph, is in Rep 120 C VIII, Nr. 119, Bd. 5, GSA. On fears that Hitler favored Opel, see Mommsen and Grieger, *Volkswagenwerk,* p. 68; also the letter of June 5, 1938, from Franz-Josef Popp of BMW to Wilhelm Kissel of Daimler-Benz in *Die Daimler-Benz AG 1916–1948. Schlüsseldokumente zur Konzerngeschichte,* ed. by Karl Heinz Roth and Michael Schmid (Nördlingen, 1987), pp. 153f.; also Gerald D. Feldman, "Die deutsche Bank und die Automobilindustrie," *Zeitschrift für Unternehmensgeschichte* 44 (1999): 13.

3. See Foreign Minister Konstantin von Neurath to the Reich Chancellery, Apr. 13, 1934, and a Chancellery memorandum confirming the meeting, R43II/1465, BAB. In 1935 and 1936 Hitler received the head of a prominent French auto firm (Laurent Dingli, *Louis Renault* [Paris, 2000], pp. 301ff.).

4. See Charles Wertenbaker, "The World and Jim Mooney," *Saturday Evening Post,* Oct. 30, 1937, p. 23. See also "James D. Mooney Discusses Automotive Industry with Hitler," *General Motors World,* June 1934, pp. 1–3, and Mooney's later recollection in the "Diary of Mr. Mooney's Visit to London and Berlin: March 27 to April 6, 1939," p. 6, box 1, folder 14, Mooney Papers, Georgetown University Library. The terms of the Opel offer are spelled out in a memorandum of Sept. 16, 1936, by R. A. Fleischer, OPR 019343.

5. For the GM magazine article and Mooney's later recollection, see note 4, above. On destruction of the magazine copies, see R. A. Fleischer to Hansen, June 11, 1934, OR 040327.

6. Mommsen and Grieger, *Volkswagenwerk,* pp. 62ff. Also, Heidrun Edelmann, *Heinz Nordhoff und Volkswagen* (Göttingen, 2003), pp. 36f.; Reichsverband der Automobilindustrie to Auto Union, June 7, 1934, Bl. 173–80, Auto Union 866, file on "Volkswagen," SHStAC. Cf. Horst Handke, "Zur Rolle der Volkswagenpläne bei der faschistischen Kriegsvorbereitung," *Jahrbuch für Wirtschaftsgeschichte,* 1962, Teil I, 37f. The quoted words are from R. K. Evans to J. D. Mooney, Nov. 16, 1934, OPR 019069.

7. On Hitler's initially negative reaction to Porsche's design, see Mommsen and Grieger, *Volkswagenwerk,* p. 93. For Keppler's offer, see R. K. Evans to J. D. Mooney, Nov. 16, 1934, OPR 019065–70.

8. See Mooney's telegram of Dec. 17, 1934, to R. K. Evans, OPR 019054; Fleischer to Keppler, with memorandum, Jan. 14, 1935, OPR 019041–4; Keppler to Fleischer, Jan. 30, 1935, OPR 019024.

9. On the P-4, see Schneider, *Autos und Technik,* p. 193; also H. C. Graf von Seherr-Thoss, *Die deutsche Automobilindustrie: Eine Dokumentation von 1886 bis heute* (Stuttgart, 1974), p. 283; also J. D. Mooney's annual report on GM's overseas operations, Feb. 20, 1936, CR 010190C.

10. Mommsen and Grieger, *Volkswagenwerk,* pp. 93–96. For Hitler's speech, see "Der Führer wünscht die Schaffung des deutschen Volkswagen," *Völkischer Beobachter,* Norddeutsche Ausgabe A, Feb. 15, 1936 (Nr. 46).

11. On Fleischer's remarks, see Mommsen and Grieger, *Volkswagenwerk,* p. 100; Handke, "Zur Rolle," p. 44; Kluke, "Volkswagenprojekt," pp. 355f. For Porsche's complaints, see "Aktennotiz über die RdA-Vorstandssitzung am 12. November 1935 in München," in the archive of MBAG, Kissel, Behörden Institutionen, 9.21. On the P-4, see J. D. Mooney's report, Nov. 12, 1936, CR 010337; also Seherr-Thoss, *Automobilindustrie,* p. 283.

12. Mommsen and Grieger, *Volkswagenwerk,* p. 99; Kluke, "Volkswagenprojekt," p. 355.

13. Mommsen and Grieger, *Volkswagenwerk.,* pp. 96ff.

14. See Fleischer's letter of Sept. 9, 1936, to Staatssekretär Lammers, Chef der Reichskanzlei, requesting an appointment for Mooney and Howard with Hitler, OPR 019345. Keppler's record of the meeting is in R26I/30, BAB: "Tageszettel vom Dienstag, d. 22. September 1936." Fleischer wrote two slightly divergent accounts of the meeting, one in German, dated Sept. 24 (OPR 019340), and one in English, dated Oct. 16 (OPR 019341). On the memorandum for Hitler, a copy of which could not be located, see Fleischer's letter to Mooney's assistant, W. B. Wachtler, Oct. 16, 1936, OPR 019336f.; on Fleischer's efforts to deliver it and the response, see the letter by his defense attorneys to the appeals court, Jan. 15, 1948, in the records of his denazification proceedings, Abt. 520, KS-Z, 3297, HHStAW. On the reduction in the price of the P-4, see Fleischer's Aktennotiz of Sept. 16, 1936, OPR 019343; also Schneider, *Autos und Technik,* p. 193.

15. Mommsen and Grieger, *Volkswagenwerk,* p. 106; C. R. Osborn to G. K. Howard, Aug. 28, 1937, GM 003730–39.

16. Mommsen and Grieger, *Volkswagenwerk,* pp. 117ff.

17. See C. R. Osborn to G. K. Howard, Aug. 28, 1937, GM 003730–9. On P-4 sales, see Werner Oswald, ed., *Deutsche Autos 1920–1945* (Stuttgart, 1982), p. 287. On the Kadett, see ibid., p. 325; Schneider, *Autos und Technik,* pp. 199f. and 208; also *Der Opel-Kamerad,* Jan. 1937, and *General Motors World,* Jan. 1937. On the employee defections to Porsche, see Mommsen and Grieger, *Volkswagenwerk,* pp. 147 and 219f. The claim that Wilhelm von Opel incurred Hitler's disfavor by proclaiming to him at the 1937 Berlin auto show that the P-4 was "our Volkswagen" is without foundation: cf. K. B. Hopfinger, *Beyond Expectation: The Volkswagen Story* (London, 1954), p. 99.

18. After consultation with Keppler, the following statement was released to the press, "In close consultation with authoritative circles of the National government, the Adam Opel A.G. has decided, because production capacity in Rüsselsheim has reached its maximum, to erect a new factory in Brandenburg a.d. Havel." R. A. Fleischer to R. K. Evans, Apr. 4, 1935, OPR 019138.

19. On the financing of the plant, see Fleischer to Keppler, Mar. 1, 1935, OPR 019010. On its opening, see the reports in *Der Opel-Kamerad,* Jan. 1936, and *General Motors World,* Feb. 1936. The figures are from GM 002673: "Opel under General Motors Management" (re-

port of 1940). The figure for the workforce is from Hans-Jürgen Schneider, *Autos und Technik*, p. 472. The designation "Blitz" was bestowed on the trucks in conformity to the winning entry in a 1931 public contest to name them: ibid., p. 467.

20. See Keppler to Fleischer, Jan. 3, 1935, OPR 019046; Fleischer to Keppler, Jan. 14, 1935, OPR 019040; R. K. Evans to J. D. Mooney, Jan. 18, 1935, GM 001064–8; Paetsch to Colonel Thomas, Feb. 27, 1935 (Abschrift), OPR 019014. Paetsch to Fleischer (Abschrift), Feb. 26, 1935, OPR 019015f. On the initial truck orders, see O. C. Mueller's circular memorandum of Mar. 21, 1936, OPR 017802. On subsequent orders, see A. Bangert to H. Grewenig, Aug. 13, 1937 (OPR 017729) and Grewenig to Fleischer, Sept. 17, 1937 (OR 042133). On the portion of truck sales to the army, see the anonymous "Gesamt-Produktion des Werkes Brandenburg der Adam Opel A.G. 1936–1940," OPR 016934ff.

21. On the profitability of sales to military, see the anonymous analysis of truck sales as of Apr. 30, 1938, OR 039891–3. See the extensive Opel correspondence of 1937–38 on the difficulties caused by the army's demands regarding a special truck project designated alternatively as P.K.W. and P.K.W. 901, esp. G. K. Howard to J. D. Mooney, Mar. 10, 1937, GM 001071–3; also OPR 031702, OR 042158–9, OR 042171–9, OR 042193, OPR 017675–77.

22. See Ludwig Hamburger, *How Nazi Germany Has Controlled Business* (Washington, 1943). On the four-year plan, see Dieter Petzina, *Autarkiepolitik im Dritten Reich* (Stuttgart, 1968); Alfred Kube, *Hermann Göring im Dritten Reich* (Munich, 1986), pp. 151ff.; R. J. Overy, *Göring: The "Iron Man"* (London, 1984), pp. 48ff. On the rubber problem, see chap. 1, above; the "veiled threat" quotation is attributed to GM's Nicholas Vansittart in a letter from American diplomat George S. Messersmith to Acting Secretary of State R. Walton Moore of Dec. 22, 1936, no. 807, Messersmith Papers, University of Delaware Library. On Opel's problems with the government's control of labor supply, see H. Grewenig to C. R. Osborn, Aug. 26, 1938, OR 043092–5. Mooney's words are from his letter to Sloan, Oct. 6, 1936, GM 003718; Howard's are from his report to J. D. Mooney, June 12, 1938, GM 001729.

23. See Howard's letter to R. A. Fleischer, Apr. 1, 1936, GM 001627–31; also his memorandum to J. D. Mooney, Apr. 6, 1936, GM 001605–26; both were submitted to GM's Finance Committee by A. P. Sloan, May 27, 1936, GM 001604.

24. Sloan's views were relayed to G. K. Howard in a letter from C. R. Osborn, Aug. 28, 1937, GM 003730–9.

25. See J. D. Mooney's speech to the Cleveland Chamber of Commerce, May 18, 1937, box 3, folder 7, Mooney Papers, Georgetown University Library; also "Secretary Hull Calls for More Liberal Trade Policy in Interests of Peace" and "Cordell Hull, Protagonist of Peace," in *General Motors World*, May 1937. Howard's speech, to the World Trade Dinner of May 25, 1939, was published under the headline "America's Foreign Policy . . . " in *German-American Commerce Bulletin* 14, no. 6 (June 1939): 3ff. On Hull's reaction, see "Summary of Discussions with Mr. Pyke Johnson and Mr. Weaver, Washington—June 4, 1940," by W. B. Wachtler, GM 003631. Howard's book was published by Charles Scribner's Sons, New York, in the fall of 1940 under the title *America and a New World Order*. In a lengthy article praising the book in the Oct. 1940 issue of *General Motors World*, its thesis was summarized as "the most-favored nation clause must go" (p. 19).

26. Howard's remarks are from his report of June 12, 1938, to J. D. Mooney, GM 001719. For Nazi accusations of Jewish ties on the part of Opel, see OPR 017302f. and O17429. On the trade board (*Wirtschaftsgruppe Fahrzeugindustrie*), see C. R. Osborn to G. K. Howard, Aug. 28, 1937, GM 003730f. On opposition to the Admiral, see OR 060944-9 and GM 002556-9.

27. Howard's words are from his report of June 12, 1938, to J. D. Mooney, GM 001719. A detailed directory of government agencies and their top personnel, along with a plan for maintaining contact with them, was submitted to R. A. Fleischer by the Berlin liaison office (*Behördenabteilung*) on Feb. 10, 1938, OR 061858–910. See also Fleischer's memorandum of Sept. 24, 1936, on the meeting of GM and Opel executives with officials of the Economics Ministry and the *Reichsbank* two days earlier, OPR 019338f. On the good relations with those officials, see C. R. Osborn to G. K. Howard, Aug. 28, 1937, GM 003732. On Mooney's cultivation of Schacht, see his letter to A. P. Sloan, Oct. 6, 1936, GM 003718–24.

28. On the rubber arrangements, see chap. 1; also R. A. Fleischer's memorandum of Sept. 24, 1936, OPR 019338f.

29. See G. K. Howard's report to J. D. Mooney, June 12, 1938, GM 001719f.; also Fleischer to R. K. Evans, Mar. 11, 1935, OPR 019144.

30. On the building materials, see the letter of Opel's Brandenburg management to the Regierungspräsident, Potsdam, Oct. 31, 1938, Rep. 2A IS/1431, BLHAP. On the steel allocations, see G. S. von Heydekampf to C. R. Osborn, May 18, 1938, OR 039924f. On Brandenburg's designation as a "vordringlicher Betrieb," see H. Grewenig to C. R. Osborn, Aug. 26, 1938, OR 043092–5. On Blomberg's visit of Apr. 23, 1936, see R. A. Fleischer to Major Klein, May 29, 1936, OR 040254; also *Der Opel-Kamerad,* May-June 1936.

CHAPTER 4. A NAZI GRASP FOR OPEL IS FENDED OFF

1. This and much of the following is based on two lengthy 1938 manuscripts by Howard: "Notes for Discussion with Prof. Dr. Karl Lüer and Dr. Franz Belitz" (GM 003752–846) and his report of June 12, 1938, to Mooney (GM 001641–1885). On Howard's background, see GM 003755; also *General Motors World,* Dec. 1935; also the biographical information in "Personnel: General Motors Export Division, May 1928," CR 010384f.

2. See Howard's "Notes for Discussion" (note 1, above), GM 003758f.; on Osborn's background, see the biographical information in *General Motors World,* Jan. 1935, pp. 5f., and July 1937, p. 5.

3. On the law creating the post of plant leader, see Werner Mansfeld, et al., *Die Ordnung der nationalen Arbeit. Kommentar* (Berlin, 1934); also Karl Arnhold, *Der Betriebsführer und sein Betrieb* (Leipzig, 1937). On Fleischer's career, see the records of his denazification trial, Abt. 520, KS-Z, Nr. 3297, HHStAW; also the biographical sketch in the 1935 company pamphlet, "Who Is Who at Opel?" Sgl. Opel I, 2.3, SMR. The quoted words appear in letters to Fleischer from Edgar W. Smith, Apr. 28, 1937 (OPR 031712) and J. D. Mooney, Dec. 17, 1937 (OPR 031718).

4. The "Betriebs-Ordnung der Adam Opel A.G." of Sept. 21, 1934 (copy in Slg. Opel I, 2.2, SMR), accorded sweeping authority to the plant leader over the employees: "Der Be-

triebsführer bestimmt die Richtlinien. Er trägt die grösste Verantwortung. Seine Anordnungen sind unbedingt zu befolgen" (p. 3). See Fleischer's numerous internal *Mitteilungen,* Abt. 112, Nr. 578, HWAD. On the security force, see W. G. Guthrie to C. R. Osborn, July 28, 1938, OR 043107. For examples of Fleischer's correspondence on behalf of Opel, see GM 001200, 001206–9; OPR 017289, 017455, 0017472–4, 019020–22, 019336f., 031038, 032823–5. For complaints about his failure to share Opel's documents, see Wilhelm von Opel to Fleischer, Feb. 1, 1936 (OPR 019086) and E. R. Palmer to Fleischer, Oct. 15, 1936 (OPR 019151). The quoted words are from the biographical sketch of Fleischer in "Who Is Who at Opel?" (note 3, above).

5. On the change in Osborn's title, see Fritz Opel to Howard, May 16, 1938, quoted in Howard's report to Mooney, June 12, 1938, GM 001680f. On Fleischer's role during the visit of Hitler's deputy Rudolf Hess, see *Der Opel-Kamerad,* Sept.-Oct. 1936; on the anniversary celebration, ibid., Sept. 1937; on the 1938 auto show, ibid., Mar. 1938. On Osborn's assembly of documentation, see the German translation of Osborn's letter to General William H. Draper, July 12, 1946, and the letter of his German aide, Karl Schäffer, to Opel's Angestelltenrat, July 30, 1946, both in the records of Fleischer's denazification trial (note 3, above). On the rumors, see Howard's June 12 report to Mooney, GM 001872f.

6. See Howard's letter to J. D. Mooney, May 4, 1938, GM 003743–51. See also Fleischer's speech as plant leader, "Wir Opel-Angehörige in unserer Umwelt," Mar. 1938 (OR 062793–823) and the testimonials in his defense by Opel employees at his denazification trial (note 3, above).

7. Howard's "Notes for Discussion" (note 1, above), GM 003766ff.; also his letter to Mooney, May 4, 1938, GM 003743–51. On the new law, see Curtis Warren Bajak, "The Third Reich's Corporation Law of 1937," Ph.D. diss., Yale University, 1986.

8. Howard's "Notes for Discussion" (note 1, above), GM 003799ff.

9. See Howard's "Notizen für die Besprechung mit dem Gauleiter," May 20, 1938, OPR 024455; also his report to Mooney, June 12, 1938, GM 001734f. At his denazification trial (see note 3), Fleischer maintained that he had departed for the Chancellery by himself only because Osborn had been late (transcript of Aug. 19, 1946). For the photograph, see p. 56.

10. Howard's "Notes for Discussion" (note 1, above), GM 003790 and 003818–33. The quoted words are from GM 003824. See also the detailed twenty-one accusations against Fleischer prepared before the Paris meeting, OPR 024459–82.

11. See Howard's transcript of his trans-Atlantic telephone conversation with Mooney, May 17, 1938, 001687–93. At his denazification trial (note 3, above) Fleischer explained that although he was registered a party member as of May 1937, his entry had been predated by a year. As verification, he provided a canceled check for the previous year's dues, which cleared his bank account on May 5, 1938 (Meine Mitgliedschaft in der NSDAP datiert vom 1.5.1937, Anlage zum Brief vom 6. August 1946).

12. Howard's "Notes for Discussion" (note 1, above); the quoted words are from GM 003755 and 003842f.

13. Howard's report of June 12, 1938, to Mooney, GM 001654–93.

14. Ibid., GM 001712. On Sprenger, see Stephanie Zibell, *Jakob Sprenger* (Darmstadt, 1999).

For an example of his control over local affairs, see the file note of Heinrich Wagner, Sept. 10, 1938, regarding land purchases by Opel, GM 002549.

15. See Howard's report to Mooney, June 12, 1938, GM 001712f.

16. Ibid.

17. Ibid., GM 001715f.

18. For translations of the *Vertrauensrat* letter and Fleischer's letter to the *Reichsverband der Automobilindustrie,* see ibid., GM 001702–10. Fleischer had written about the colonel in his capacity as Opel's *Wehrwirtschaftsführer,* a title bestowed on him by the army that carried no formal authority and soon lapsed into disuse. See Berenice A. Carroll, *Design for Total War: Arms and Economics in the Third Reich* (The Hague, 1968), p. 139, n34.

19. See Howard's report to Mooney, June 12, 1938, GM 001715–7.

20. Ibid., GM 001719–22.

21. Ibid., GM 00722–40.

22. Ibid., GM 001731.

23. Ibid., GM 001736–40.

24. Ibid.

25. Ibid., GM 001741f. For the quotations, see ibid., GM 001742 and 001757.

26. Ibid., GM 001750–55. For the German text of Sprenger's letter, see OPR 024441–7.

27. See Howard's report to Mooney, June 12, 1938, GM 001756f and 001844.

28. Ibid., GM 001759–63.

29. Ibid., GM 001765.

30. Ibid., GM 001767f.

31. The minutes are in ibid., GM 001771–5. For the settlement with Fleischer, see the English translations of his letter of resignation and Geheimrat von Opel's letter to him, both dated May 25, 1938, GM 001816ff.

32. See the minutes in Howard's report to Mooney, June 12, 1938, GM 001779–87; see also the revised Articles of Association, with Howard's commentary, ibid., 001797–802.

33. Ibid., GM 001875–8; for Howard's comments to Mooney on Richter's appointment, see ibid., GM 001789f.

34. Ibid., the quotations are from GM 001873 and 001769.

CHAPTER 5. THE GAULEITER IS THWARTED BUT NOT WITHOUT CONSEQUENCES

1. For Howard's report, accompanied by his letter to Mooney of June 12,1938, see GM 001641–1885.

2. Ibid., GM 001816ff. See GM 001828–30 for an English translation of Howard's letter to the Gauleiter. For the German text, see OPR 024439–40.

3. For an English translation of Sprenger's letter, dated May 28, see GM 001840–42. For the German text, see OPR 024436–38.

4. Howard to Sprenger, May 30; Sprenger to Howard, June 2; Howard to Sprenger, June 3: GM 001843–55.

5. For Howard's letter of June 3, see note 4, above. For his report to Mooney about the Berlin trip, see GM 001832–4.

6. Howard to Thomas, June 17: GM 001193.

7. GM 001833. See also Howard's letters of thanks to Thomas, Milch, and Udet, from London, June 17, GM 001193–6.

8. On the gear plant project, see p. 9 of "Report on the Opel Works of General Motors Corporation," by George P. Alt, Antitrust Division of the U.S. Justice Department, Oct. 24, 1942, which was based on interviews with former American executives at Opel, RG 169, box 1652, #408950, NARA. Also, p. 2 of "Comments of Former American Directors of the Opel Werke, Germany" (1942), ibid., #137252. On access to GM's American technology, see the communications of Heinrich Wagner, production manager at Opel, to Karl Schäffer, July 12, 1938 (OR 043111) and to Osborn, Dec. 15, 1938 (OR 043077) about the assignment two Opel employees to the United States to study transmission gears at GM plants there.

9. Osborn to Howard, Feb. 9, 1939, with funding request: GM 001240–3.

10. Howard to Sprenger, June 3, GM 001850–55 (English); OPR 024425–9 (German).

11. Sprenger to Howard, June 4, GM 001856–8 (English); OPR 024421–4 (German). Howard to Sprenger, June 6, GM 001859 (English); OPR 024419 (German).

12. See Howard's report to Mooney, June 12, 1938, GM 001863–7. On Howard's concession, see Osborn's "Anlage zum Schreiben vom 10. August," OPR 024393.

13. Howard's report to Mooney, June 12, 1938, GM 001866–7. On the introduction of Avieny, see OPR 024570: Osborn's "Notes on the meeting with Gauleiter Sprenger at his house in Frankfurt, Zeppelinallee 8 on Thursday, July 28, 1938, at 8:30 a.m." On Avieny's career, see Office of Military Government, United States, *Ermittlungen gegen die Deutsche Bank,* bearbeitet von der Hamburger Stiftung für Sozialgeschichte des 20. Jahrhunderts (Nördlingen, 1986), pp. 216ff.

14. See the English text of Osborn's prepared remarks, "To the Gauleiter," OPR 024564–9. On the ensuing conversation, see Osborn's "Notes" (note 13, above).

15. OPR 024570–8, Osborn's "Notes" (note 13, above).

16. OPR 024411f., "Ausführungen, die Mr. Osborn dem Gauleiter am 29. Juli 38 machte". See also the English text of Osborn's prepared remarks, dated July 29, 1938, OPR 024551–7.

17. OPR 024558–63, "Notes on meeting with Gauleiter Sprenger at his house in Frankfurt am Main on July 29, 1938, at 11 a.m."

18. Sprenger to Osborn, Aug. 4, OPR 024408–10 (German); OPR 024549f. (English).

19. Osborn to Brinkmann, Aug. 10, OPR 024394, with accompanying "Anlage zum Schreiben vom 10. August 1938," OPR 024391–3. On Brinkmann, see Willi Boelcke, *Die deutsche Wirtschaft 1930–1945* (Düsseldorf, 1983), pp. 189–93.

20. Osborn to Funk, Aug. 10, OPR 024386–9.

21. Osborn to Sprenger, Aug. 10, OPR 024390; Sprenger to Osborn, Aug. 16, OPR 024384f.

22. Osborn to Howard, Aug. 26, GM 003725–9.

23. Winter to Osborn, Aug. 22, with drafts of the letter to Sprenger, one incorporating Brinkmann's suggestions, OPR 024372–83; Osborn to Sprenger, Aug. 25, OPR 024365–70 (German); OPR 024520–3 (English).

24. Sprenger to Osborn, Sept. 5, OPR 024362f.

25. See the letters from BMW's Franz Josef Popp to General Udet, Sept. 5, 1938, and State Secretary Milch, Sept. 9, 1938, BA/MA, RL3/52; draft letter from Göring to Wilhelm Kissel of Daimler-Benz, Sept. 24, 1938, RL3/55, BA/MA. GM 001189–91: "Memoran-

dum concerning the visit of Mr. Knudsen to Field-Marshall Göring . . . Sept. 18, 1938";
Norman Beasley, *Knudsen: A Biography* (New York, 1947), pp. 192–95.

26. Osborn to Sprenger, Sept. 22, OPR 024359–61.

27. Sprenger to Osborn, Nov. 23, OPR 024357f.; Akten-Notiz by Wilhelm von Opel, "Besprechung mit dem Reichsstatthalter in Frankfurt a/M. am Donnerstag, den 22. Dezember 1938 um 10 Uhr vormittags," OPR 024356; Elis Hoglund to Osborn, Feb. 6, 1939, TX 011004–7.

28. See the records of Stief's 1947 denazification trial, Abt. 520 Gross-Gerau, Nr. 2745/46, HHStAW.

29. For correspondence and memoranda about the Stief arrest, see OPR 025044–69. See also Mooney's account of his meeting with Meissner on April 1 in "Diary of Mr. Mooney's Visit to London and Berlin, March 27 to April 6, 1939," in box 1, folder 14, Mooney Paper, Georgetown University Library. As a commissioned naval reserve officer, Mooney followed the regulations regarding decorations by foreign governments and turned over to the Navy Department the Order of Merit of the German Eagle medal bestowed on him in June 1938 by the German consul in New York. It was then forwarded by the Navy Department to the State Department; see the State-Navy correspondence of October 1938, RG 59, 093.622/43, NARA. After Mooney's death in 1957, the medal was sent to his widow, box 6, folders 6, 9, and 10, Mooney Papers. On the bestowal of similar German medals on other Americans at that time, see Neil Baldwin, *Henry Ford and the Jews* (New York, 2001), pp. 283–85.

CHAPTER 6. OPEL IS CONSCRIPTED FOR THE GERMAN WAR EFFORT

1. Hoglund to Osborn, Feb. 6, 1939, TX 011004–7.

2. Ibid. On Brinkmann's incapacitation, see Willi A. Boelcke, *Die Deutsche Wirtschaft 1930–1945* (Düsseldorf, 1983), pp. 191f. On the visit to the GM proving grounds, see "Bericht über die Amerikareise der Kommission des Generalbevollmächtigten für das Kraftfahrwesen (7.4–12.5.1939)" by Oberstleutnant v. Mühlenfels, Kissel Behörden-Institutionen, 9.26, MBAG. See also Heidrun Edelmann, *Heinz Nordhoff und Volkswagen* (Göttingen, 2003), pp. 46–47. The industry's advisory board bore the name Wirtschaftsgruppe Fahrzeugindustrie.

3. See the minutes of the meeting of Mar. 13, CR 008886.

4. Osborn to Howard, Feb. 9, 1939, with his appropriations request dated Feb. 8, GM 001240–3.

5. Ibid. Knudsen's approval on the appropriations request form was dated May 19, 1939, GM 001243. On the beginning of operations at the plant, see p. 9 of "Report on the Opel Works of General Motors Corporation," by George P. Alt, Antitrust Division of the U.S. Justice Department, Oct. 24, 1942, which was based on interviews with former American executives at Opel, RG 169, box 1652, #408950, NARA; also "Comments of Former American Directors of the Adam Opel Werke," which record the responses of Cyrus Osborn, Elis Hoglund, and R. K. Evans to questions posed to them by an American intelligence officer in Jan. 1942, box 1232, #137252, NARA; see also Philip W. Copelin (formerly of GM) to Coordinator of Information, Jan. 9, 1942, RG 226, box 203, folder 23537,

NARA. (I indebted to Prof. Richard Breitman for bringing the latter document to my attention.) The Air Ministry eventually reimbursed Opel for the start-up cost of the gear plant; see the memorandum, "Vorgeschichte der ersten Zahlungen des RLM," by W. E. Niegtsch of Opel's finance office, Jan 27, 1941 (erroneously dated 1940), which records a request to the Ministry on Sept. 28, 1939, for funds to cover Anlaufkosten for LF 3, which was apparently the designation for the gear plant, and receipt of 2.9 million marks by Mar. 19, 1940, OR 048597.

6. Osborn to Howard, July 19, TX 011013–25.

7. Osborn reported on these and other developments in a lengthy letter to Mooney of Nov. 22, 1939, GM 000719–42.

8. Ibid. See also Osborn to Mooney, Oct. 3, 1939 (TX 011033–8), forwarded by Mooney to GM president William Knudsen on Oct. 6 (TX 011032).

9. Ibid.

10. Ibid.

11. Ibid. See also Osborn to von Hanneken, Sept. 11, TX 010947f.; Osborn to von Schell, Sept. 16, TX 010949f.

12. Von Hanneken to Osborn, Sept. 15, OPR 031219. Gerd von Heydebrand to Osborn, Sept. 16, OPR 031218; Osborn to Mooney, Nov. 22, GM 000728.

13. For Göring's interest in using Opel, see chap. 5, n25. Hitler's order of Aug. 21, 1939, is in RL3/1496, BA/MA. On the meeting of Sept. 18 and the inspection at Rüsselsheim, see RL3/571, BA/MA, record of report by Major Henker, Sept. 20. On the inspection and Wagner's report, see Osborn to Mooney, Nov. 22, GM 000729. See also Lutz Budrass, *Flugzeugindustrie und Luftrüstung in Deutschland 1918–1945* (Düsseldorf, 1998), pp. 561, 594f., 638, 645f. Budrass relies on a baseless claim to the effect that Mooney agreed to Opel's conversion to war production in the course of meeting with Hitler and Göring in Berlin on Sept. 19 and 20 (Anita Kugler, "Die Behandlung des feindlichen Vermögens in Deutschland und die 'Selbstverantwortung' der Rüstungsindustrie. Dargestellt am Beispiel der Adam Opel AG von 1941 bis Anfang 1943," in *1991. Zeitschrift für Sozialgeschichte des 20. und 21. Jahrhunderts,* Jg. 3 [1988], Heft 2, p. 51). In two contributions on the same subject in " . . . *ohne Rücksicht auf die Verhältnisse,*" ed. Bernd Heyl and Andrea Neugebauer (Frankfurt a.M., 1997), Kugler dated the alleged meeting varyingly as Sept. 19 and 20 on p. 41 and as Sept. 19 on p. 69. None of the documents cited in support of these claims contains any information about such a meeting, and mention of it has been omitted from Kugler's most recent publication on the subject, "Airplanes for the Führer," in *Working for the Enemy,* by Reinhold Billstein et al. (New York, 2000), pp. 33–81. Contemporaneous documentation indicates that Mooney was in Rüsselsheim on Sept. 19 and left the next day for Switzerland, Osborn to Mooney, Nov. 22, GM 000729f.

14. See the two alternative leasing plans drawn up at Opel, TX 010953–7. Also, Osborn to Mooney, Nov. 22, GM 000729f.

15. Osborn to von Hanneken, Sept. 23, TX 010951f. Also, Osborn to Mooney, Nov. 22, GM 000730–32.

16. Osborn to Mooney, Oct. 3, TX 011031.

17. Ibid. Also Osborn to Mooney, Nov. 22, GM 000732.

18. GM 000737f.

19. GM 000738f.

20. GM 000740.

21. GM 000740f. For the board meeting, see the agenda and minutes, TX 010975–86.

22. TX 010991f. The initial proposal called for only one German member on the executive committee, agenda for the board meeting, TX 010977. See also Wilhelm von Opel and Osborn to Heinrich Wagner, Feb. 7, 1940, GM 001419–21.

23. "Annual Report of General Motors Corporation for the Year Ended December 31, 1939," BR 035679; the quotation is from Howard's report to GM's Administrative Committee, July 25, 1940, CR 009536.

24. On war materials, see Wagner to Osborn, Oct. 12, 1939, with notes by the latter of same date, OR 042998–301.

25. Osborn to Mooney, Mar. 26, 1940, GM 002644–64.

26. Ibid.

27. On the end to car production and the shift to aircraft components, see enclosure 3, minutes of the Supervisory Board, June 11, 1940, GM 001402; also "Opel in der JU 88-Fertigung: Ein Kurzbericht in Wort, Bild und Zahl," LR 02622, Deutsches Museum, Munich. On the uses of the Ju 88, see Edward L. Homze, *Arming the Luftwaffe* (Lincoln, Neb., 1976), pp. 163ff.; James S. Corum, *Luftwaffe* (Lawrence, Kan., 1997), pp. 266f.; Herbert Molloy Mason, Jr., *The Rise of the Luftwaffe* (New York, 1973), p. 378.

28. On the fuses, see W. E. Niegtsch to H. Hansen, Dec. 29, 1939, OR 48912–4; also OR 048679. On the ordinance contracts, see Rüstunginspektion des Wehrkreises XII, Wiesbaden, to Wehrwirtschafts-und Rüstungsamt im Oberkommando der Wehrmacht, Berlin, Feb. 7, 1940, RW20–12/18, BA/MA; also the memorandum by O. Jacob, Aug. 27, 1940, regarding the army's cancellation of some of those contracts after the fall of France, OR 049025f. On the allocation of workers to munitions production, see "Opel in der JU 88-Fertigung" (note 27, above). On pending contracts, see W. E. Niegtsch to E. Lachmann, Feb. 7, 1941, OR 048570f. On the Blitz trucks, see Osborn to Mooney, Mar. 26, 1940, GM 002656f.; on the military uses of the trucks, see Eckart Bartels, *Opel at War* (West Chester, Penn., 1991) and *Opel Military Vehicles, 1906–1956* (Atglen, Penn., 1997).

29. See Günter Neliba, *Die Opel-Werke im Konzern von General Motors (1929–1948) in Rüsselsheim und Brandenburg* (Frankfurt a.M., 2000), pp. 92f. On the separate bookkeeping system, see K. Mees to W. E. Niegtsch, Jan. 28, 1941, OR 048572f. At the Supervisory Board meeting of Mar. 10, 1941, GM was represented by Osborn, Mooney, and Hoglund (GM 001408ff); at that of June 11 by Hoglund, Albin Madsen, and David Ladin (GM 001367ff); at that of Nov. 11 by Hoglund alone (GM 001346ff).

30. Osborn to Mooney, Mar. 26, 1940, GM 002654; in discussions during May about possible reassignment of plant leader Hanns Grewenig in which Osborn participated, consideration was given to placing him him in charge of the "ammunition program": memorandum by Karl Schäffer, June 4, 1940, OPR 025113. The quotation is from p. 4 of "Comments of Former American Directors" (note 5, above).

31. See Howard's notes for Jan. 15, GM 001486. For Mooney's report of Jan. 30, see CR 009472. For Knudsen's remark, see the text of his speech of Mar. 5: BR 075951.

32. Mooney to Knudsen, Mar. 27, GM 002642. His remarks at the Supervisory Board meeting of Mar. 10 are recorded in the minutes, GM 001445.

33. GM 003518f.: "Summary of Conversation with Mr. Sloan, Thursday, March 28, 1940."

34. BR 004817: "Annual Financial Report for the Business Year 1939, May 15, 1940." For Howard's report of July 25, see CR 009535f; for that of Feb. 15, 1941, see CR 009571.

CHAPTER 7. MR. MOONEY TRIES TO STOP THE SECOND WORLD WAR

1. These events are related in the second chapter of a typescript of an unpublished memoir written by Mooney after the Second World War with the close assistance of Louis Lochner, hereafter cited as Memoir. One copy, entitled "Lessons on War and Peace," is located in the Mooney Papers at the Special Collections Division of the Georgetown University Library, boxes 3 and 4. Another copy, untitled, is located in the Lochner Papers at the State Historical Society of Wisconsin, Madison, box 7, folder 39. Lochner subsequently published his own version of the events described in this chapter in his book, *Always the Unexpected* (New York, 1956), pp. 262ff. The versions of Mooney and Lochner are confirmed by the earlier account of Richter in a letter to Staatssekretär Krohn of June 17, 1942, R87/236, BAB. On Mooney's celebrity status, see "The Export Genius behind General Motors," *Forbes,* Aug. 15, 1928; "Faces of the Month," *Fortune,* Feb. 1930; "A Panel of General Motors Executives," *Fortune,* Apr. 1930; "The World and Jim Mooney," by Charles Wertenbaker, *Saturday Evening Post,* Oct. 30, 1937; see also the numerous newspaper clippings and speech manuscripts in the Mooney Papers. In William Stevenson, *A Man Called Intrepid: The Secret War* (New York, 1976), p. 108, Mooney is erroneously described as an unofficial agent who reported, under the codename "Stallforth," to Stevenson, a British intelligence officer in New York. In several other books, Mooney is also alleged to have used that name even though Frederick (a.k.a. Federico) Stallforth was a different person, a businessman who met with German officials on several visits to Berlin prior to United States entry into the war and was interviewed afterward by American officials; see Ulrich von Hassell, *Vom Anderen Deutschland* (Frankfurt a.M., 1964), pp. 179, 190, 199–200, 203; also memorandum by Joseph Flack of the State Department on a conversation with Stallforth in Washington, Aug. 19, 1940, RG 59, 740.001/6061, NARA; also memorandum by W. D. Whitney to President Roosevelt, Oct. 1, 1941, on his meeting with Stallforth in Washington on Sept. 30: President's Secretary's File (hereafter PSF), Safe File, Germany, box 3, HP. A collection of Stallforth's papers is in RG 200, entry 19710, NARA. On Stallforth, see also Mary Alice Gallin, *German Resistance to Hitler,* 2nd ed. (Washington, 1969), pp. 123f. The confusion with Stallforth may have arisen from Mooney's activities as a lieutenant commander in the U.S. Naval Reserve. In a letter of Sept. 30, 1946, to the denazification court hearing the case of Rudolf Fleischer, Mooney stated that during the years 1937–39 he had performed intelligence work—which he specified was "open" rather than covert—in Europe for the navy, Abt. 520 K-Z, Nr. 3297, HHStAW.

2. See Bernd Martin, *Friedensinitiativen und Machtpolitik im Zweiten Weltkrieg* (Düsseldorf, 1974), pp. 57ff.

3. On Mooney's war service, see Memoir, p. 5. The quoted words are from his "Remarks made on board the U.S.S. *Enterprise,*" July 31, 1938, box 3, folder 14, Mooney Paper, Georgetown University Library.

4. The quoted speech, delivered on April 17, 1937, was published in the July issue of *Annals of the American Academy of Political and Social Science* under the title "American Economic Policies for the Impending World War," and in *Vital Speeches the Day* 3, no. 14 (May 1, 1937) under the title "What World War Will Mean for Us and What We Can Do about It."

5. For Howard's remarks, see his speech to the World Trade Dinner, May 25, 1939, published in the June issue of the *German-American Commerce Bulletin.* For Mooney's views, see his speech of May 18, 1937, to the Cleveland Chamber of Commerce, box 3, folder 7, Mooney Papers, Georgetown University Library. The manuscript of his Rochester speech of January 25, 1937, is in box 3, folder 3.

6. The first quotation is from his 1937 speech to the American Academy of Political and Social Science (note 4, above). His speech to the Council on Foreign Affairs, "The Economic Aspects of Recognition of Russia," delivered on Jan. 22, 1931, is in box 2, folder 10 of the Mooney Papers; see also the text of his radio broadcast of April 21, 1931, under the sponsorship of the National League of Women Voters, ibid. The second quotation is from a letter to Sloan of Oct. 20, 1930, in David R. Farber, *Sloan Rules. Alfred P. Sloan and the Triumph of General Motors* (Chicago, 2002), p. 144.

7. George S. Messersmith to William Phillips, Nov. 16, 1934, item 442, Messersmith Papers, University of Delaware Library. Earlier that year, Mooney had sought to promote German-American barter transactions by serving as intermediary between German Economics Minister Hjalmar Schacht and George N. Peek, president of the Export and Import Bank, who was for a time Roosevelt's special adviser on foreign trade. Their correspondence is in C2270, Peek Papers, Western Historical Manuscript Collection, Elis Library, University of Missouri. See also the memorandum of Assistant Secretary of State William Phillips on his conversation with Mooney and Peek, June 1, 1934, RG 59, 611.6231/347, NARA, and Mooney to Phillips, June 20, 1934, ibid., 862.51/4130.

8. For the quoted words, see Patrick J. Hearden, *Roosevelt Confronts Hitler* (DeKalb, Ill., 1987), p. 120. On Mooney's view of Germany as a bulwark against Communism, see the reports on his press interviews upon his return from Europe: "France to Give U.S. Order for Tools," *New York Times,* Dec. 15, 1939; "Finds Europe Wants Peace," *Daily News* (N.Y.), Dec. 15, 1939. See also "James D. Mooney Returns from Europe," in *German-American Commerce Bulletin,* June 1939. On economic appeasement, see Hearden, *Roosevelt Confronts Hitler,* pp. 88–122; Gustav Schmidt, *The Politics and Economics of Appeasement* (New York, 1986), pp. 31–225.

9. Memoir, pp. 21–32; "James D. Mooney Returns from Europe" (note 8, above). On Kennedy's role, see *Hostage to Fortune: The Letters of Joseph P. Kennedy,* ed. Amanda Smith (New York, 2001), p. 331; David E. Koskoff, *Joseph P. Kennedy* (Englewood Cliffs, N.J., 1974), p. 221.

10. The interview article, by Walter Duranty, appeared in the *Detroit News* of Oct. 3 under the headline "Peace Hopes Still Remain" and was syndicated nationally by the North American News Alliance.

11. Memoir, pp. 37–41; Lochner, *Always the Unexpected,* pp. 262f.

12. Memoir, pp. 43–53.

13. Ibid., pp. 55–57. For Bullitt's report to Hull and the latter's reply, see *Foreign Relations of the United States: Diplomatic Papers, 1939,* vol. 1 (Washington, 1956), pp. 519f. On the parallel German overtures through other American businessmen, see Charles Tansill, *Back Door to Power* (Chicago, 1952), pp. 558–61; Saul Friedländer, *Prelude to Downfall* (London, 1967), pp. 37f., and Nicholas Bethell, *The War Hitler Won* (London, 1972), pp. 288f. See also William L. Langer and S. Everett Gleason, *The Challenge to Isolation, 1937–1940* (New York, 1952), p. 258.

14. Memoir, p. 57. For Lothian's telegram of Oct. 24, see C17220/13005/18, PRO/FO.

15. Memoir, pp. 58–61.

16. Sir Robert's report of Oct. 26 to Halifax is in 371/23099, PRO/FO.

17. Ibid.

18. Memoir, pp. 62–68.

19. Ibid., pp. 69–71.

20. Ibid., pp. 72–78.

21. Ibid., pp. 79–81. According to Mooney, the meeting, which he dated as Dec. 22, was not entered into the president's calendar and thus escaped notice by the press.

22. Ibid., pp. 81–84. See also the notes he made immediately after the meeting, box 1, folder 12, Mooney Papers, Georgetown University Library; an edited version forms appendix 2 to the Memoir.

23. Ibid., pp. 84–7. A carbon copy of the note is in President's Personal File, 6448, HP.

24. Memoir, pp. 88–91. See also entry for Jan. 30, 1940, in Berle's diary, Adolf Augustus Berle Papers, HP; microfilm copy in Sterling Memorial Library, Yale University, roll 2.

25. Memoir, pp. 93, 114–17. The newspaper report appeared in the *Daily Express* on Feb. 17 under the headline "Hitler would resign to stop the war." For the quoted British reaction, see 371/24406, PRO/FO.

26. Memoir, pp. 115–20.

27. Ibid., p. 99.

28. Memoir, pp. 96–103, 107–13, 121. Lochner, *Always the Unexpected,* p. 269.

29. Ibid., pp. 121–24. The report by Welles of Mar. 2 is in *Foreign Relations of the United States, 1940,* vol. 1 (Washington, 1959), pp. 43ff.

30. Memoir, pp. 121–30. See also the memorandum on the meeting by translator Paul Schmidt, Andreas Hillgruber, ed., *Staatsmänner und Diplomaten bei Hitler,* 2 vols. (Frankfurt a.M., 1967), 1:80–86. An English translation of Schmidt's record of Hitler's responses is in box 1, folder 16, Mooney Papers, Georgetown University Library. The presentation that Mooney prepared in advance of the meeting is in box 1, folder 17.

31. See Dieckhoff's memorandum of Mar. 5, *Documents on German Foreign Policy,* ser. D (Washington, 1954), vol. 8, pp. 865f.

32. Memoir, pp. 139–41.

33. These letters, dated Mar. 11, 12, 13, 14, and 15, are in PSF, Safe File, Italy, box 3, HP; also RG 59, file 740.0111, NARA. Slightly variant paraphrases are in box 1, folder 13, Mooney Papers, and in the Memoir, pp. 142–4, and appendixes 6 and 7.

34. Memoir, pp. 148–50. A copy of the president's telegram of Mar. 25 is in President's Personal File, 6448, HP; a carbon of the president's letter of Apr. 2 is in PSF: Departmental File, Navy, May-June 1940, box 58, HP.

35. Memoir, pp. 149–60. The letter, dated May 10, is in May-June 1940, box 58, PSF, Departmental File, Navy, HP.

36. The text of the speech, which Mooney delivered on June 1, was published in *Vital Speeches of the Day* 6, no. 17 (June 15, 1940): 542–44; also in *Congressional Record*, vol. 86, appendix, pt. 16, pp. 4056f. It was broadcast nationally by the American Broadcasting Company, as indicated by the radio program of the *New York Times* of June 1, p. 27. The article for the *Saturday Evening Post*, "War or Peace in America?" appeared in the Aug. 3, 1940, issue.

37. Memorandum for "Doc" O'Connor, June 27, 1940, PSF, Subject File, O'Connor Basil, 1940–41, HP.

38. The two telegrams, sent by the president's secretary, Edwin M. Watson, on June 28 and 29, are in President's Personal File, 6448, HP. Hopkins' letter of June 29 is in ibid., PSF, Subject File, O'Connor Basil, as is Mooney's letter of July 1. Mooney later learned of Hopkins' intervention, Memoir, pp. 164–66.

39. See the articles by Henry Paynter in *PM*, Aug. 9, 12, and 13, 1940; also "General Motors Chief Leads U.S. Clivenden Set," *New Leader*, Aug. 17, 1940. For the responses of Mooney and his colleagues to the *PM* articles, see box 1, folder 24, Mooney Papers. The allegation that he had attended the Waldorf-Astoria banquet was retracted in an article by James H. Wechsler in *PM* two years later (note 42, below). On *PM*, see Paul Milkman, *PM: A New Deal in Journalism* (New Brunswick, N.J., 1997).

40. See the telegram of July 18, 1940, to the Foreign Ministry from chargé d'affaires Hans Thomsen in Washington, *Akten zur Deutschen Auswärtigen Politik, 1918–1945*, ser. D, Bd. 10 (Frankfurt a.M., 1963), p. 201. Mooney's records of his discussions with Wiseman are in his Papers, box 1, folder 22. The text of a letter by Mooney of Feb. 21, 1941, addressed to Roosevelt, is in box 1, folder 11. No such letter could be located at the Roosevelt Library at Hyde Park.

41. The FBI reports are in RG 59, 862.20211, NARA, "Alleged Nazi subversive activities in US of James D. Mooney," as are Messersmith to James B. Stewart, Mar. 4 and to Fletcher Warren, Mar. 5, 1941; Berle to Hoover, May 31, 1941. See also Farber, *Sloan Rules*, pp. 232f.

42. See "Another 'Heil!' by Jas. Mooney," by James H. Wechsler, *PM*, Apr. 30, 1942. Kennedy's pessimism is amply recorded in his published letters (note 9, above). As for O'Connor, he wrote in a letter to Hopkins of June 25, 1940, that the war had been effectively over since the evacuation of the British troops from the Continent at Dunkirk in late May, PSF, Subject File, O'Connor Basil, 1940–41, HP.

43. For Roosevelt's remark to Welles, see the latter's *The Time for Decision* (New York, 1944), p. 73. On the president's aims at the time, see Stanley E. Hilton, "The Welles Mission to Europe, February-March 1940: Illusion or Realism?" *Journal of American History* 58 (1971): 93–120.

44. Wachtler to Mooney, Sept. 12, 1947, box 4, folder 14, Mooney Paper, Georgetown University Library. In Sept. 1939 GM requested the State Department to inquire at the American Embassy in Berlin regarding "present whereabouts of James Mooney," telegram for Geist from Messersmith, Sept. 11, 1939, RG 59, 340.1115/2278A, NARA. On the proposal of a leave of absence, see the memorandum of Apr. 4, 1940, by Edward Riley, GM 003590–601.

45. "Summary of Conversation with Mr. Sloan, Thursday, Mar. 28, 1940," by Wachtler, GM 003518f; Sloan to Mooney, Aug. 27, 1940, box 1, folder 24, Mooney Papers, Georgetown University Library.

CHAPTER 8. GM LOSES CONTROL BUT TAKES WARTIME PROFITS

1. See the excerpt from the report of July 16, 1940, by Gauhauptstellenleiter Dr. Schlie in the records of Karl Stief's denazification trial, Abt. 520, Gross-Gerau, Nr. 2745/46, HHStAW. On the hostility of Opel Angestellten, see the memorandum sent to Heinrich Wagner by G. S. von Heydekampf, Apr. 5, 1941, OPR 024489. On Osborn's departure, see the letters of Howard, Osborn, and Hoglund, Aug.-Sept. 1940, GM 001515–19.

2. Hoglund to Howard, Sept. 16, 1940, GM 001515; F. L. Hopkinson to Osborn, Oct. 4, 1940, GM 001514. See the proxy for Hoglund of Mar. 12, 1940, OPR 016015; and the Untervollmacht for Richter of Nov. 4, 1940, OPR 016026 (English translation, OR 016015). For the minutes of the Supervisory Board meeting of Nov. 11, 1940, see GM 001346–66. See also Hoglund's instructions to Richter in his letter of Feb. 14, 1941, copy in Wagner denazificiation trial records: Abt. 520, Gross-Gerau, Nr. 2135/46, HHStAW. The April 1941 issue of *General Motors World,* the monthly magazine of the overseas division, reported that Hoglund arrived in New York by sea on Mar. 10, having driven for five days from Geneva to reach Lisbon, which would place his departure soon after his letter to Richter was written at Rüsselsheim.

3. On the decree of Jan. 15, 1940, see Stephan H. Lindner, *Das Reichskommissariat für die Behandlung feindlichen Vermögens im Zweiten Weltkrieg* (Stuttgart, 1991), pp. 29ff. On the "arrangement" to back Lüer for the custodianship, see Richter to Hoglund, June 13, 1941, GM 000747ff.

4. Ibid., GM 000751ff.

5. Ibid. Everyone was obviously reluctant to commit to paper comments about the uniformed Nazi incursion, but it is alluded to in two documents: Commissar Johannes Krohn's Vermerk of Apr. 8, 1942, R87/233, BAB; and ibid., "Die Entwicklung der Verwalterfrage bei der Adam Opel A.G." by Lüer (undated).

6. On the buyout of Winter's dealership, see "Die Entwicklung" (note 5, above); Osborn to Mooney, Nov. 22, 1939 (GM 000723) and Mar. 26, 1940 (GM 002661); also minutes of the Opel Supervisory Board, Mar. 21, 1941 (GM 001325); Aktennotiz by Karl Mees, July 13, 1940 (OPR 030299f.). On Winter's actions as commissar, see David F. Ladin to E. C. Riley, Dec. 9, 1940, GM 004085ff.; Philip W. Copelin to A. J. Wieland, Feb. 7, 1941, with enclosures, GM 004094ff. On Hanneken's report, see Richter to Hoglund, June 13, 1941, GM 000754.

7. GM 000755–8.

8. GM 000758–62; and also GM 000775f., Richter to Hoglund, July 12, 1941. For a translation of Lüer's letter, addressed to Richter, dated May 7, 1941, see GM 004123. On the lengthy negotiations and settlement with Grewenig, see OPR 025109–94.

9. Richter to Hoglund, June 13, 1941, GM 000758, 000765; Aktenvermerk by Reichkommissar Ernst, May 24, 1941, R87/6335, BAB; Ernst to Sprenger, Sept. 17, 1941, ibid., R87/236.

10. Richter to Hoglund, June 13, 1941, GM 000751, 000762f. Richter's remarks appeared in the report on the birthday celebration in the May-June issue of *Der Opel-Kamerad.*

11. On the U.S. actions on assets and German retaliation, see William L. Langer and S. Everett Gleason, *The Undeclared War, 1940–1941* (New York, 1953), p. 515. On the ceremony at Rüsselsheim, see "Der schaffende Deutsche—unser Höchstwert," *Mainzer Anzeiger,* July 15, 1941, clipping in records of Heinrich Wagner's denazification trial (note 2, above). Also, "Opel-Betriebsappell am 14. Juli 1941," *Der Opel-Kamerad,* July-August. On the Gauleiter's denunciation of Osborn, see p. 5 of Karl Stief's postwar manuscript, "Mein Verhältnis zu Partei und Wehrmacht," in the records of his denazification trial, Abt. 520, Gross-Gerau, Nr. 2745/46, HHStAW; also the anonymous Aktennotiz on a conversation with the Nazi in charge of surveillance at the Rüsselsheim factory, Dr. Hildebrandt, Oct. 1, 1941, OPR 024952ff.

12. On Lüer's Brandenburg speech, see the report in the *Brandenburger Beobachter,* undated clipping, OPR 018472. Suggestions for the speech in a letter of Sept. 16 to Lüer from Gerd Stieler von Heydekampf, manager of the truck plant, indicate that it was delivered sometime thereafter, OPR 018481.

13. See the letter of Nov. 15, 1940, sent "via trans-Sibiric rail" by Opel treasurer Hermann Hansen to GM's Edward Jenkins at GM's New York office, regarding royalty payments to American owners of patents used by Opel, OR 042593ff.

14. See Richter's reports to Hoglund of June 13, July 12, and Sept. 2, GM 000772, 000778f., 000785ff. For the minutes of the board meeting, see GM 001269–75.

15. On the tardy arrival by pouch of Richter's reports of June and July, see Hoglund to Howard, Aug. 29, 1941, GM 000780. Richter's final written report of Sept. 2 did not reach New York until shortly before the American diplomat Paul H. Pearson conveyed his last message orally to F. L. Hopkinson of GM on Oct. 21, GM 000799–802. The quotation is from Richter's final written report, GM 000793.

16. There is no basis for the assertions that GM "was in complete management control of its Rüsselsheim warplane factory for nearly a full year after Germany's declaration of war against the United States" and that "communications as well as materiel continually flowed between GM plants in Allied countries and GM plants in Axis-controlled areas": Bradford C. Snell, "American Ground Transport" appendix to pt. 4 of U.S. Senate, *The Industrial Reorganization Act: Hearings before the Subcommittee on Antitrust and Monopoly of the Committee on the Judiciary on S. 1167,* 93rd Cong., 2nd sess. (Washington, 1974), pp. A-22 and A-85. Citing only Snell's paper, Ludolf Herbst has written that GM controlled Opel throughout the war via Switzerland: "Der Krieg und die Unternehmensstrategie deutscher Industrie-Konzerne in der Zwischenkriegzeit," in *Die deutschen Eliten und der Weg in den Zweiten Weltkrieg,* ed. Martin Broszat and Klaus Schwabe (Munich, 1989f), p. 74.

17. On Nazi doubts about Wagner, see the letter from the Kreisobmann to the Gauverwaltung of the Deutsche Arbeitsfront, Frankfurt, Aug. 22, 1941, in records of Wagner's denazification trial, Abt. 520, Gross-Gerau, Nr. 3125/46, HHStAW. On the arrests, see the minutes of Opel's Nazi-controlled Vertrauensrat, Dec. 18, 1941, OPR 020531; also minutes of Opel Supervisory Board, Feb. 27, 1942, GM 004034f; also Chef der Sicherheitspolizei und des SD to Reichskommissar für die Behandlung feindlichen Vermögens, July 20, 1942, R87/6347, BAB; also Schäffer to M. Mauer, July 30, 1946, and an affidavit by Hansen, Aug. 17, 1946, in Fleischer's denazification trial records, Abt 520, KS-Z, Nr. 3297, HHStAW.

18. R87/233, BAB: von Schell to Krohn, Dec. 12, 1941; Krohn's memorandum of Dec. 15, 1941.

19. Krohn's extensive correspondence and memoranda about these matters are in R87/233, BAB. See in particular his memorandum of Jan. 10, 1942, on the visit from Winter and Werlin's letter to Göring of Apr. 22, 1942.

20. Ibid., Krohn's memo of Jan. 7, 1942, on that day's visit by Richter and Heinz Nordhoff, together with the lengthy written proposal submitted by Richter; Krohn's memo of Feb. 2, 1942, about Richter's report of Sprenger's promotion of Avieny's candidacy. On the shareholder meeting of Mar. 30, see Berlin Kammergericht Urkundenrolle, Nr. 22, Jahr 1942, OR 064716–19; also Richter's letter of Mar. 30 to Wilhelm von Opel, Lüer, Madsen and Belitz: R87/6335, BAB. There is no basis for the assertion in note 135 on p. A-85 of Snell's "American Ground Transport" (note 16, above) that four GM executives served on Opel's board throughout the war. On Madsen's exclusion from sensitive discussions, see Richter to Hoglund, June 13, 1941 (GM 000772) and the board minutes of May 11, 1942 (GM 003990ff.). On Madsen's inadequate German, see Richter's letter to Wilhelm von Opel of Sept. 5, 1942, R87/6336, BAB. He wrote to Richter in English: letter of Dec. 10, 1942, ibid. Anita Kugler's suggestion on p. 74 of Reinhold Billstein et al., *Working for the Enemy* (New York, 2000), that Madsen might have served as a clandestine wartime message-bearer between GM and Opel is untenable, as there is no evidence of any such contact. During the war GM received news of its subsidiary in occupied Denmark, which Madsen headed, from one of that firm's managers, Hakon D. Skafte, who could travel to neutral Sweden. In a report of Dec. 13, 1943, Skafte recounted developments at the Danish subsidiary but made no mention of Opel: "The Position of G.M. International A/S, under the German Occupation of Denmark," CR 008943–46. Far from avoiding American scrutiny, Skafke communicated with GM through the U.S. legation in Stockholm. In advance of one of his visits, GM informed the State Department that he would be available to provide information: Edward Stettinius, acting secretary of state to American Legation, Stockholm, Oct. 27, 1943, RG 59, 740.00112A/28205, NARA. For information provided to the legation by Skafke, see Herschel V. Johnson, Stockholm, to the Secretary of State, Mar. 25, 1944, with enclosed report on GM's Danish subsidiary, RG 59, 740.59112A/1, NARA.

21. See the account of information obtained from the late-returning employee, William J. Epstein, by George P. Alt, Antitrust Division of the U.S. Justice Department, in his "Report on the Opel Works of General Motors Corporation," Oct. 24, 1942, pp. 13–16, RG 169, box 1652, #408950, NARA. Epstein was probably the "returning refugee" mentioned in Hoglund's letter of July 7, 1942, to G. Edward Buxton, Office of Strategic Services, Washington, ibid.

22. See Commissar Krohn's memos on meetings with Wagner, Apr. 8, and Richter, June 29, with the latter's memo, "Betrifft: Erweiterung Brandenburg," submitted to Krohn, June 26, R87/233, BAB. For the complaints of Belitz and Geheimrat von Opel against Lüer, see the minutes of the Supervisory Board meeting of May 11, GM 003996f.

23. See Richter's memo, "Betrifft: Erweiterung Brandenburg" (note 22, above); also Lüer's memo of May 15 on his meeting with Werlin at the Reichskanzlei on May 13, R87/233, BAB; on the Riga project, see the record of Hitler's conference with Albert Speer on May

15: *Deutschlands Rüstung im Zweiten Weltkrieg,* ed. Willi A. Boelcke (Frankfurt a.M., 1969), p. 114; Heidrun Edelmann, *Heinz Nordhoff und Volkswagen* (Gottingen, 2003), p. 50.

24. See Commissar Krohn's memo on communications from Richter, May 22, 1942, R87/ 233, BAB. For Himmler's designs on Opel, see Albert Speer, *Der Sklavenstaat* (Stuttgart, 1981), pp. 37f., 164f.

25. On the negotiations with Daimler-Benz, see Richter's memo, "Betrifft: Erweiterung Brandenburg" (note 22, above) and the records in file Kissel Protokolle 1942, I/15, MBAG. On Richter's support for Winter, see his letters to Krohn, Sept. 6, 1942 (R87/ 6336, BAB). The quoted words are from a Fernschreiben of July 14, 1942, by Gestapo chief Heinrich Müller to Heinrich Himmler (Andreas Seeger, *"Gestapo Müller"* [Berlin 1996], p. 27); see also Speer, *Sklavenstaat,* pp. 164–66.

26. R87/233, BAB, Krohn's memos of July 7, with copies of Göring's letters of June 30 to Lüer, Sprenger, and Wagner; R87/6335, BAB, Wilhelm von Opel to Wagner, July 8.

27. On Lüer's grievance, see Krohn's memo of July 9, R87/233, BAB. Göring's order to withhold action on Wagner's appointment, conveyed by an aide to Richter, is quoted in Krohn's memo of July 23, ibid. See also the minutes of the Supervisory Board, July 24, GM 003965ff.

28. R87/6336, BAB, Wagner's memo of July 27 on a meeting with Göring on July 25 and Göring's letter to Krohn of Oct. 31; Supervisory Board resolution, Sept. 9, GM 003953. See also Krohn's memos of Aug. 14, 26, and 29, R87/233, BAB.

29. Lindner, *Reichskommissariat,* pp. 97ff., 126. See also Krohn's memorandum of Sept, 1, 1943, R87/236, BAB.

30. The Internal Revenue Service permitted a deduction of $34,890,024; see *Thirty-Fourth Annual Report of General Motors Corporation: Year Ended December 31, 1942,* GM 002995. Throughout the war, GM continued to be identified as the sole "Grossaktionär" of Opel in the authoritative publication on German corporations: *Die Grossunternehmen im Deutschen Reich 1943,* Jahrgang 48 (Berlin, 1943), Band 6, p. 6217.

31. See the correspondence in R87/233, 6336, and 6337, BAB.

32. On monitoring of the firm by Richter and Krohn, see the latter's extensive correspondence, as well as the commissar's frequent memoranda, in R/87, files 233 and 6336–41, BAB. Richter served as custodian of two smaller firms that were owned by GM, Frigidaire G.m.b.H, and General Motors G.m.b.H, Berlin, as well as of the American corporation's patents; see ibid., files 6342, 6347–48, and 6403. He was paid an honorarium of 50,000 marks by Opel out of GM's dividends in 1942, OPR 044376.

33. RG 243, NARA, U.S. Strategic Bombing Survey, European Survey, Munitions Division, Adam Opel, Rüsselsheim, Germany, 2nd ed., January 1947 (NARA microfilm publication M1013, roll 7). For Milch's intercession, see RL3/860, GL-Besprechung, Mar. 24, 1942, BA/MA. On the citations as "Kriegsmusterbetriebe," see the minutes of the joint meeting of the Beirat and Vertrauensrat, May 25, 1943, R87/6338, BAB.

34. See Nordhoff's report, "Entwicklung seit Kriegsbeginn. Opel-Brandenburg," of Feb. 10, 1943, R87/6337, BAB; also Edelmann, *Heinz Nordhoff und Volkswagen,* pp. 52ff. The truck production figures were extrapolated from data in Lüer's quarterly reports of Mar. 1, 1944 (R87/6338) and Jan. 5, 1945 (R87/6340). Rights to production of the Blitz truck

would prove an important advantage for Daimler-Benz after the war, when Opel's Brandenburg plant was lost to the Russians; see Neil Gregor, *Daimler-Benz in the Third Reich* (New Haven, 1998), p. 149. On establishment of the eastern repair shops, see the minutes of the joint meeting of the Beirat and Vertrauensrat, May 25, 1943, R87/6338, BAB.

35. For the workweek and hours, see Rüstungsinspektion XII Wiesbaden, Kriegstagebuch, Nr. 3, May 20, 1940, RW 20–12/3, Bl. 56f. BA/MA; also Lüer's speech of July 14, 1941, *Der Opel-Kamerad,* July-Aug. 1941, p. 160. Much information on Nazi disciplinary measures can be found in the records of the denazification trial of Artur Liebermann, Abt. 520, Darmstadt-Zentral, Nr. 519 683, HHStAW. On worker opposition at the Rüsselsheim plant, see Arnold Busch, *Widerstand im Kreis Gross-Gerau 1933–1945* (Gross-Gerau, 1988), pp. 110–25; Axel Ulrich, "Betrieblicher Widerstand gegen die NS-Gewaltherrschaft am Beispiel der Opelwerke in Rüsselsheim," and Bernd Heyl, "Vergesst mich nicht" in *". . . ohne Rücksicht auf die Verhältnisse,"* ed. Bernd Heyl and Andrea Neugebauer (Frankfurt a.M., 1997). See also Geheimrat von Opel's expression of concern at the Supervisory Board meeting of May 11, 1942, about denunciations and harassment of Opel workers by the Gestapo, GM 003999f.

36. See the minutes of the Vertrauensrat meeting of Nov. 10, 1941, OPR 020540. On Wagner's role in protecting those targeted by the Nazis on racial grounds, see the records of his denazification trial, testimony of Dr. H. Schächer, Jan. 15, 1948, Abt. 520, Gross-Gerau, Nr. 3125/46, HHStAW. On the role of Wilhelm von Opel, see the records of his denazification trial, affidavits by Dr. Hanns Schächer, Nov. 10, 1945, Dr. W. G. Behrens, Dec. 8, 1945, Karl Mees, Dec. 8, 1945, Abt. 520, Wiesbaden Neuablage, Nr. 167, HHStAW. On demotions and dismissals, see the records of the denazification trial of Artur Liebermann (note 35, above). On other wartime developments at Rüsselsheim, see the anonymous manuscript of autumn 1945: "Die Adam Opel AG im Dritten Reich," OPR 024924–55. Internal evidence, as well as an attached Aktennotiz on a meeting of Oct. 1, 1941, with a Nazi agent of Gauleiter Sprenger at the factory, indicates that this manuscript was probably written after the war by Heinrich Wagner.

37. The figures are from Lüer's fourth quarterly report for 1942, dated Feb. 6, 1943, RG87/6337, BAB. See also the Arbeiter Database in the General Motors–Opel Collection, Manuscripts and Archives Division of Sterling Memorial Library, Yale University, which contains the employment records of 7,025 foreigners who worked at the Rüsselsheim factory during the war. The records of the Brandenburg truck factory were apparently seized and sent to the Soviet Union by the Russian occupation authorities after the war and attempts to locate them as part of the GM-Opel documentation project were unsuccessful. On the treatment of foreign workers at Rüsselsheim, see the testimony and affidavits presented at the denazification trial of Betriebsleiter Artur Wilhelm Liebermann (note 35, above); for conditions at Brandenburg, see Edelmann, *Heinz Nordhoff und Volkswagen,* pp. 59–61.

38. See the workforce statistics as of the end of September 1944 in Lüer's last quarterly report, submitted on Jan. 5, 1945, R87/6340, BAB. On the recruitment of volunteer labor for Opel in the Soviet Union, see RW 20–12/12, Bl. 162–164, BA/MA, Anlage 19 to Kriegstagebuch der Wehrwirtschaftsinspektion im Wehrkreis XII, June 1–Sept. 30, 1942. On the treatment of foreign workers, see Klaus Pflügner, "Ich wollte alles, nur kein Soldat werden: Opel im Zweiten Weltkrieg," in *"Morgen Kommst Du nach Amerika": Erin-*

nerungen an die Arbeit bei Opel, 1917–1987, ed. Peter Schirbeck et al. (Bonn, 1988), pp. 230ff. See also the records of the denazification trial of Artur Liebermann (note 35, above). On the foreign-worker casualties of the air raid of the night of Aug. 25–26, 1944, see Lüer's report to Commissar Krohn, Aug. 29, R87/6339, BAB. Two German "fire watchers" reported that during the raid of the night of Sept. 8, 1942, the French prisoners of war "did not heed the order to take cover in trenches and shelters and were therefore themselves responsible" for the twenty deaths; see "Plant Report of Damage from Attack of 8/9 September 1942," exhibit D of U.S. Strategic Bombing Survey. Physical Damage Division, plant report no. 45, July 1945, RG 243, box 946, NARA.

39. The largest number of Jews reported in the surviving records as working at the Warsaw shop was 53: Gefolgschaftsbericht, Nov. 30, 1942, OPR 022365f. By May 1943 the number had declined to 35, and for the next month none were listed; see the financial reports for the Warsaw shop, OPR 021212–588. For Riga the largest number mentioned was 36, of whom 16 were women: Bangert to Wagner, Aug. 28, 1942, OPR 025291. For other reports on Jewish labor at the two shops, see OPR 018650f., 18820f., 022357f., 022369f., 029821, 29839f. In response to an order by Hitler, Opel was assigned responsibility for establishing and operating a repair shop at Pleskau in White Russia beginning in the summer of 1942 (OR 058142ff.), but no employment records for it could be found for this study. Fragmentary evidence of Opel's use of Jews at Riga is located in the records of the Nazi administration of that city, R91/164, BAB.

40. On Opel's mounting liquidity, see the audit for 1942 by Dr. Carl Brauns (R87/6341, BAB) and the report of Obersteurinspektor Hiller, Sept. 26, 1943 (R87/67, BAB). On the increase in capitalization, see "Jahresbericht und Bilanz für das Geschäftsjahr 1941," OPR 030280f. On Nazi pressure for Gewinnabschöpfung in the case of Opel, see the letter from an aide of Reichsleiter Martin Bormann to Commissar Krohn, Apr. 3, 1944, R87/67, BAB. On bombing damage and Richter's efforts to obtain compensation for it, see the correspondence in R87/6339 and 6340, BAB. In a letter of Jan. 11, 1945, Richter informed Kellermann of the Reichskommisariat that Heinz Nordhoff, manager of Opel's Brandenburg truck factory, had gained from the Armaments Ministry a pledge of up to thirty-five million marks for repairs to that factory, to be paid out on a monthly basis in line with expenditures, of which eighteen million marks were already available (R87/6340, BAB). No funds had been allocated to the Rüsselsheim plant, Richter added, because of failures on the part of its management. It is unlikely that any significant government compensation subsequently reached Rüsselsheim in view of the increasingly chaotic conditions of the final months of the war. Since the Brandenburg factory was promptly seized by the Russians and dismantled for shipment to the Soviet Union, none of the repairs made there and paid for by Armaments Ministry funds redounded to the benefit of GM when it reclaimed Opel in 1948. On the bombing guidance by GM executives, see the affidavit of retired Lt. Col. Edward L. Barlow, former member of the War Department General Staff, Dec. 19, 1975, GM 000452ff. On dividends: OPR 044376.

41. "Background, Outlook and Post War Plans for Adam Opel A.G," presented to the Overseas Policy Group War Administration Committee, Feb. 23, 1944, CR 036357–87. On the returning employee, see note 21, above. The allegation that GM maintained clandes-

tine communications with Opel after American entry into the war is baseless: Anita Kugler, "Airplanes for the Führer: Adam Opel AG as Enemy Property, Model War Operations, and General Motors Subsidiary, 1939–1945" in *Working for the Enemy*, Reinhold
Billstein et al. (New York, 2000), pp. 74f. In support of that allegation, Kugler quotes two
sentences, neither of which establishes any wartime communication between GM and
Opel. One sentence, in a report by custodian Lüer to the Opel advisory council of May
13, 1943, records a tax write-off in Germany of Opel machinery and does not reveal any
knowledge of GM's war-loss write-off of Opel in the United States, R87/6337, Bl. 283,
BAB. The second quoted sentence appears in Heinrich Richter's memorandum on a
meeting he and Lüer had with Dr. Saager, an official of the Economics Ministry, on Jan.
30, 1943, ibid., Bl. 74ff. Richter wrote that he had pointed out to Saager (Bl. 76) that GM
had written off its ownership of Opel down to the last cent ("Die General Motors Corporation hat den Opel-Besitz längst auf den letzten Cent abgeschrieben"). This was interpreted by Kugler as revealing knowledge of GM's write-off of Opel that could have resulted only from communications between Richter and GM. In the context of the
meeting recorded by the memorandum, however, Richter's words amounted to rhetori-
cal hyperbole aimed at thwarting a proposal by some officials at the Economics Ministry
to create a German company that would buy the physical assets of Opel, thereby in effect
expropriating GM. Richter's aim was to counter the claim behind that plan to the effect
that GM's ownership of Opel represented an American economic-imperialist threat to
Germany. The sentence directly following contains the even more hyperbolic assertion
that GM's executives had shown little interest in foreign business. If Richter had somehow learned of GM's tax write-off, he would, as a meticulous lawyer, not have claimed
that it involved a renunciation of ownership of the firm's stock, which was not the case.
His memorandum and subsequent correspondence with Commissar Krohn clearly indicate that he believed GM was still the owner of Opel. It would, in any case, have been
foolhardy of him to reveal knowledge of a recent action by GM in the United States in a
meeting with a German government official, since that would have left him vulnerable to
a charge of communicating with an enemy country in wartime, an offense that carried a
dire penalty in the Third Reich. Also without validity is the contention of Bradford C.
Snell in note 135 on page A-85 of his "American Ground Transport" that during the Second World War "Communications as well as materiel continually flowed between GM
plants in Allied countries and GM plants in Axis-controlled areas." The State Department document of July 7, 1943, cited on that point by Snell (RG 59, 740.00112A/33034,
NARA) concerned only questions arising from compliance by GM's subsidiary in neutral Switzerland with pressure from Swiss clearing authorities to discharge a small debt to
a German company for earlier purchases, a matter quickly cleared up; see the State Department correspondence with GM on this and other matters concerning the Swiss subsidiary, RG 59, CDF 740.00112A, nos. 28133D, 28241A, 28473A, 31350, 33134, NARA; also
GM 000893–901. GM communicated with GM Suisse via the State Department:
Charles G. Stradella to State Department, Mar. 24, 1943, RG 59, 740.00112A/28205 and
31350, NARA. The Opel financial report of 1944 cited by Snell in his note 135 records only
uncollected accounts receivable from prewar transactions with other GM subsidiaries,
not current transactions, as erroneously assumed by Snell.

42. See Neliba, *Opel-Werke,* pp. 152–57; "Historischer Rückblick auf die Entwicklung der Personalabteilungen der Adam Opel AG," by Dr. H. Schäcker, Mar. 1961, OR 066946ff.; also Hans-Jürgen Schneider, *125 Jahre Opel: Autos und Technik* (Cologne, 1987), pp. 220ff.; Jürgen Lewandowski, *Opel* (Bielefeld, 2000), pp. 83ff. On Wagner's role, see the records of his denazification trial, Abt. 520, Gross-Gerau, Nr. 3125/46, HHStAW. On the Russian dismantlement and shipment of the Brandenburg factory to the Soviet Union, see the report of July 10, 1946, by former Opel employee Jacob, with attached record of his responses to questions posed to him, TX 010605–11.

43. Sloan, *My Years with General Motors,* pp. 330ff. In 1949, the Internal Revenue Commission assessed the recovery value of Opel at $4,801,636.50, a figure that reflected the heavy war damages at Rüsselsheim, the total loss of the Brandenburg factory and other facilities in the Soviet zone, and the uncertain economic conditions in Germany; that resulted in a tax of $1,824,622, Internal Revenue Commissioner to General Motors Corporation, Aug. 1, 1949, and F. G. Donner's memo, Aug. 11, 1949: GM 002009ff. In 1967, under federal legislation to compensate American firms for overseas wartime losses from funds generated by liquidation of enemy property confiscated in the United States, GM was assigned $16,386,500 for losses at Opel after $16,831,806 had deducted from the full award because of previous tax benefits; see Foreign Claims Settlement Commission of the United States, *Annual Report to Congress for the Period January 1–December 31, 1967* (Washington, D.C., 1968), p. 189. According to an internal GM memo of 1974, because of limited funds, the commission's awards were reduced when the Treasury Department made payment, so that GM actually received $10,048,795, GM 004880. Many of the publications cited in the preface to this book erroneously assert that GM received compensation of $33,000,000. GM's claim included machinery and equipment at Opel's eastern repair shops, where slave labor was used, despite reservations registered by Elis Hoglund, who succeeded in having the construction costs of barracks for prisoners of war at Rüsselsheim excluded: John C. Schluer, GM Legal Staff, to T. A. Murphy, July 14, 1966, GM 002853. On GM's acceptance of Opel's wartime dividends in 1951, see the worksheet for GM's Federal Income Tax return for 1951, CR 000078919 (supplemental CD of General Motors–Opel Collection).

CHAPTER 9. CIRCUMSTANCES AND OPTIONS—RESPONSIBILITY AND GUILT

1. The minutes of GM's Financial Policy Committee for 1951 contain no mention of the Opel wartime dividends, CR 000078681–917 (supplemental CD of General Motors–Opel Collection). Whereas those dividends amounted to $261,061, GM's net income for 1951 was $506,199,560: General Motors Corporation, *Forty-Third Annual Report: Year Ending December 31, 1951,* p. 43. After resuming control of Opel in 1948, GM may also have indirectly derived material benefit from the much larger portion of the firm's wartime profits not declared as dividends but retained by Opel as reserves. It would, however, be difficult, if not impossible, to establish the extent to which GM benefited. Those reserves, mingled with some from the prewar period, were heavily drawn upon during the years 1945–48 by the U.S. military government custodial administration in charge of Opel to repair bombing damage at the Rüsselsheim factory and put it into production. By

the time GM resumed control, the reserves had been much depleted and their value drastically reduced by the currency reform of 1948. No attempt seems to have been made by GM at the time it resumed control to establish the various sources of those reserves, GM 013682–715, report to Operations Policy Committee, Aug. 10, 1948. The commitment to the compensation fund was made in a letter from Robert W. Hendry, chairman and managing director of Adam Opel AG, to Dr. Manfred Gentz of the Stiftungsinitiative der deutschen Wirtschaft "Erinnerung, Verantwortung und Zukunft" in Stuttgart, Apr. 14, 2000, OPR 000078920 (supplemental CD of General Motors–Opel Collection). On the fund, see Susanne-Sophia Spiliotis, *Verantwortung und Rechtsfrieden* (Frankfurt a.M., 2003).

APPENDIX

1. This allegation was first made in 1974 by Bradford C. Snell on p. A-22 of his "American Ground Transport," appendix to pt. 4 of U. S. Senate, *The Industrial Reorganization Act: Hearings before the Subcommittee on Antitrust and Monoploy of the Committee on the Judiciary, on S. 1167,* 93rd Cong., 2nd sess. (Washington, D.C., 1974).

2. See the letter of E. W. Webb, president of Ethyl Gasoline Corporation, New York, to the Chief of the Army Air Corps, Washington, D.C., Jan. 12, 1935, with appended "Statement of Facts," exhibit 145 in U.S. Senate, *Scientific and Technical Mobilization: Hearings before a Subcommittee of the Committee on Military Affairs,* 78th Cong., 1st sess., pt. 6 (Washington, D.C., 1944), pp. 939–42. The text of the agreement establishing Ethyl G.m.b.H is exhibit 147, ibid., pp. 943f. The text of the Italian government decree is exhibit 148, ibid., p. 944. In a letter of Sept. 17, 1942, to the chairman of the Senate Subcommittee to Investigate the Use of Farm Products, W. S. Farish, president of Standard Oil, stated that Ethyl Gasoline Corporation had agreed to approve German production of TEL only after receiving "a statement from our Government that there was no objection, on the ground [*sic*] of military secrecy, in its relation to the national defense, to the establishment of such a plant." See U.S. Senate, *Utilization of Farm Products: Industrial Alcohol and Synthetic Rubber: Hearings before a Subcommittee of the Committee on Agriculture and Forestry on S. Res. 224,* 77th Cong., 2nd sess., pt. 4 (Washington, D.C., 1942), pp. 1198f. According to a book by another Standard Oil executive, the licenses for the TEL plants built in Germany by Ethyl G.m.b.H. were "approved by the American State Department after consultation with the War and Navy Departments." See Frank A. Howard, *Buna Rubber* (New York, 1947), p. 66.

3. For the IG Farben communication, see "Comments on Professor Haslam's Article in the Petroleum Times of 12/25/1943," submitted to Dr. August von Knieriem of IG Farben by Dr. Goldberg, May 30, 1944; English translation in U.S. Senate, *Elimination of German Resources for War. Hearings before a Subcommittee of the Committee on Military Affairs, pursuant to S. Res. 107 and S. Res. 146,* 79th Cong., 2nd sess., pt. 10 (Washington, D.C., 1946), exhibit 7, pp. 1302–6. On the importance of the TEL plants for the German war economy, see Peter Hayes, *Industry and Ideology. IG Farben in the Nazi Era* (Cambridge, 1987), pp. 139–41; Edward L. Homze, *Arming the Luftwaffe* (Lincoln, Neb., 1976), p. 147; Wolfgang Birkenfeld, *Der synthetische Treibstoff, 1933–1945* (Göttingen, 1964), pp. 63–

66. On the 1939 sale of EGC's Ethyl G.m.b.H. holdings to Associated Ethyl Co., Ltd., see the letter of W. S. Farish cited in note 2, above. On GM's role with regard to Ethyl G.m.b.H. and Associated Ethyl Co., Ltd., see GM 004385ff, 004513ff. In 1937 the 600,000-mark share of Ethyl G.m.b.H. purchased by Opel for GM in 1935 was sold to Ethyl Gasoline Corporation by Opel for the same amount: R. A. Fleischer to Edward Jenkins, Sept. 3, 1937, OR 063363. On the antitrust suit, see the finding of the U.S. District Court of New Jersey, March 1942: U.S. Senate, *Investigation of the National Defense Program: Hearings before a Special Committee Investigating the National Defense Program, pursuant to S. Res. 71,* 77th Cong., 1st sess., pt. 11 (Washington, D.C., 1942), pp. 4677–87. The quoted words are from Dr. Goldberg's "Comments."

Bibliography

Arnhold, Karl. *Der Betriebsführer und sein Betrieb.* Leipzig, 1937.

Bajak, Curtis Warren. "The Nazi Corporation Law of 1937." Ph.D. diss., Yale University, 1986.

Baldwin, Neil. *Henry Ford and the Jews.* New York, 2001.

Bartels, Eckart. *Opel at War.* West Chester, Penn., 1991.

———. *Opel Military Vehicles, 1906–1956.* Atglen, Penn., 1997.

Bethell, Nicholas. *The War Hitler Won.* London, 1972.

Billstein, Reinhold, et al. *Working for the Enemy: Ford, General Motors and Forced Labor in Germany during the Second World War.* New York, 2000.

Boelcke, Willi, ed. *Deutschlands Rüstung im Zweiten Weltkrieg.* Frankfurt a.M., 1969.

———. *Die Deutsche Wirtschaft 1930–1945: Interna des Reichswirtschaftsministerium.* Düsseldorf, 1983.

Budrass, Lutz. Flugzeugindustrie und Luftrüstung in Deutschland 1918–1945. Düsseldorf, 1998.

Busch, Arnold. *Widerstand im Kreis Gross-Gerau 1933–1945.* Gross-Gerau, 1988.

Carroll, Berenice A. *Design for Total War: Arms and Economics in the Third Reich.* The Hague, 1968.

Casey, Steven. *Cautious Crusade: Franklin D. Roosevelt, American Public Opinion, and the War against Nazi Germany.* New York, 2001.

Corum, James S. *Luftwaffe.* Lawrence, Kansas, 1976.

Dingli, Laurent. *Louis Renault.* Paris, 2000.

Douglas, Paul F. *Six upon the World.* Boston, 1954.

Drobisch, Klaus. "Hindenburg-, Hitler-, Adenauerspende." *Zeitschrift für Geschichtswissenschaft* 15 (1967): 447–58.

Edelmann, Heidrun. *Vom Luxusgut zum Gebrauchsgegenstand: Die Geschichte der Verbreitung von Personenkraftwagen in Deutschland.* Frankfurt a.M., 1989.

———. *Heinz Nordhoff und Volkswagen.* Göttingen, 2003.

Ellis, Howard S. *Exchange Control in Central Europe.* Cambridge, Mass., 1941.

Farber, David. *Sloan Rules: Alfred P. Sloan and the Triumph of General Motors.* Chicago, 2002.

Feldman, Gerald D. "Die deutsche Bank und die Automobilindustrie." *Zeitschrift für Unternehmensgeschichte* 44 (1999): 3–14.

Friedländer, Saul. *Prelude to Downfall.* London, 1967.

Gallin, Mary Alice. *German Resistance to Hitler.* Washington, 1969.

Gregor, Neil. *Daimler-Benz in the Third Reich.* New Haven, 1998.

Hamburger, Ludwig. *How Nazi Germany Has Controlled Business.* Washington, 1943.

Hamburger Stiftung für Sozialgeschichte des 20. Jahrhunderts, ed. *Das Daimler-Benz Buch.* Nördlingen, 1987.

Handke, Horst. "Zur Rolle der Volkswagenpläne bei der faschistischen Kriegsvorbereitung." *Jahrbuch für Wirtschaftsgeschichte* (1962): Teil I, 22–68.

Hassell, Ulrich von. *Vom Anderen Deutschland.* Frankfurt a.M., 1964.

Hauser, Heinrich. *Opel: Ein deutsches Tor zur Welt.* Frankfurt a.M, 1937.

Hearden, Patrick J. *Roosevelt Confronts Hitler.* DeKalb, Ill., 1987.

Henning, Hansjoachim, "Kraftfahrzeugindustrie und Autobahnbau in der Wirtschaftspolitik des Nationalsozialismus 1933 bis 1936." *Vierteljahrschrift für Sozial- und Wirtschaftsgeschichte* 65 (1978): 217–42.

Herbst, Ludolf. "Der Krieg und die Unternehmensstrategie deutscher Industrie-Konzerne in der Zwischenkriegszeit." In *Die deutschen Eliten und der Weg in die Zweiten Weltkrieg,* ed. Martin Broszat, et al. Munich, 1989.

Heyl, Bernd, and Andrea Neugebauer, eds. *". . . ohne Rücksicht auf die Verhältnisse": Opel zwischen Weltwirtschaftskrise und Wiederaufbau.* Frankfurt a.M., 1997.

Higham, Charles. *Trading with the Enemy: An Exposé of the Nazi-American Money Plot, 1933–1945.* New York, 1983.

Hillgruber, Andreas, ed. *Staatsmänner und Diplomaten bei Hitler.* 2 vols., Frankfurt a.M., 1967.

Homze, Edward. *Arming the Luftwaffe: The Reich Air Ministry and the German Aircraft Industry, 1919–39.* Lincoln, Neb., 1976.

Hooton, E. R. *Eagle in Flames: The Fall of the Luftwaffe.* London, 1997.

Hopfinger, K. B. *Beyond Expectations: The Volkswagen Story.* London 1954.

Horkenbach, Cuno, ed. *Das Deutsche Reich von 1918 bis heute.* Berlin, 1935.

Howard, Graeme K. *America and a New World Order.* New York, 1940.

Kluke, Paul. "Hitler und das Volkswagenprojekt." *Vierteljahrshefte für Zeitgeschichte* 8 (1960): 341–83.

Knickerbocker, Hubert R. *The German Crisis.* New York, 1932.

Koskoff, David E. *Joseph P. Kennedy.* Englewood Cliffs, N.J., 1974.

Kugler, Anita. "Die Behandlung des feindlichen Vermögens in Deutschland und die 'Selbstverantwortung' der Rüstungsindustrie: Dargestellt am Beispiel der Adam Opel AG von 1941 bis Anfang 1943." *1991. Zeitschrift für Sozialgeschichte des 20. und 21. Jahrhunderts* 3 (1988): 46–78.

———. "Das Opel-Management während des Zweiten Weltkrieg: Die Behandlung 'feindlichen Vermögens' und die 'Selbstverantwortung' der Rüstungsindustie." In *". . . ohne Rücksicht auf die Verhältnisse,"* ed. Bernd Heil and Andrea Neugebauer. Frankfurt a. M., 1997, pp. 35–68.

———. "Flugzeuge für den Führer. Deutsche Gefolgschaftsmitglieder und ausländische Zwangsarbeiter im Opelwerk in Rüsselsheim 1940 bis 1945." In *". . . ohne Rücksicht auf die Verhältnisse,"* ed. Bernd Heil and Andrea Neugebauer. Frankfurt a. M., 1997, pp. 69–92.

———. "Airplanes for the Führer: Adam Opel AG as Enemy Property, Model War Operation, and General Motors Subsidiary." In Billstein et al. *Working for the Enemy.* New York, 2000, pp. 33–82.

Langer, William L., and Gleason, S. Everett. *The Challenge to Isolation, 1937–1940.* New York, 1952.

Levinson, Charles. *Vodka Cola.* New York, 1978.

Lewandowski, Jürgen. *Opel.* Bielefeld, 2000.

Lindner, Stephan H. *Das Reichskommissariat für die Behandlung feindlichen Vermögens im Zweiten Weltkrieg.* Stuttgart, 1961.

Lochner, Louis P. *Always the Unexpected: A Book of Reminiscences.* New York, 1956.

Mansfeld, Werner et al., eds. *Die Ordnung der nationalen Arbeit: Kommentar.* Berlin, 1934.

Martin, Bernd. *Friedensinitiativen und Machtpolitik im Zweiten Weltkrieg.* Düssdeldorf, 1974.

Mason, Timothy W. *Arbeiterklasse und Volksgemeinschaft.* Opladen, 1975.

Michel, Alexander. *Von der Fabrikzeitung zum Führungsmittel: Werkszeitschriften industrieller Grossunternehmen von 1890 bis 1945.* Stuttgart, 1997.

Milkman, Paul. *PM: A New Deal in Journalism.* New Brunswick, N.J., 1997.

Miller, Douglas. *You Can't Do Business with Hitler.* Boston, 1941.

Mommsen, Hans, and Manfred Grieger. *Das Volkswagenwerk und seine Arbeiter im Dritten Reich.* Düsseldorf, 1996.

Neliba, Günter. *Die Opel-Werke im Konzern von General Motors (1929–1948) in Rüsselsheim und Brandenburg.* Frankfurt a.M., 2000.

Offner, Arnold A. *American Appeasement: United States Foreign Policy and Germany, 1933–1938.* Cambridge, Mass., 1969.

———. "American Appeasement Revisited: The United States, Great Britain and Germany, 1933–1940." *Journal of American History* 64 (1977): 373–93.

———. "The United States and National Socialist Germany." In *The Fascist Challenge to the Policy of Appeasement,* ed. Wolfgang J. Mommsen and Lothar Kettenacker. London, 1983.

Oswald, Werner, ed. *Deutsche Autos, 1920–1945.* Stuttgart, 1982.

Overy, R. J. *Göring: The "Iron Man."* London, 1984.

———. *War and Economy in the Third Reich.* Oxford, 1994.

———. "Transportation and Rearmament in the Third Reich." *Historical Journal* 16 (1973): 389–409.

Petzina, Dieter. *Autarkiepolitik im Dritten Reich.* Stuttgart, 1968.

Pohl, Hans et al., eds. *Die Daimler-Benz AG in den Jahren 1933 bis 1945.* Stuttgart, 1986.

Roth, Karl Heinz, and Michael Schmid, eds. *Die Daimler-Benz AG 1916–1948. Schlüssel-dokumente zur Konzerngeschichte.* Nördlingen, 1987.

Schirmbeck, Peter, ed., *"Morgen kommst Du nach Amerika": Erinnerungen an die Arbeit bei Opel, 1917–1987.* Bonn, 1988.

Schmidt, Gustav. *The Politics and Economics of Appeasement.* New York, 1986.

Schneider, Hans-Jürgen. *Autos und Technik: 125 Jahre Opel.* Weileswist, 1987.

Schröder, Hans-Jürgen. *Deutschland und die Vereinigten Staaten, 1933–1939.* Wiesbaden, 1970.

Schweitzer, Arthur. "Business Power under the Nazi Regime." *Zeitschrift für Nationalökonomie* 20 (1960): 414–42.

Seeger, Andreas. *"Gestapo Müller."* Berlin, 1996.

Seherr-Thoss, Graf H. C. *Die deutsche Automobilindustrie: Eine Dokumentation von 1886 bis heute.* Stuttgart, 1974.

Sloan, Alfred P. *My Years with General Motors.* New York, 1963.

Smith, Amanda, ed. *Hostage to Fortune: The Letters of Joseph P. Kennedy.* New York, 2001.

Snell, Bradford C. "American Ground Transport," pt. 4A—appendix to pt. 4 of U.S. Senate, *The Industrial Reorganization Act: Hearing before the Subcommittee on Antitrust and Monopoly of the Committee on the Judiciary, on S. 1167,* 93rd Cong. 2nd sess. on S. 1167 (Washington, D.C., 1974).

Speer, Albert. *Der Sklavenstaat.* Stuttgart, 1981.

Spiliotis, Susanne-Sophia. *Verantwortung und Rechtsfrieden: Die Stiftungsinitiative der deutschen Wirtschaft.* Frankfurt a.M., 2003.

Tansell, Charles. *Back Door to Power.* Chicago, 1952.

Turner, H. A. *German Big Business and the Rise of Hitler.* New York, 1985.

Welles, Sumner. *The Time for Decision.* New York, 1944.

Zibell, Stephanie. *Jakob Sprenger.* Darmstadt, 1999.

Index